ATOM

ATOM

It Is Time to Upgrade the Economy

Second Edition

Kartik Gada

BEP

BUSINESS EXPERT PRESS

Leader in applied, concise business books

ATOM: It Is Time to Upgrade the Economy, Second Edition

Copyright © Business Expert Press, LLC, 2021.

Cover design by Kartik Gada

Interior design by Exeter Premedia Services Private Ltd., Chennai, India

First published in 2021 by
Business Expert Press, LLC
222 East 46th Street, New York, NY 10017
www.businessexpertpress.com

ISBN-13: 978-1-95334-950-7 (paperback)
ISBN-13: 978-1-95334-951-4 (e-book)

Business Expert Press Service Systems and Innovations in
Business and Society Collection

Collection ISSN: 2326-2664 (print)
Collection ISSN: 2326-2699 (electronic)

First edition: 2021

10 9 8 7 6 5 4 3 2 1

Printed in the United States of America.

Description

The accelerating pace and diffusion of technological change has taken control of an ever-growing fraction of the world economy. This fraction is being assimilated into a different set of economic fundamentals, such as the rapid and exponential price deflation inherent to technology. The effect of this was insignificant until recently, but is now beginning to create conspicuous distortions in many economic metrics, and is just years from being the dominant force across the entire economy.

In response to technological deflation, the central banks of the world will have to create new money in perpetuity, increasing the stream at an exponentially rising rate much higher than is currently assumed. This now-permanent need for monetary expansion, if embraced, can fund government spending more directly. This in turn creates a very robust, dynamic, and efficient safety net for citizens, while simultaneously reducing and even eliminating most forms of taxation by 2025–30. Alternatively, this monetary expansion can be a means to create Sovereign Venture Funds that can hedge a country's risk far more effectively than existing sovereign wealth funds.

Failure to recognize that technological deflation mandates permanent and ever-rising central bank monetary expansion that can and should gradually become the primary source of government spending could result in countries falling behind more enlightened countries in a very short time.

The nature of current worldwide technology is to link various disruptions with each other, consume monetary liquidity to generate deflation, and lower the effective prices of most goods and services over time. Therefore, the entirety of worldwide technology has to be seen as a holistic economic entity, and can be defined as the 'Accelerating TechnOnomic Medium', or 'ATOM'.

Keywords

accelerating change; artificial intelligence; technological progress; technological deflation; technological unemployment; automation; robotics; data science; quantitative easing; federal reserve; machine learning; deep learning; GDP; universal basic income; UBI; atom; European Central Bank; Bank of Japan; singularity; tax; income tax; monetary policy; deficit; national debt; sovereign venture fund; Andrew Yang; modern monetary theory; exoplanet

Contents

Welcome. This is a book/whitepaper about how technology has created new economic forces that are reshaping society. Contained within is guidance on how individuals, organizations, and nations have to adapt to these transformations in order to prosper.

If you are interested in any of the following, this is the reading material for you:

- Accelerating, exponential technological progress
- Technological disruption and its social and economic impact
- How artificial intelligence and robotics are affecting employment
- Why most mainstream economists are unable to measure the economic impact of technology and no longer understand monetary forces
- Navigating the next recession/financial crisis
- Creating a dynamic safety net that replaces outdated government programs and is simultaneously the destination of central bank easing
- A path toward migrating the tax burden away from humans and onto technological productivity
- How a country can hedge against technological disruption of its core industries
- How the data you generate can be monetized for your benefit
- How to harness technological forces for yourself

I hope this content changes how you view the world, in the present and the future.

Kartik Gada
Version 1.0: February 26, 2016
Version 2.0: February 29, 2020
May 31, 2020

Executive Summary

The accelerating pace and diffusion of technological change has taken control of an ever-growing fraction of the world economy. This fraction is being assimilated into a different set of economic fundamentals, such as the rapid and exponential price deflation inherent to technology. The effect of this was insignificant until recently, but is now beginning to create conspicuous distortions in many economic metrics and is just years from being the dominant force across the entire economy.

In response to technological deflation, the central banks of the world will have to create new money in perpetuity, increasing the stream at an exponentially rising rate much higher than is currently assumed. This now-permanent need for monetary expansion, if embraced, can fund government spending more directly. This in turn creates a very robust, dynamic, and efficient safety net for citizens, while simultaneously reducing and even eliminating most forms of taxation by 2025–30. Alternatively, this monetary expansion can be a means to create Sovereign Venture Funds that can hedge a country's risk far more effectively than existing sovereign wealth funds.

Failure to recognize that technological deflation mandates permanent and ever-rising central bank monetary expansion that can and should gradually become the primary source of government spending could result in countries falling behind more enlightened countries in a very short time.

The nature of current worldwide technology is to link various disruptions with each other, consume monetary liquidity to generate deflation, and lower the effective prices of most goods and services over time. Therefore, the entirety of worldwide technology has to be seen as a holistic economic entity, and can be defined as the 'Accelerating TechnOnomic Medium', or 'ATOM'.

CHAPTER 1

Prologue

Time is the fire in which we burn.

—Delmore Schwartz

I once had a dream in midsummer, 2015. I was in a dark and humid basement one afternoon, and I came across a very large book. Upon slapping away the dust from the cover of this grand tome, its title became visible, a title both grand and vague—*Exponential and Accelerating.* The mildew and centipedes aside, this was just too interesting to pass up. I hastily proceeded to peruse through its yellowed pages to see what was contained within; to imbibe the compilation of events from eons long past to see how we got to today.

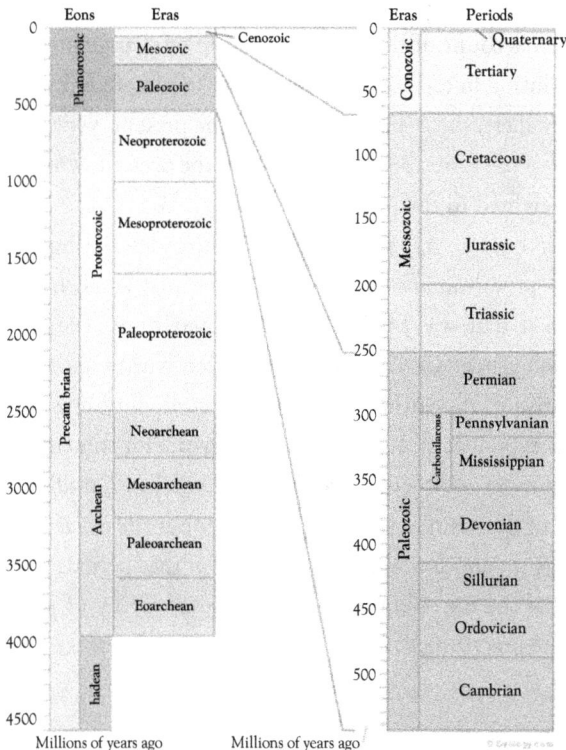

Eons	Eras	
	0	
Phanerozoic	Mesozoic	Cenozoic
	Paleozoic	
	500	
Proterozoic	Neoproterozoic	
	1000	
	Mesoproterozoic	
	1500	
	Paleoproterozoic	
	2000	
Precambrian	2500	Neoarchean
Archean	3000	Mesoarchean
	Paleoarchean	
	3500	
	Eoarchean	
	4000	
Hadean	4500	

Millions of years ago

Eras	Periods
0	
Cenozoic	Quaternary
	Tertiary
50	
100	Cretaceous
Mesozoic	
150	Jurassic
200	
	Triassic
250	
	Permian
300	Pennsylvanian
Carboniferous	Mississippian
350	
Paleozoic	Devonian
400	
	Sillurian
450	Ordovician
500	
	Cambrian

Millions of years ago

The first few chapters of the book described the origin of the Earth, the evolution of early life and the progress through the geologic periods. The arrival of multicellular creatures, vertebrates, and advanced animals was described, but what stood out was the unstated subtext that the rate of evolutionary change was inherently accelerating, and that this accelerating gradient has been present all along, and evident at all points from 4.5 billion years ago to the present. It is almost as though there is an inherent recursive loop of acceleration within the genetic code of all life.

The first full 88% of the time since the origin of life on Earth represented very little advancement relative to what happened immediately thereafter, described as the 'Cambrian Explosion' 540 million years ago. But it was an 'explosion' only to the extent that a linear perception would depict it as such. Under a logarithmic scale, it was right on schedule. Additionally, the rate of change was faster from that point onward; there was never a return to the pre-Cambrian slower rate of evolution. Even the subsequent dinosaurs of the Mesozoic era, which we think of as having lived very long ago, existed 95–98.5% of the way to the present in a linear time scale since the origin of life. Notice how each era becomes smaller in duration, on account of the accelerating rate of change inserting a rising level of evolution in each unit of time closer to the present. The Cenozoic era is the smallest, since it is the closest to the present, yet has the greatest differential of life forms between its start to the present, with the differential itself weighted to the present.

Then, it became apparent that the entire description of evolution through to protohumans only occupied the first small fraction of this book, even if that was 99.9% of the elapsed time. The emergence of human intelligence (see illustration) occurred within an extremely brief period relative to the entire evolutionary record, almost as though intelligence was exponential. It took 4.5 billion years for something as intelligent as a chimpanzee to evolve, and then it took just 5 million more years for the size of the brain to triple. After that, the entire existence of modern humans was yet another miniscule fraction of that period. It seemed that the events of the last 40,000 years were more worthy of prose than the events of the preceding 4.5 billion years.

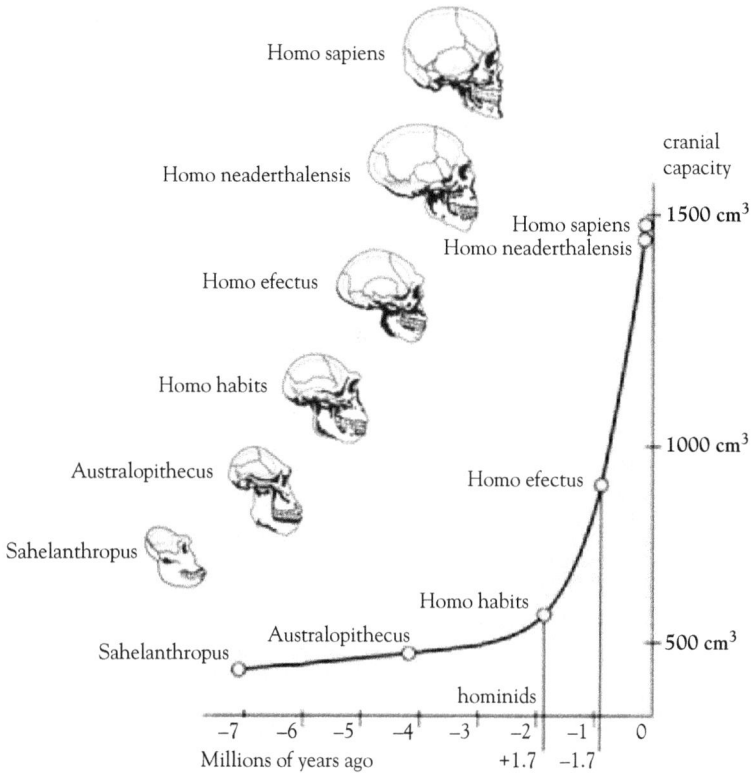

On to the Age of Man, I read about the earliest agriculture, the great ancient civilizations, and continued on through the Middle Ages. It was apparent that each century occupied more pages of the book, or rather, that each century was more filled with noteworthy events. The last five centuries received the most detail, and the twentieth century itself had more content than the entirety of eons prior to that point. I continued to read on about the Industrial Revolution, the beginnings of space exploration, and the computer age. The common theme was that we live in a time where events occur at an increasingly rapid rate.

Yet, I was only halfway through the book when I reached the present, and this puzzled me. I looked at the copyright date of the book and was stunned. The book in my dream was written in the early 22nd century, and the remaining few hundred pages were a description of the 21st century! I could barely contain my excitement at the prospect of reading the second half of this volume, but the pages seemed to be welded shut, and I could not turn to the pages past what described my present day. I tried to pry it open with a screwdriver, but to no avail. My dream did not allow me to see the most interesting section of this book from the future. I could only ponder the profound possibility that the latter 85 (now 80 as of 2020) years of the century were so eventful that it occupied half of the book; the same length as all of Earth's noteworthy events from the start until 2015.

I awoke suddenly, and the next morning went straight to the bookstore to peruse some of the latest books on futurism. A few volumes from renowned thinkers in various fields occupied the shelves, some on the future of artificial intelligence, other books on space exploration, and still others on biotechnology. However, each of those books described a future saturated predominantly with only their specified technology, thereby making each book mutually exclusive with the others. The more holistic and multidisciplinary books were over a decade old, a situation entirely inconsistent with the accelerating rate of technological progress. Lastly, there was little in the way of practical applications such as policy recommendations for economic and political leaders, or guidance for ordinary people seeking to adapt to this tsunami of technological change. Many questions of contemporary importance were left unaddressed.

This vacuum convinced me that the time had come for a compact publication that weaves these rapidly accelerating but seemingly disparate strands into a single tapestry of our destiny. To transcend the mere theoretical, the publication must provide multiple solutions for the increasingly stifling bottleneck created by the outdated econo-political apparatus. For ages, the default assumptions have been built around tradeoffs between safety nets and higher taxes, or guaranteed minimum incomes and business friendliness. But times are changing, and we are on the brink of an era where technological diffusion will be pervasive and pronounced enough to make some of these tradeoffs recede. The churn of fortunes and prosperity will increasingly be governed by how much an individual, business, or government grasps the concepts of exponential, accelerating economic and technological progress.

There comes a rare time when a seemingly unrelated tangle of very complicated problems that continues to vex all established assumptions can be addressed with a comprehensive, elegant, yet simple solution. If ever there was a time and place for 'outside the box' ideas of grand scope, it is here and now. As a society, we could be on the brink of taking prosperity to a new level with some remarkably straightforward economic and monetary adaptations. But if we do not embark on these reforms, we will soon have another financial crisis within the next few years, which may be worse than the previous one.

To describe the multiple interlocking forces between technology, economics, finance, and government in as simple and concise a manner as possible, I have embedded brief introductory videos at the start of major chapters. This layer is for the benefit of those who would like a summary of a particular topic in the publication before they decide to read a formidable wall of text. The goal of this publication is to reach a large and diverse audience of people on some very complicated subject matter, among whom learning speeds and styles can vary greatly.

What you are about to read and watch might change the way you look at the world, and fully change every assumption you have about the future, mostly for the better. At a minimum, you might never look at certain slices of life the same way again.

To begin, let us first consider the many complicated trends, policies, and interconnections that govern the world today. Perhaps you are worried about technology replacing your job or the jobs of people close to you. Perhaps you feel that your taxes are too high, and that government spending patterns do not reflect your values. Perhaps you are troubled as to why interest rates are nearly zero, yet there seems to be deflation spreading across many sectors of the economy. Perhaps you just feel that technology is creating a new type of inequality that is hard to describe by old-fashioned criteria, yet palpable on an instinctual level.

If you feel any or all of the above questions are a source of personal uncertainty, then this is the reading material for you. You may start thinking about many important topics that have very little written about them. Even better, perhaps you can get behind some of the ideas I have presented here, since many of these challenges can be addressed in highly complementary ways. As we embark on this unpacking process, we must divide the body of knowledge into sections. There are multiple concepts that tie together to form the grand unified set of analyses and recommendations I am presenting here.

To begin, we will first establish the case that economic growth is and always has been exponential and accelerating, and has been throughout all of human civilization, even as it is being partly stifled at present. Secondly, we will examine the deepening scope of technological penetration into an ever-widening share of the economy, how this is creating accelerating deflation, and why this is not necessarily a negative thing. After that, we will arrive at a policy solution for governments and central banks to assess and implement, designed to remove the drag effect of the current set of policies and set the stage for the next era of economic ascendance. Finally, we will detail some case studies and ideas that you can benefit from on a personal level, and claim a greater slice of the ATOM economy, since, after all, some others already are.

CHAPTER 2

The Exponential Trendline of Economic Growth

Study the past, if you would divine the future.

—Confucius

The future influences the present just as much as the past.

—Friedrich Nietzsche

The first and most important concept to internalize is the accelerating rate of change. This is a very under-discussed subject even though it increasingly affects almost everything about modern life. One of the best places to read about this is Ray Kurzweil's 2001 essay, despite the age of the article (the conspicuous dearth of more recent writings by multiple people is itself a problem that this publication aims to correct). From his essay, we see how technological progress is accelerating, multi-faceted, and diverse. The essay also proves that technological progress is not in stagnation or reversal, as some claim. It is important to note how exponentially accelerating processes have been going on since the dawn of life on Earth, and through the evolution of life, with each unit of change taking even smaller intervals of time. That process has continued through measures of progress within human society as well, especially in economics and technology. In this chapter, we will specifically focus on the economic evidence of accelerating change, for no other metric does more to demonstrate how fortunate we are to be alive in the 21st century.

For now, we will use the customary metric of 'Real' GDP growth rates (i.e. inflation adjusted), while later explaining why the less famous but more natural measurement of Nominal GDP (NGDP), despite including inflation, is the more relevant measurement for the future. 'Real' GDP overstates the dangers of moderate inflation, while understating the dangers of negative inflation (deflation), ironically making it less real, in an era of high technology. Furthermore, is GDP even the correct metric anymore? <u>GDP is calculated in a manner that favors doing 'even more with more' to a greater degree than it favors doing 'the same with less',</u> <u>while technology is primarily about the latter.</u> It is also true that GDP does not always provide the most precise measure of prosperity, for which indices like the <u>Human Development Index</u> are more comprehensive.

Asset prices (the stock market, real estate, etc.) are a far better metric of actual progress, since both the positive (exponential growth) and the negative (inequality of gains) are captured more accurately. Plus, the combined price of assets cannot be distorted by deficit spending. But for lack of a better alternative in tracking centuries of progress as stock market data does not go back nearly as far, we will use GDP for the purposes of these calculations.

Economic Growth Through the Ages: Everyone has studied historical events in school, passing exams and even writing papers. Contemporary schooling barely describes the greatest historical transformation of all time—the very recent upliftment of the human condition. An education about historical events is utterly incomplete without a sufficient illustration of the prosperity levels of the era. This backdrop has to go far deeper than a 'there were no airplanes in those days' level of cursory mention, for only then can the conditions precipitating wars over resources, slavery, etc. be truly grasped. Romanticizing the imagery of some past society invariably necessitates a selective focus on the topmost aristocrats, while ignoring the brutal and brief lives that the other 99% were condemned to. Effectively, any lament about 'how good things were then' is an inaccurate fictionalization.

We are presently accustomed to per capita real growth rates of almost 3%/year for the world economy and consider this to be a status quo cruising speed, as though such a growth rate has always existed. In reality, such growth rates did not begin until the middle of the 20th century. In the 19th century, the average world growth rate was much lower, at about 1%/year. Before that, annual growth rates were a fraction of 1% from the 16th through the 18th centuries, and virtually 0% for the thousands of years of human civilization before that. The accelerating rate of economic growth (which is the *second* derivative, mind you) has not stopped, despite how lackluster present conditions may feel.

GDP (current US$)

World Bank national accounts data, and DHD National Accounts data hies

License CC OY 40

Line	Bar	Map		v	Share	Details

Tick bill

LABEL

WORLD

90
80
70
60
50
40
30
20
10
0

xxx   xxx   xxx   xxx   xxx   xxx

1960–2018

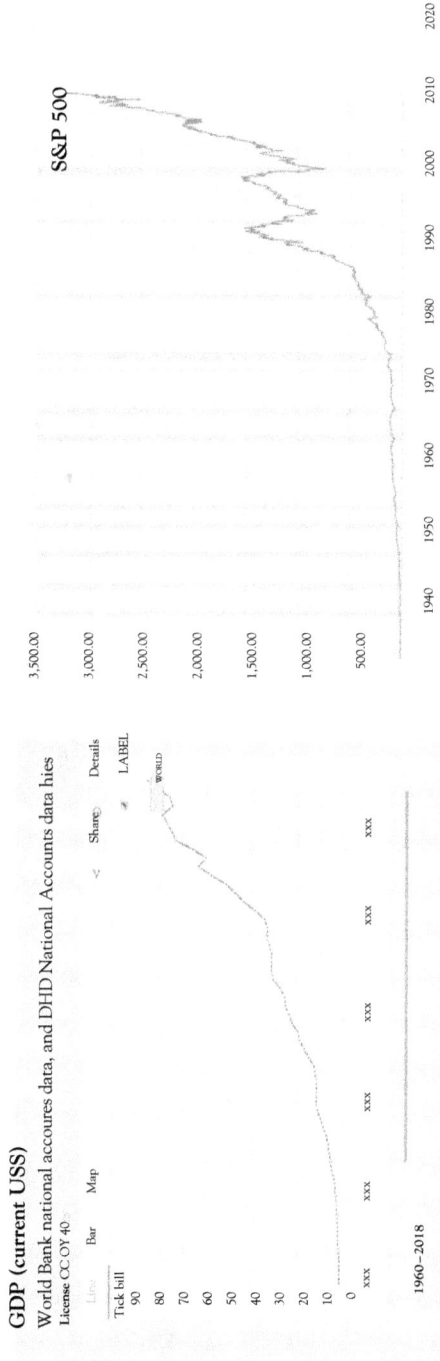

3,500.00

3,000.00

2,500.00

2,000.00

1,500.00

1,000.00

500.00

S&P 500

1940   1950   1960   1970   1980   1990   2000   2010   2020

Let us examine the above two charts (click to expand), which indicate world GDP in current dollars on a linear scale 1960–2018, and then the S&P500 stock market index, 1939–2019. The exponential nature of economic growth is apparent from both charts, but each depicts the trajectory in a different light. If you projected the same trend forward just a few more years, we can see that a much higher level of prosperity arrives in force, particularly with the more accurate indicator of the stock market. The topic of adjusting for inflation may arise, but as we will see in a later section, current methods of calculating inflation overstate inflation rates, and are thus starting to become obsolete.

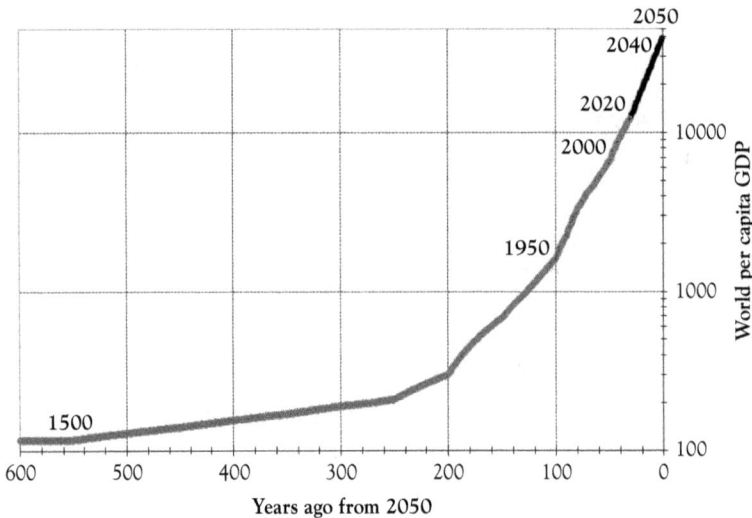

We have world GDP estimates going back centuries, and if we take a simple linear regression of past data and project it until the year 2050, on a third chart with a logarithmic scale on the vertical axis, we get a window into the future. We can examine this even more effectively with the horizontal axis oriented as looking backwards from the present, with green as what has actually occurred, and blue as a mere projection of the trendline. Note the parabolic curve despite the scale being logarithmic, effectively exhibiting a second derivative of exponential growth. The accelerating nature of economic growth, going back centuries, is apparent when the chart is presented in this way, and proves that it could not have existed until recently.

Imagine if 3% annual growth rates in per capita GDP, implying a doubling every 24 years, had started from 500BC, resulting in over 105 doublings by now. Or imagine if it had started from 1500 AD or even from just 1800 AD, which would still have yielded nine doublings since then, resulting in a growth factor of an incredible 512x. The evidence is indisputable that the current growth rates have only begun very recently. Since growth rates of this nature were never possible before the modern era, the second-derivative indicates that there is no reason to think the trendline has stopped or even plateaued. The key word here is *trendline*, as distinct from actual data.

If thousands of years of nearly 0% growth can be followed by a century of 1%, several decades of 2%, and then another few decades of 3% growth, simple mathematical extrapolation of that trend implies much higher growth rates in the near future. This fourth chart is an extension of the same chart backwards 2500 years. As we can see, the steep trajectory of growth has never, at any time, halted or reversed. In terms of simple multipliers, the rise from 1% to 3% trendline growth is no different, proportionally, than a rise from 3% to 9% growth later on in the curve. Mathematically, this should not seem any more rapid for the estimated year the curve intersects than today's growth rates would have seemed in the 19th century. You may be skeptical about this if you have not read the later chapters in this publication yet. Is an unstoppable progression of ever-rising growth rates a believable outcome? Since past performance is not always a predictor of future outcomes, surely we cannot just project the trendline to a point where in just a few decades even ordinary people are destined to have great prosperity. Is there some ceiling of human productivity that we have arrived at? How will most people acquire the skills to produce that much output? Is it not inevitable for the law of large numbers to eventually catch up, even if an identical skeptic in the 19th century would have been proven wrong had he dismissed an accurate prediction of 2020 prosperity as too optimistic?

The crucially unpredictable ingredient in such projections is that of nation-state risk. Economic growth within an individual country does not just happen without the right set of conditions. Sometimes, the wrong policies, centralized micromanagement, or ossified assumptions can lead to economic declines such as the Great Depression. Recoveries since these calamities have generally returned world GDP back to the trendline as though the crisis never happened, with the more accurate metric of asset prices rebounding to the trendline even faster.

But some nations often leapfrog others in the process of the global mean-reversion, capturing a disproportionate share of the recovery. The most prominent example is of how China and India jointly declined from being 40% of world GDP in 1820 to just 2% in 1975, even as the aggregate world GDP trendline was a smooth exponential curve throughout that period. This period was essentially the 'Dark Ages' for China and India, precisely coinciding with when the West was outperforming by the greatest margin. The rapid recoveries of China and to a lesser extent India since then can be seen as the start of a process of mean reversion to historical norms of GDP share, assisted by the steeply rising world trendline. The two nations are now jointly 20% of world GDP, and may very well recover all the way up to the traditional 40% in a matter of just years, not decades or centuries.

There is reason to believe that the economy may force a toppling of obstacles preventing the trendine from reverting back to its natural state. So far, this trajectory has reverted to the exponential trendline through world wars, economic depressions, plagues, and the dissolution of empires.

Yet most advanced and even middle-income countries today somehow appear to be stuck in a lengthy malaise of sub-par GDP growth, combined with little or no inflation. There seems to be a resigned acceptance of a melancholy 'Real' per capita growth rate of under 2% in the US, and under 1% in Europe, even though this is less than what was seen in the 1990s. The default assumption appears to be that this will be the norm for the foreseeable future, in direct violation of the expected accelerating gradient of growth. Even worse, the Nominal GDP that the US normally sees has fallen from over 6% prior to 2007 to under 4% now, which adds a poorly understood but nonetheless substantial damper on economic vibrancy and the pace of innovation. As more years of this divergence accumulate, the opportunity cost is rising. The world can no longer afford to continue to ignore how technology has altered the fundamentals of macroeconomics.

CHAPTER 3

Technological Disruption is Pervasive and Deepening

There is a single light of science, and to brighten it anywhere is to brighten it everywhere.

—Isaac Asimov

Any sufficiently advanced technology is indistinguishable from magic.
—Arthur C. Clarke

The ATOM has Already Enveloped Your Life: If we are to begin to believe that a centuries-old trend of accelerating economic growth is ongoing and about to take us to very high growth rates, we have to take the analysis to a much more personal and precise level. We have to observe and measure how this trend has enveloped your life.

The ubiquitous meme embedded into most discussions of technological progress is <u>Moore's Law</u>. The iconic observation by the great Gordon Moore of Intel traces its origins back to 1965, where an article in Electronics Magazine described how the number of transistors in an integrated circuit is destined to double every year (later revised in 1975 to double every two years). Now, half a century later, this publication aims to introduce a next-generation, two-axis concept to the venerable and still-valid but nearly-succeeded Moore's Law.

Anyone who has purchased computers over the years has come to expect the price of computing power to halve every 18–24 months, making the expanding constellation of gadgets cheaper and smaller. But for most people, the observation stops there. They don't see the true long-term implications of this pricing phenomenon beyond the need to upgrade their computer or smartphone every few years. This oversight is akin to missing the forest from fixating on an individual tree.

Since Moore's Law is limited to semiconductors, and specifically to comparing one chip to the next one chip, the unknown sister of Moore's Law must be mentioned alongside it. Data storage technologies have improved in a manner identical to Moore's Law, even though it involves different technologies only indirectly related to semiconductors, in entirely different companies. One dollar purchases more storage than one billion dollars could have purchased forty years ago, and that storage occupies much less space today.

But there is yet another layer to this exponential progress, which transcends even Moore's Law and the equivalent for storage. Consider that on top of the approximate 18-month doubling times of both computational power and storage capacity, both of these industries have grown by a combined average of approximately 14% a year for the last fifty years. Individual years have registered much higher or lower growth than that, but let us say that the trend growth of both industries continues to be 14% a year. Software price-performance doubles at a much slower rate (6–9 years per doubling, by many estimates), but nonetheless is an exponential improvement in its own right.

This revenue growth rate is a general indicator of device proliferation and technology diffusion, and many visible examples of this surging wave present themselves to the observant eye. Consider the television programs of the 1970s, where the characters had all the household furnishings and electrical appliances that are common today, except for any product with computational capacity. Yet, prosperity has risen greatly since that time, and it is obvious what the only catalyst could have been.

Closer to the present, among 1990s sitcoms, how many plot devices would no longer exist in the age of mobile phones and Google Maps? Take a program as widely viewed as *Seinfeld*. Refer to the episode entirely devoted to the characters not being able to find their car, or each other, in a parking structure (1991), <u>or this legendary bit from a 1991 episode in a Chinese restaurant</u>. These situations are simply obsolete in the era of mobile phones. The 'Breakfast at Tiffany's' situation (1994) created by George Costanza would be obsolete in an era of Netflix, Wikipedia, and YouTube. The <u>'Soup Nazi'</u> of 1995 could avoid aggravation today by exclusively taking and fulfilling online orders for pickup. He would never have to see a customer face to face, just as well since he now has to contend with Yelp reviews.

In the 1970s, there was virtually no household product with a significant computing component. In the 1980s, many people bought basic game consoles like the Atari 2600 and had digital calculators. They purchased their first VCR, but only a fraction of the VCR's components were exponentially deflating semiconductors, so VCR prices did not drop that much per year. In the early 1990s, many people began to have home PCs. For the first time, a major, essential home device was pegged to the curve of 18-month halvings in cost per unit of power. In the late 1990s, the PC was joined by the Internet connection and the DVD player. In the 21st century, dozens of new devices have been added, many of which constituted the high-tech augmentation of traditionally low-tech appliances.

We can now proceed to the real-world test. Everyone reading this can tally up all the items in their home that qualify as 'technological deflation' devices, which is any hardware device where a much more powerful/capacious version will be available for the same price in 2 years. You will be surprised at how many devices you now own that did not exist in the eighties or even the nineties, but you just cannot imagine living without today (this poll started with the first version of this publication in 2016).

Include: Actively used PCs, LED TVs and monitors, smartphones, tablets, game consoles, VR headsets, digital picture frames, LED light bulbs, home networking devices, laser printers, webcams, DVRs, Kindles, robotic toys, and every external storage device. Count each car as 1 node, even though modern cars may have $4000 of electronics in them.

Exclude: Old tube TVs, film cameras, individual software programs and video games, films on storage discs, any miscellaneous item valued at less than $5, or your washer/dryer/oven/clock radio just for having a digital display, as the product is not improving dramatically each year.

How Many Techno-Deflating Devices Does Your Household Own?
- Under 10
- 11–20
- 21–30
- 31–40
- 41–50
- 51+

By my estimation, the approximate number of devices in an average US home that are on this curve, by decade:

1970s and earlier: 0

1980s: 1–2

1990s: 2–4

2000s: 5–10

2010s: 12–30

2020s: 50–100

2030s: Hundreds?

This progression is even more striking when you consider how many devices are simultaneously consolidating. A smartphone now has a camera, storage, music player, calculator, alarm clock, and GPS system within it, removing all of those as separate devices. Despite the understatement inherent to counting nodes, more and more nodes, themselves rising in average complexity, continue to enter daily life. There was no metric of technological advancement before the modern era that was progressing so rapidly and widely.

iPhone, iPad and iPod sales from 1st quarter 2006 to 4th quarter 2018 (in million units)

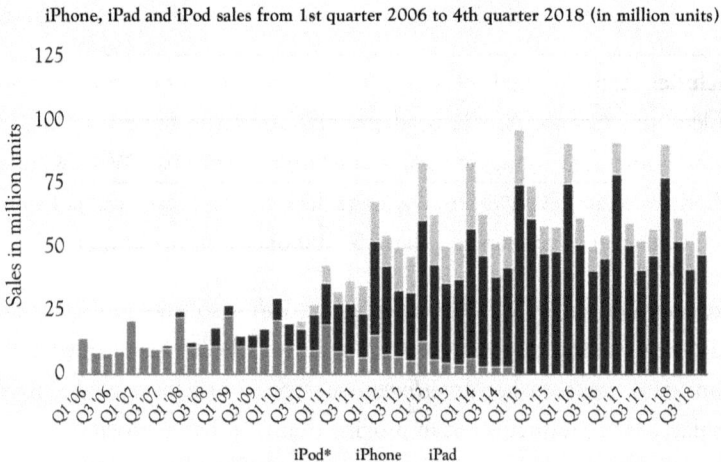

This effect is visible across every type of electronic device. Take a look at this chart of Apple iPod unit sales in relation to iPhones and iPads. There is great beauty in a chart like this. It initially encapsulated how when a combination of technologies (storage, batteries, music software, processing, etc.) finally becomes inexpensive and compact enough to be combined into a device of the right price, size, and utility, the sales of the novelty skyrocket. Yet when the functionality becomes mature just a few years later, the entire iPod becomes a subset of the more advanced iPhone or iPad. Individual iPods no longer sell at that point, much like individual calculators no longer sell. The entire lifecycle takes little over a decade, despite the multiple generations of improvement within this period.

Extrapolating a bit, we can project that the average home of 2025 will have various wonders. Multiple ultrathin TVs hung like paintings, robots for menial cleaning, VR-ready goggles and gloves, sensors and microchips embedded into clothing, table-sized surface computers, intelligent LED lightbulbs with motion-detecting sensors, and server-class home computers, to name a few. The home network of at least 15 nodes manages the entertainment, security, and energy systems of the home simultaneously.

At the industrial level, the changes are even greater. Just as with telephony, photography, video, and audio before them, we will see medicine, energy, manufacturing, media, and legal industries become information technology industries, and thus set to advance at rates much faster than before. The economic impact of this is staggering. Deflation has traditionally been a bad thing, but the ATOM has introduced a second form of deflation—a benevolent one.

Another way to look at it is to chart how many units of a certain technology can be purchased relative to GDP per capita. In an article from Prof. Mark J. Perry, we have a comparison of what was available to consumers in 1964 vs. 2016 (let alone 2020). This is an incredible illustration of how much quality has improved relative to purchasing power over a 50-year span, even though merely inflation-adjusted dollars are used, rather than Nominal GDP per capita. If NGDP per capita were used, then the impact is further quadrupled.

Now, when one expands the scope of this observation about proliferating deflationary nodes, we can add up the revenues of the semiconductor, electronic storage, software and other such technologically deflating industries. As of 2020, this calculation comes to about $2.7 Trillion/year, or 3% of World GDP. This figure was just 2% of World GDP when the first version of this publication was released in 2016, just 1% in 2004, and only about 0.5% of World GDP in 1992, so rapidly deflating products and components are becoming an ever-rising percentage of all economic output. If the proportion doubles again in the same pattern, then it could be 6% of World GDP by 2030 or so, and continuing to rise after that.

This progressing convergence of World GDP with technology is exceedingly important to every aspect of the future economy, from central bank monetary easing to inflation/deflation to the fiscal health of governments. Since almost every product or service created and delivered through a process that uses increasing levels of technology, this phenomenon is getting woven into the fabric of everything.

The Panoply of Creative Destruction: Words like 'disruption' and 'destruction' are usually associated with negative events. This consequently leads many to have a subconscious aversion to technological progress. There is insufficient understanding of Joseph Schumpeter's concept of 'Creative Destruction', where the process of technological change topples existing norms and replaces them with new ones in a new power hierarchy. A great book and documentary series to examine is 'How We Got to Now' by Steven Johnson. Mr. Johnson chronicles the iterative and messy process through which light, sound, time, and other fundamentals were eventually harnessed for modern human use. The accelerating rate of change is visible across his narration of historical events, and his work is an excellent prequel to the subject matter we are about to examine.

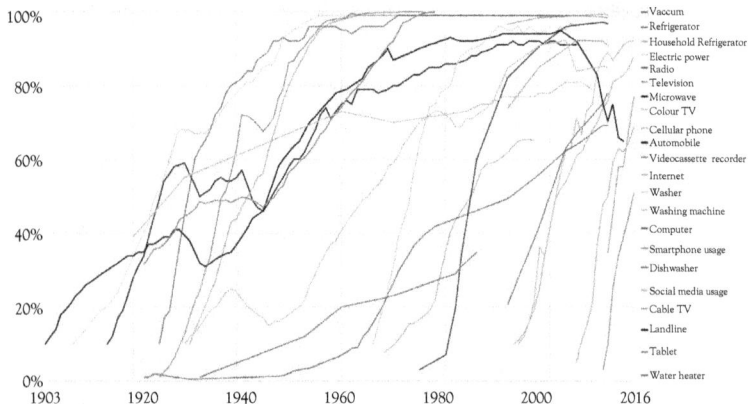

Technology adoption by households in the United States

Proceeding to the present, it is not technological disruption that is new, but the exponentially rising *rate* of change means more sectors, businesses, and lives are being transformed at greater speed through an ever-widening cascade of disruptions. This chart from BlackRock displays the rising speed of proliferation of each new disruptive technology. The effect is not even fully captured in this US-only chart, since a worldwide chart, which I could not locate, would reveal an even faster acceleration. The accelerating rate of change is visible here as well, and a continuation of this trend indicates that upcoming technologies will vault from 0% to 50%–80% penetration within just a few years.

This effect can be across industries that have been unperturbed for decades, or by the creation of entirely new industries altogether. Furthermore, for the very first time, evidence is emerging that seemingly unrelated disruptions have some degree of interconnectedness with each other.

Incumbents often go to great lengths to suppress disruptions, even if they themselves attained the position through some previous disruption. Whenever an incumbent industry has a misguided belief that disruption can be prevented outright by going to the government to get protectionist barriers erected around it, that industry merely experiences a temporary delay in the disruption, after which the reversion to the trendline is necessarily sharper. The script unfolds predictably. The incumbents focus more on political favors than innovation, which is usually a poor strategy when multiple industries are simultaneously seeking favors from the same government. In the meantime, the successors ascend to great heights at a speed the regulatory complex cannot handle, and the entire situation becomes more headline-grabbing than it otherwise may have been. Examples of such industries include publishing, taxis, and universities, all of which predictably ended up seeing their disruption happen in a compressed time, with the post-disruption landscape ending up where the general trendline would have predicted anyway.

Silicon Valley continues to be 'ground zero' for creative destruction, but there are many other innovators in various locations across the globe, quietly tinkering on something that could topple a major incumbent thousands of miles away. Quite a bit of disruption happens from incremental refinements crossing a certain threshold, rather than a radical new product category, and hence Asia is a major source of disruptive sparks in its own right.

Just a few of the examples of creative destruction that are currently underway include:

1. Artificial Intelligence (AI), after decades of quiet progress unnoticed by those outside the field, is now on the brink of making an immense economic impact, due to both parallel computing and big data both reaching cost effectiveness as enabling technologies. Many aspects of productivity can be greatly accelerated in a manner that is orthogonal and complementary to most other professions and industries. This empowers one person to do the job of four in some cases, or to embark on an entirely new type of career in others. On one hand, it is exciting to anticipate the trillions of dollars of output that will soon be generated with minimal input. On the other hand, input-optimization is a fancy way of saying that millions of jobs might get displaced. While new, higher-paying jobs will be created in different fields and different countries, the same workers cannot simply transition to those new jobs, nor is the creation immediate after the displacement of the old jobs.

    AI is the single biggest disruption on the horizon, as it directly affects the greatest number of jobs across almost all industries. It could simultaneously lead to a dividend of productivity that can flow more freely across borders than most other types of productivity. The dichotomy of AI will cause great confusion to readers of media output from the dueling camps. This topic will be specifically addressed in more detail later in this publication, for AI is the conduit via which fundamental modernization of the state's function and fiscal flows will become inevitable.

2. 3D Printing accelerates many aspects of design, prototyping, and manufacturing, enabling greatly improved or even entirely new processes, products, and services. From this, the thresholds of fixed cost and economies of scale can lower to unprecedented levels, decentralizing and democratizing all aspects of manufacturing. This transforms everything from commodity consumer goods to international supply chains to the production of aircraft, spacecraft, and buildings.

    The technology can now print in over 200 different materials representing a wide range of cost and durability. 'Personal Manufacturing' will soon be accessible to average households. An individual could download a design and print it at home or the corner store, rather than be restricted to only those products that can be mass produced. Many complicated shapes that could never have been produced as single units can now be printed, greatly increasing the speed and flexibility of manufacturing. Certain aspects of construction can take a major leap forward, and it is quite possible that by 2025, construction of basic structures takes less than one third the time that it does today. This, of course, will deflate the value of all existing buildings in the world at that time, as is expected of any commodity in the ATOM age.

3. Computing itself is on the brink of its first major transition in about 60 years. Semiconductors may no longer be able to further shrink transistors after around 2021 or so, finally retiring the venerable trend described by Moore's Law. This is not the obituary of technological progress, as Moore's Law is not the first, but rather the fifth paradigm of computing (as Ray Kurzweil has elaborated upon in detail in his books). The low-cost parallel computing enabled by NVidia's GPU allowed computing to advance on a vector no longer bottlenecked by transistor sizes (neural networks that run AI are more suited for parallel computing). Hence, transitioning to a successor to semiconductors is just the next handoff. Integration of discrete computing components such as the CPU, GPU, Memory, and Storage into a single unit will be another revolution in computing efficiency, enabled by new computing paradigms. Technologies like memristors may have a major role in this consolidation, as well as capturing an additional dimension of gains (literally) from their suitability for 3D chipsets.

Quantum Computing, an entirely different approach to computing, is no longer mere science fiction. Quantum computing functions by chaining together 'qu-bits', which unlike digital bits, can reside in a state of '0' and '1' at the same time. The power of the chain rises as an exponent of the number of the qu-bits that are chained together, and as the ability to create longer chains arises, quantum computing can greatly surpass the power of any conceivable digital computer. By some estimates, this may be possible by the 2030s, enabling multiple branches and technologies of computing to reside in different niches.

Class central

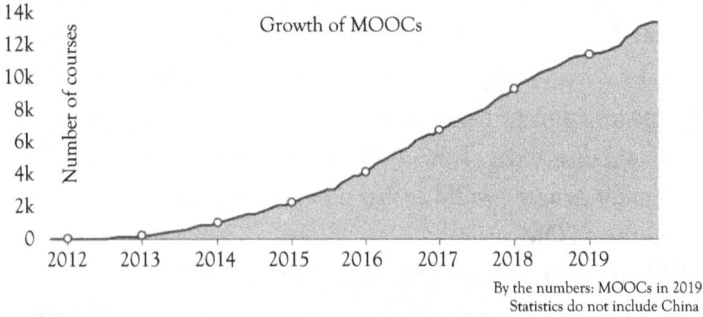

By the numbers: MOOCs in 2019
Statistics do not include China

4. <u>Education, both higher and lower, is being disrupted by the day</u>. The education sector has long operated under the fundamentally flawed principle that the cost of the same educational program can rise over time. To the contrary, costs should naturally decline over time, *since education is just another form of information and thus governed by the same forces of transmission as other information technologies*. Compounding the certainty of their imminent disruption, many universities, overconfident about their irreplaceable status in American society, have bloated their cost structures with excessive administrative personnel. These administrators have, in turn, taken on a role of political activism that has muddled the priorities of many universities away from education and career preparation.

In the meantime, several companies have produced courses and even entire degrees that can be completed online at the fraction of the cost of an in-residence degree and without the need for relocation. Employers such as Google have moved quickly to recognize these alternatives as legitimate substitutes to traditional credentials when evaluating potential hires. Such employers effectively indicate that a debt-free candidate at age 19 might have the same chance of getting an entry-level position as a debt-laden candidate at age 22. After initial resistance, other industries will gradually follow suit when they see enough LinkedIn profiles of successful Google employees without degrees. Eventually, many high-paying careers will require educational preparation that need not be expensive at all. These careers will in turn pull away bright adolescents from careers that may require massive student loan debt.

This example is particularly effective in demonstrating how the ATOM is self-reinforcing. The fields that among the most relevant to technological progress, such as Computer Science, are the ones most suitable for being delivered via low-cost, online degrees, attracting more students away from less ATOM-infused fields. Additionally, the coronavirus pandemic of 2020 may just be the tipping point that moves a large portion of education to the more efficient and pragmatic online model, since many schools and universities have been forced to shutter for months.

The other dimension of ATOM acceleration of education is personalization through AI. Classroom-based methods are suited to only one learning style, when there are in fact over 50 different learning styles. As online educational tools use AI to customize to a student's learning style, the software draws from the experience of all other students of that style to adapt to each successive student, removing the problem of geographical dispersion of people with similar learning styles. As this sort of AI progresses, the speed of learning for users of such AI could rise 25–50% or more.

5. The transportation sector is currently a nexus of several simultaneous technological overhauls. <u>Strong, light nanomaterials are entering the bodies of cars to increase fuel efficiency and safety</u>. Engines are migrating to hybrid and electrical forms and reducing energy wastage through new design innovations, with electric vehicles now comprising 3% of new cars sold in 2020. New models of ride-sharing such as Uber will alter assumptions about car ownership while monetizing unused seats. The declining price of computing ensures that the timeline for luxury features to trickle down to average cars continues to compress. The $25,000 car of 2025 will be superior to the $50,000 car of 2000 in almost every technical measure.

By many accounts, consumer behavior has altered to where people consider it normal to 'upgrade' their perfectly functioning 8-year-old cars to a newer model with better electronic features. This may seem odd, but people did not tend to replace fully functional television sets before they failed until the 2004–05 thin-TV disruption, and the same product lifecycle dynamic will manifest with automobiles.

By 2032, self-driving cars will be readily available to the average US consumer, and will constitute a significant fraction of cars on the highway. The savings from self-driving cars will be manifold, from quicker commutes to fewer traffic fatalities to less pressure to widen roads (at a cost of $10M/mile or more). Self-driving cars will revise existing assumptions about highway speeds and acceptable commute distances. This effect of a 'longer leash' will whittle down real estate prices of expensive areas, which are expensive partly due to pre-ATOM transportation assumptions.

6. The financial services industry currently charges $600 Billion in fees for the $20 Trillion in annual worldwide credit/debit card transactions. This is a legacy of a structure established in an era when computing power needed to process transactions was expensive. Today, several ventures are seeking to modernize transactions to eliminate this cut that ensconced incumbents take. Major financial services companies may see shrinkages in revenue, and will have to innovate and create new value-added services. The companies that do a better job of this than their competitors will accrue all of the industry profits, while the others will go bust.

Other product areas of 'Fintech' involve reducing the hefty costs and fees associated with mutual funds, custom portfolios, and mortgage processing, where a number of startups have already emerged. On the systemic side, an area of disruption is 'distributed ledger' technology. A distributed ledger enables the formation of Smart Contracts. Such a capability provides a degree of transparency and incorruptibility that may dramatically reduce the cost of transactional security and contract integrity. Smart Contracts can automate many forms of contracts that are both expensive and available only in very granular, retail forms. For example, a lawyer may have a certain contract template, and then charges clients $6000 for each one, with only minimal customization. If he has 1000 clients over a few years, that is 1000 x $6000, or $6 million in fees. If 1000 such lawyers all do the same thing, then that is $6 billion in fees charged by 1000 lawyers to 1 million clients. Instead, a Smart Contract automates all this and delivers it at less than 1/1000th of the cost, eliminating almost $6 billion in cost across the economy, generating technological deflation, and increasing access of this sort of contract to people who were not willing or able to pay $6000 in the old order. This can be applied to a wide range of contracts, as well as government transactions such as registrations, filings, and the disbursement of benefits and grants. Many aspects of government efficiency (federal, state, local) could rise 25% or more.

7. In the healthcare sector, <u>there are a number of disruptions seeking to crack the innovation-obstructing walls erected across the industry in country after country</u>. This is a major front in the battle between technology and excessive graft/cronyism. The endless frustration that technology has not yet overcome these barriers to bring cost-deflation and market competition to an industry notoriously averse to them may be at a turning point within a few years.

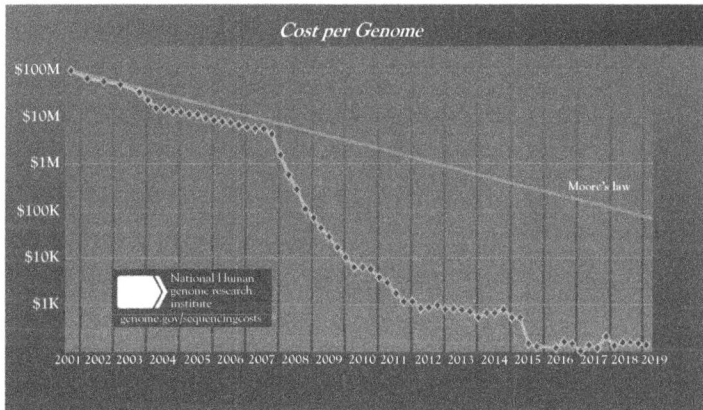

The cost of genome sequencing <u>plunged by a factor of 1000 in an extraordinary 4-year burst from 2007 to 2011, and is still dropping further</u>. While this has not yet created proportional cost reductions across other parts of the healthcare sector due to the enabling components being more static, as those costs inch down, more people will sequence their genomes. From this, networks of common genetic patterns will form by the 2020s. This will accelerate research around the genetics of disease as medicine begins to take on a 'search engine' flavor. When AI enters the equation, as patients feed symptoms and photographs into some deep learning engine, the engine becomes better at diagnosing ailments, which increases broader usage, which increases the engine's precision further in a self-reinforcing loop. A human doctor cannot assimilate the input of thousands of patients dispersed across various geographies, and the engine serving as the AI doctor can be accessed from home, at any hour, and certainly at much lower cost. As some physicians realize they need to practice medicine in collaboration with these new technologies, the more genome and AI savvy MDs will thrive, while those who still adhere to the paternalistic paradigm will be left behind. As the medical profession transforms from the greater proliferation of the 'for patients, by patients' medium of knowledge, this will begin to lower costs.

Another disruption is surgical robotics, where incisions can be small and precise instead of large enough for the surgeon's hands. This minimally invasive approach reduces risks and recovery times of major surgeries by 50–90%. Intuitive Surgical, the premier manufacturer of surgical robots, currently holds many key patents in this sector. As their patents expire, the cost of surgical robots will drop greatly as more entrants into the marketplace generate competition and make up for lost time. As more surgical robots connect to the cloud and begin to incorporate AI, the learnings of any one robot will immediately be available to every other robot accessing that repository of algorithms.

The persistent problem of healthcare innovation being obstructed by excessive government involvement in each transaction is the creation of the perverse situation where technological changes actually increase costs in the short term. This is because the weight of disruption is not yet enough to generate 'cracks in the dam' levels of pressure. As the scope of technological disruptions eventually becomes too much to regulate, the present disgrace will be overcome and will then finally see costs decline.

Solar PV prices vs. cumalative capacity, 1976 to 2016

Solar photovoltaic (PV) module prices (measured in 2016 US$ per watt-peak) versus cumulative installed (measured in megawatts-peak, MWp). This represents the 'learning curve' for solar PV and approximates a 22% reduction in price for every doubling of cumulative capacity.

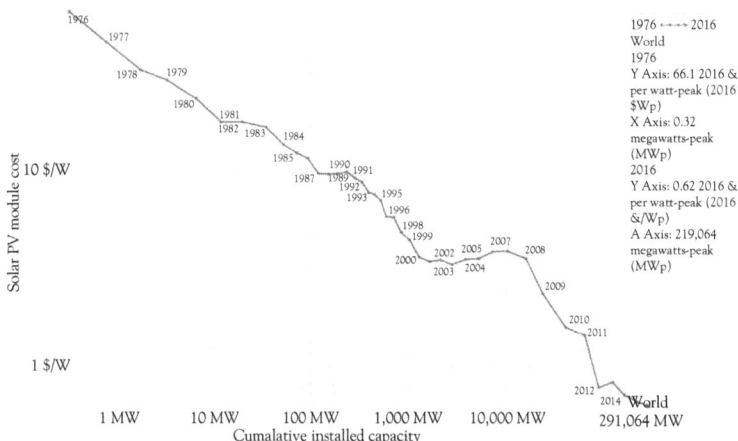

Source: Lafond et al. (2017); IRENA; Solarserver   Ourworldindata.org/energy-production-and-changing-energy-sources/ CC BY-SA

8. The energy sector is in the midst of numerous long-overdue disruptions that would take several pages to fully describe. The compound effect of multiple disruptions has introduced competition between sectors that were previously unrelated, in a superb example of how the ATOM works.

In one of the most important predictions at The Futurist, I predicted, in early 2011, the permanent decline in oil prices, on account of ATOM principles. Oil is unlikely to rise above $70/barrel for a very long time, if ever.

Electrical vehicles displace oil consumption with electricity, even while the electricity itself starts to be generated through solar, wind, and ultra-low-cost natural gas from hydraulic fracking technology. Photovoltaics (PV), in particular, has been following a steady price decline trend for over 40 years under Swanson's Law, and is soon going to be the most cost-competitive form of electricity in the lower latitudes that contain most of the world's population. Note the logarithmic scales on both axes of this chart, indicative of exceptionally rapid progress even by ATOM standards.

Average lighting efficacy (light output per unit of energy consumed) and cost per bulb

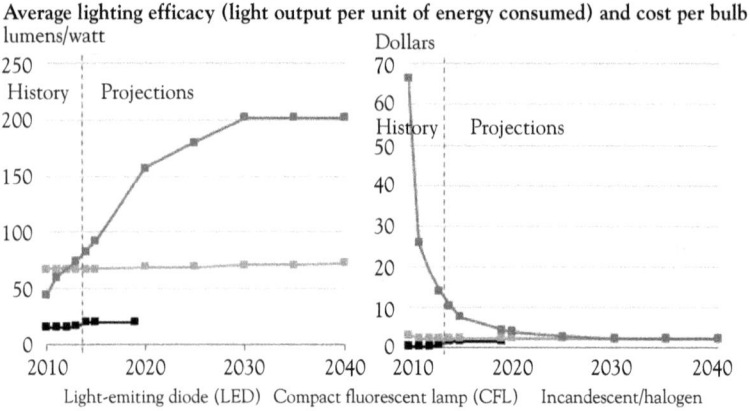

Light-emiting diode (LED)   Compact fluorescent lamp (CFL)   Incandescent/halogen

The electrical economy will be further transformed by revolutions in lighting and batteries, which will lower electrical bills, enable more accessibility to electricity in developing nations, and smooth out spikes that arise from supply-demand mismatches.

The creative destruction in energy will extend to the geopolitical landscape, where we see many petrostates much weaker in 2020 than they have been in decades. Eventually, very few countries will be reliant on energy that originates further than 2000 miles from their own borders, and the practice of transporting liquid hydrocarbons to another hemisphere will be seen for the strange historical aberration it is.

9. After decades of stagnation, space exploration is finally seeing a hand-off from being the exclusive endeavor of 3–4 major governments to being a target for private enterprise. Private spaceflight is becoming cost-effective through companies like Elon Musk's SpaceX. From these flight capabilities, asteroid mining might be a decade away from yielding trillions of dollars of valuable elements from nearby asteroids, which will of course crush the price of valuable metals on Earth, facilitating new industrial applications and more technological deflation. There is a particular interest in heavier (i.e. precious) elements that are rare in the Earth's crust (having sunk to the center) but more common within certain asteroids due to lower mass and thus gravity. This could collapse the price of gold, platinum, and other metals due to the supply increase.

3D Printing adapted for space can construct elaborate structures in space itself merely by refilling the orbiting printer with printing filament, which is far easier than launching finished products from Earth. Large, orbiting mirrors might serve to reflect sunlight towards a desired location on the Earth's surface, such as onto a major city during nighttime. The progress in semiconductors, storage, batteries, and data transmission is particularly valuable for space as it permits satellites and probes to shrink down to a mass that can be launched without rockets, while wireless software updates can upgrade them continuously from Earth. We are about to have thousands of times as many images from space, of objects never before imaged in such detail, as we have had in the past.

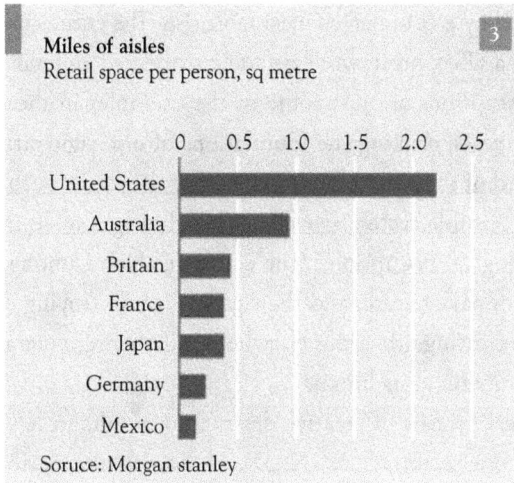

Miles of aisles
Retail space per person, sq metre

	0	0.5	1.0	1.5	2.0	2.5
United States						
Australia						
Britain						
France						
Japan						
Germany						
Mexico						

Soruce: Morgan stanley

10. E-commerce is not new, and was the basis of the 'dot-com bubble' of the Y2K era. However, the real value of e-commerce is not the mere ability to save retail overhead costs and have products delivered to the home. There is a second layer of value that is only being realized now, twenty years after the first wave. This value is from the data collection inherent to e-commerce. It has been long known that companies like Google and Facebook provide their products and services for 'free' because they monetize user data. Amazon does this too, even though its products are not free. Amazon and other e-commerce retailers thus have the ability to undercut brick and mortar retail even further without incurring a loss, as the data layer is a second source of money.

E-commerce, prior to the coronavirus crisis, was about 12% of total US retail, and the coronavirus quarantine pushed it higher. Even after the crisis abates, it may stay at a permanently higher level on account of this fast-forwarding of growth. The shift away from brick and mortar retail has many effects, particularly in the United States, where allocation of land to physical retail is far higher than in most other countries. This land will have to be repurposed, which is a huge dividend of new land available for pressing contemporary uses, such as housing. Local governments are not dynamic enough to modernize zoning ordinances and permits to enable the free market to repurpose this resource at market speeds, so there could be disruptive pressure on this front as well, due to the gales of creative destruction unleashed by e-commerce's inexorable rise. The entire concept of suburbia, within a US context, will have to be reoriented and reimagined.

These disruptions are just some of the examples in the pipeline for the next few years, shaking the foundations of old, rigid structures. The ATOM Award of the Month (ATOM AotM) chronicles such disruptions across every possible sector, as well as their linkages to seemingly unrelated technological disruptions. The common theme among all of them is their deflationary nature, and their process of destroying certain types of jobs while creating other jobs elsewhere at higher renumeration. This is creative destruction at its finest.

The typical process of creative destruction results in X wealth being destroyed in one sector, while 2X, 3X, or more wealth is created instead by different people in different sectors. For each of the disruptions listed above, 'X' might be a trillion dollars or more. Yet that is not even the best part, for each disruption exerts a reinforcing effect on every other nascent disruption, as each are dynamic components of the broader ATOM.

All Technological Disruptions are Interconnected: In the midst of a technological disruption, neither the incumbents nor the disruptors pay much attention to parallel creative destruction in distant industries and countries, under the assumption that it is entirely unrelated. On the contrary, my proprietary research has discovered that all technological advancement, and all creative destruction, is interlinked by varying degrees of distance. It is not a constellation of many isolated techno-centers operating in different industries and geographies, but one unified

ATOM, where one successful cycle of creative destruction strengthens the prospects of each subsequent candidate technology in the pipeline, and the aggregate economic volume of such disruption rises exponentially.

One of best examples of this can be illustrated by returning to the example of the crude oil market. When oil prices began to rise around 2004, various people who project every trend linearly from a rear-view mirror analysis descended into hysteria about 'peak oil', with some going so far as to insist that economic prosperity would regress back to that of the 19th century once oil became 'too expensive'. By contrast, technologically and economically literate observers were untroubled, since they knew that higher oil prices would necessarily cause a market response across the entire phalanx of mitigating technologies from every direction. Drillers worked to improve their hydraulic fracking methods. Material scientists worked on lighter yet stronger materials for cars. Battery innovators worked to increase charge duration. Engine designers worked to increase engine efficiency through a re-imagining of the humble spark plug. Each group represented a component of a holistic response to expensive oil prices. As each column advanced on the problem from a different direction, speeding up as oil got more expensive, there was never any real chance of oil staying significantly above $110/barrel for a lengthy period, and as of early-mid 2020, it is down to a mere $20–25/barrel after years of ongoing disruption of oil supply *and* demand. Gold and copper may seem to have no relation to oil, but the same process of disruption manifested there as well. The high price of gold created a larger market window to prospect for more supply, and aerial drones increased prospecting efficiency by orders of magnitude in remote locations.

A second example, which happens to be imminent, is the retail sector of India. Anyone acquainted with India knows that the retail experience is still of a 19th century nature, with inconvenient layouts, cash payments, rude haggling, and prices varying by over 50% between merchants less than 100 meters apart. The supply chain is so inefficient that half of all fruits and vegetables rot before reaching the point of sale, and routine shopping that may take an hour in the US takes half a day in India. Since these 'mom and pop' operations are a powerful voting block, the government has erected steep barriers to obstruct the entry of foreign retail chains such as Wal-Mart and IKEA. These multinationals would, by their very operating presence, improve infrastructure, logistics, and price competition across India, yet this overdue progress is being thwarted through electoral politics. The ATOM, in response, has merely redirected to move the disruption to a higher, broader plane. If international-grade brick and mortar retail is being obstructed, that makes it simultaneously easier for e-commerce to emerge. If landline Internet proliferation was not rapid enough, the smartphone delivered wireless Internet access deep down the pyramid, which in turn made e-commerce accessible. This is one of the great examples of how the ATOM invariably bypasses obstructions in proportion to how stifling they are. In India today, the e-commerce sector is projected to grow at over 30%/year for the next few years, enabling an improvement across roads, consumer finance, and marketing, that otherwise was progressing at the most sclerotic of rates.

The same principles apply to more widely dispersed areas of innovation. As described above, many poorer countries are resistant to the implementation of even 20th century technologies. But as one product, the smartphone, managed to percolate through the dense barriers to reach people with no prior Internet access, cracks began to emerge in the technological time-capsules that such societies represent. Many other technologies are now gaining a long-overdue foothold even there through this new conduit of ATOM transmission. Apps to facilitate education, health, agriculture, and transportation can easily spread to a huge number of people who were far below the economic threshold one previously associated with advanced technology usage. Since the smartphone is often the first electricity-consuming device for some of these rural users, it forces the emergence of a power grid where there was none before. The government ineptitude that failed to provide electricity is bypassed by the decentralized nature of photovoltaics and the rapid price declines seen under Swanson's Law. This in turn creates electrical power that in turn enables other devices to be used in these areas for the first time.

What this demonstrates is that the ATOM has a certain aggregate amount of disruptive capacity that rises each year with accelerating rates of technological progress. More specifically, the magnitude of each individual disruption in at a particular time determines how much of the ATOM is occupied until the disruption manifests, after which that portion of the ATOM moves on to the next disruption. By monitoring and measuring the various instances of creative destruction underway at any given time, one can estimate both the size of the ATOM and the force it will exert on subsequent disruptions once the completion of current disruptions frees up ATOM capacity. If toppling a formidable problem like $110+ oil occupied a substantial fraction of the ATOM for over 7 years, then the completion of that disruption frees up that portion of the ATOM for the next one. This could be one similarly huge obstacle or a dozen smaller ones.

Under the concept of human civilization merging with technology prophesized by Ray Kurzweil, this could be the early evidence of a unifying fabric of technology that leads to a 'Technological Singularity' in a few decades time. While that topic is beyond the scope of this publication, what is apparent now is how a pipeline of disruption, and the allocation of the ATOM between them based on how sweeping, complex, and 'due' the disruption is, can be estimated. This provides a path to more precise forecasts.

Creative Destruction and Human Collateral Damage: While the gains of wealth and productivity look excellent at the highest level of macroeconomic statistics, the human cost incurred by the sifting sands are a different matter. By current trends, the US economy seems mired in a long-term status quo where vanishing industries force many laid off workers to start in new industries at the entry level for half of their previous compensation. The net new wealth created by the new industries often does not reach the average household.

One could declare that income diversification is the golden rule of the early 21st century, and those who fail to create and maintain multiple streams of income are imperiling themselves. In such a climate, the best career one can embark on, which will never be obsolete, is that of the serial entrepreneur. This is true, but not everyone is cut out to be an entrepreneur, or has the cushion of savings that could enable them to pursue entrepreneurship. Furthermore, the current tax code is not friendly towards entrepreneurship at all. Hence, only a fraction of the people who could succeed as entrepreneurs are in fact full-time entrepreneurs.

The US citizenry often sees a baffling paradox of weak employment and low labor force participation despite high corporate earnings growth. Technological disruption is blamed for this without simultaneously being praised for the new jobs it creates. Big paydays for entrepreneurs will make the headlines frequently, right alongside stories of people who saw their entire profession vanish and have not found new employment for years. This has been sheepishly designated as the 'new normal', complete with an industry devoted to directing opprobrium to designated scapegoats. But given what we have seen about the accelerating rate of economic growth, this is certainly not where the trendline should have delivered us by now.

Amidst these sweeping waves of technology, human society is stratifying. Some people find this creative destruction to be exhilarating, while others find this to be extremely stressful. Given how complicated and unpredictable these economic reorientations appear to the majority of people, the role of government has to be to cushion the process of creative destruction in a very agnostic yet acceleration-aware manner.

Ultimately, the ATOM has an economic effect analogous to a double-edged sword. Technology leads to ever-rising rates of economic growth, but also causes disruptions that lead to stress and uncertainty. If only there were a set of ideas that could enhance the former while minimizing the latter properties of technology. If we could monetize the accelerating rate of technological change in a manner that reduces, rather than increases, the dislocation stresses that workers face from this process of creative destruction. Despite this, the last thing the government should do is attempt to pick winners and losers, for this is a moral hazard that weakens the system and the faith that people have in it. Fortunately, there are a few solutions available, both comprehensive and efficient.

CHAPTER 4

The Overlooked Economics of Technology

A box without hinges, key, or lid. Yet golden treasure inside is hid!
—JRR Tolkien

There have been a number of previous instances where talk of a 'new economy' has emerged, only for the suggestion to be shot down whole-sale when the subsequent market crash arrived. This condemns the valid observations to get buried in the frenzy of retroactive rejection, hedging, and caveats as perma-pessimists are given media exposure. More specifi-cally, the missing ingredient in most prior debates and analyses of tech-nological economics is a sufficient examination of the technology-driven convergence of previously unrelated forces, and whether we are far enough along the exponential megatrend described in Chapter 2.

We have established earlier that while people have grown accustomed to seeing all forms of consumer technology continuously decline in price, very few take the next step and observe the ever-widening array of prod-ucts that continue to merge into this river of exponential technological deflation. Fewer still contemplate the effect this has on the broader macro-economy, and why this was too insignificant to matter until recently, but no longer. It is surprising how little thought is given to this even by estab-lished economists and governments, despite how it affects nearly every-thing of economic and social consequence. Why might this be?

The Intertwining of Disparate Phenomena: To approach the nexus that this publication seeks to address, we must first map the roads leading to it. There are three unrelated groups of experts who do not yet see that their fields are beginning to overlap significantly for the first time.

The first are the futurists and technology forecasters watching tech-nological progress and predicting technological disruption (Ray Kurzweil being the most illustrious among them, even if his best output was in 1999–2008). They have done yeoman work in evangelizing why the rate of technological change is exponential and accelerating, and tracking examples that demonstrate this.

The second group is one of monetary policy experts observing every word uttered by the central banks of the world. They try to assess the impacts of various monetary expansion programs, and whether the style administered by one central bank is as effective as that done by another.

The third group consists of macroeconomists and fiscal policy 'experts' (i.e. they possess credentials) who keep track of government spending, taxation, debt levels, the Laffer Curve, bond yields, and so on across each major nation-state. The budgetary process of their government is very important to their professional work and annual calendar.

But here we are in 2020. Even after four years of media appearance by me for the first version of this publication, each of these three groups are still baffled as to why their models and assumptions can no longer explain the peculiar disconnects that are appearing across financial markets, central bank liquidity actions, and economic indicators that steer government fiscal policy. The latter two groups are part of the establishment and prevailing zeitgeist, while the first group is small, seen as eccentric, mostly tied to the field of computer science, and has insufficient marketing expertise to generate mainstream awareness of their work. To my knowledge, no Western politician or central banker has ever uttered a single sentence about the accelerating rate of technological change and how governance has to mirror it in both agility and scope.

I have seen brilliant and acclaimed thinkers in each discipline figuring out a fraction of the composite body of knowledge presented here, but not an entire holistic view, much like the old story of a few blind men and an elephant. Part of this is due to not knowing where to continue the investigation. Why should a budgetary analyst read about accelerating technological change and Moore's Law? Why should an AI expert dive deeply into central bank balance sheets?

When the spaces between previously unrelated fields begin to ignite the sparks of new knowledge, it is usually from an outside agent. I am not part of the formal establishment in any of these three groups, and perhaps that might just be what can enable a vision of what is to come.

Accelerating Technological Deflation, and the Federal Reserve: The primary discovery that every recommendation here rests on is that if rapidly-deflating technological products are now an impressive 3% of GDP as of 2020, there must be some resultant deflation affecting the broader economy. To detect this, we turn to the customary actions that governments take if they find inflation to be too low. If the government has been taking actions to fight deflation, and this deflation appears to be exponential, perhaps it has origins in the spread of technology through the economy.

In the United States, the Federal Reserve controls the Fed Funds Rate, which it raises when it expects inflation to be higher in the future, and lowers when the economy is weakening and/or inflation is trending too low. Until the end of the 20th century, this process was relatively straightforward, with the Fed Funds Rate very rarely ever going below 3% or so. Inflation was discussed as though it could fall in only two categories; 'high' and 'very high'. It was further assumed that whenever employment reaches a threshold of 'full employment' that inflation was certain to accompany this. Many practices that require inflation to succeed, such as taking on mortgage debt, were assumed to be indisputable wisdom that had no such dependency.

However, after the technology boom and bust at the turn of the century, inflation was conspicuously missing. The Federal Reserve had the freedom to lower the Fed Funds rate all the way down to 1% in 2004, and while observers expected this would finally cause inflation, it still did not. Relatively few economists were particularly curious about why that might be, since the rate was still above zero, and the possibility of rates at zero did not seem realistic. Japan had lowered its own rate to zero, and still struggled with deflation. But since Japan has lower birth and immigration rates than the US, this explanation was deemed sufficient and Japan was not seen as an indicator of a broader phenomenon that could also emerge in the US.

As the economy strengthened, The Federal Reserve, expecting inflation, steadily increased the 1% Fed Funds rate all the way up to 5.5% by 2007, only to find that this was too high and that the housing market, and with it the entire economy, was weakening precipitously. The Fed reacted with a rapid reversal of rates all the way down to not just the 1% of 2003–04, but to nearly 0%. However, to the surprise of observers, even 0% was not enough to create inflation, so they began a form of monetary expansion known as 'Quantitative Easing' (QE). QE was designed to simulate the conditions of negative rates without deposits actually being docked an interest charge by banks. Some liken QE to 'money-printing', but that is not quite accurate, as the impact of each dollar can vary based on the method of QE.

Effectively, the Federal Reserve embarked on a campaign to expand the monetary supply via a process of asset purchases. They would buy bonds, and hold the bonds on the balance sheet, with the implied under-standing that the bonds would be 'sold' into the open market at some future time. By purchasing bonds, the Federal Reserve lowers interest rates even for longer-term loans, which would make borrowing attractive for consumers and corporations. The Federal Reserve thought that the first program of QE would be the only one, but when equities could not sustain any gains after the conclusion of the easing program, economic indicators weakened. In response, the Fed had to embark on a second program, calling in QE2. When the conclusion of QE2 promptly led to yet another major equity correction, a third bout, QE3, was ramped up and later concluded. After that, they thought they could start unwinding the balance sheet, embarking on a reversal of QE. This caused predictable economic deterioration and the Federal Reserve quickly reversed course with a new wave of QE. As of early 2020, there is still an assumption that QE can end, be reversed, and that even the Fed Funds rate can be increased and kept above zero. Under ATOM principles, we know that this can not be the case. The coronavirus pandemic ended up being the black swan event that exposed the reality that the Federal Reserve was unequipped to face.

Traditionally, money-printing has caused inflation in times before technology was an offsetting force. The Weimar Republic of Germany (1919–33) is often cited as an example of such peril. When the first round of QE started, a crowd of hyperinflation fearmongers arose, committed to a narrative that we were doomed to repeat the Weimar experience if we embark on this slippery slope. This group found a natural synergy with the technophobe movement, which is built around an insistence that technology has not created any real economic changes in the last century. Strident opposition to QE became quite fashionable, with all QE being equated to the mismanagement of Venezuela under Hugo Chavez. Some expended considerable effort to assert their supposed expertise by insisting that inflation was much higher than the data indicated.

As QE commenced, however, the inflation was minimal and transitory at best. There has certainly not been any sustained 'high' inflation to this day despite the immense amount of QE. Whether one looks at the official Consumer Price Index (CPI) or the MIT Billion Prices Project, inflation is far below the zone where it could be considered adequate, let alone high. The hyperinflation cult has seen membership shrink, but new questions have emerged amidst the ashes of their failed predictions. Where is all that QE vanishing to? At what rate? Is this pattern of disappearance permanent? Is the QE turning up somewhere else?

Cynthia Wu and Fan Dora Xia have published research on what is termed as the Fed Funds Shadow Rate. While this research is little-known outside the immediate field, the discovery has profound significance, perhaps even greater than Ms. Wu and Ms. Xia realize. The shadow rate, which was updated monthly while the FF rate was near zero, roughly tracks the effect of US QE on generating negative FF rates.

When it was active, this shadow rate revealed at the time that increasing levels of QE still did not generate noteworthy inflation, and this may be synchronous with concurrent ATOM deflation. The rounds of QE temporarily pushed the Wu-Xia shadow rate not merely to zero, but negative. The movement from 0% to –1% and –2% was swift, and the trajectory seemed to indicate that the trend of increasingly negative rates was not linear, but exponential. When the US stopped

Fed slashes rates to shield economy from pandemic
U.S. federal funds target rate*

Recession

6%
5%
4%   0.00% – 0.25%
        Mar 15, 2020
3%
2%
1%
0%
     '07 '08 '09 '10 '11 '12 '13 '14 '15 '16 '17 '18 '19

*starting Dec. 16, 2008 the chart shows the upper limit
of the federal funds target rate range

QE, the Wu-Xia shadow rate quickly rose back to 0%, and this coincided with increased deflation and a massive crash in the price of almost every commodity. This crash was despite the fact that excluding the US, the other central banks of the world were creating a combined total of over $200B/month as of early 2016, which has continued on a rising gradient through 2020.

Hence, if the Wu-Xia shadow rate is one of the possible tools to indirectly estimate the current ATOM deflation rate, then perhaps the measure of sufficient vs. insufficient QE is the gap between the two. Accordingly, when the rate is above where the ATOM indicates technological deflation to have reached by that point, then liquidity is insufficient and deflation manifests. When the rate is the same or lower than the ATOM deflation rate, then there is sufficient liquidity and a proportional level of inflation. This means that if there is to ever be significant inflation, the Wu-Xia shadow rate has to be more deeply negative than the estimated ATOM deflation rate. This itself is impossible when the FF Rate is above zero, pinning the Wu-Xia shadow rate to the same.

Now, if technology is rising as a percentage of world GDP, this could mean that the progression of the ATOM deflation rate from –1% to –2% is an ongoing trend. The rate could similarly double again from –2% to –4%, and, amazingly, from –4% to –8% by the 2030s, merely by technology rising from the current 3% of GDP to 4% very soon, and then 8%, and beyond. This sounds extraordinary, but unless one thinks that technology will shrink as a share of GDP, it is the course we are presently on. The level of monetary expansion needed to truly generate inflation is thus far higher than most economists think.

This theory, while still somewhat speculative at the time of ATOM v1.0, has since seen a torrent of evidence pile up in its favor. The amount of cumulative 'QE' by all the central banks of the world is accelerating exponentially despite no apparent aggregate quota being agreed to by the banks, which is exactly the opposite of what the establishment of Economists has continued to predict. The more cumulative monetary creation is done without hyperinflation rearing its head, the more the ATOM thesis is strengthened with this accumulating proof. Each central bank is reacting to the conditions in its own country, but as the ATOM is global, the deflationary effect concentrates into countries with high technology density.

Even if one particular bank, like the US Federal Reserve, declared that it did not intend to conduct more QE (only to reverse that position shortly thereafter), other central banks moved to fill the gap, inadvertently ensuring that the combined total continues to rise. While the US Federal Reserve was still the laggard in terms of moving towards permanent and exponentially-rising QE, the coronavirus crisis forced them to do what they should have been doing anyway. On the seminal date of March 15, 2020, the Federal Reserve lowered the Fed Funds rate from 1.5% just days earlier to 0%, where it should have been all along, and then pledged to restart QE and to do it in more direct forms rather than just the purchases of Treasuries and Mortgage Backed Securities (MBSs), moving precisely in the direction recommended by this publication for years. Given the sheer magnitude of the position change the Federal Reserve was forced to undergo in a matter of days (whether they still understand the new economics of technology or not), it is safe to say that March 15, 2020 was when the ATOM genie fully escaped from its bottle, and the economics of technology began in earnest. I have henced named that date as the 'Netscape Moment' in Economics, after the original 'Netscape Moment' on August 9, 1995, where the IPO of Netscape was a catalyst for an acceleration of the Internet revolution. Similarly, March 15, 2020 is the day where ATOM economics were fully ratified.

Despite the most recent grand total of over $30 Trillion in monetary expansion as of 2020 ($14 Trillion more than when the first version of The ATOM was published), the crash in commodity prices even more emphatically buries since ATOM v1.0 the fears of inflation, 'peak oil', and 'a return to the gold standard' that incorrectly arose from outdated, pre-software assumptions about supply and demand. It is obvious that all this newly created money has merely offset deflation, even after the temporary coronavirus pandemic subsided. As structural deflation accelerates, the level of world QE has to keep rising and be more diffuse and broad than current programs.

Figure 2.

Major central banks: Total assets
(Trillion dollars, nsa)

Total of
Fed, ECB, BOJ, & PBOC (25.2)

Jun

Total assets of major central banks

Figure 3.

Major central banks: Total assets of FED, ECB, BOJ, & PBOC
(yearly percent change)

Latest (28.8)   Jun

Source: Haver analytics.   Yardeni research

While not every type of monetary creation has the same impact per dollar, the rising total is indicative of an all-important phenomenon which the Economics establishment has still been unwilling to comprehend, let alone accept. Note how the next chart bears an uncanny resemblance to the exponential curves found in the writings of Mr. Kurzweil and other futurists. If this exponentially rising monetary expansion is associated with the trend of technological deflation, then monetary expansion, far from ending, has to be made permanent across all major world economies, be declared as such, and rise at a rapid rate each year. From the second chart, we see that the total amount of cumulative balance sheet addition also rises at an annual percentage rate much higher than simple

NGDP. It is apparent that the notion of ever selling purchased assets on central bank balance sheets back into the market (a reversal of monetary expansion) is entirely out of the question, making the balance sheet itself a moot concept.

So if all this newly created money does not cause inflation, is it utterly vanishing? On the contrary, the nature of technology is such that the liquidity is being metabolized by the ATOM. This increases the size and scope of the ATOM, which in turn demands more liquidity, which then produces yet more technology. This self-reinforcing process generates new productivity and economic growth, and is in fact an indicator of the macro economic growth trend seeking to return to the long-term trendline. Hence, this pattern of exponentially rising monetary expansion is itself the fuel that will keep the economic growth trend going. Over time, as technology becomes a sufficiently large portion of the economy, these two exponents will begin to merge. For this reason, there is a crucial prediction for the 2020s that I will put forth. The Economics establishment still thinks that the $23T in world monetary creation done up until December 31, 2019 will be unwound, effectively meaning that the amount of net monetary creation they predict will be -$23T, reducing balance sheets to zero. By contrast, it is obvious to me that this is another accelerating, exponential trend, and that the amount done in the 2020s will be an additional $100T or so, above the first $23T. This is before even adding the dimension of the monetary creation moving more towards cash sent directly to people, rather than the esoteric buying of Treasuries and MBSs. The first few months of 2020 certainly favor my prediction being the one that turns out to be correct.

As we will see in a later section, this perpetual process can be modified into an exceptionally good circumstance and inaugurate a new age of prosperity. Unfortunately, central banks of the world are very far from internalizing this ATOM-reinforcing paradigm on multiple levels. Current monetary easing programs lead to the money accumulating disproportionately in the largest banks and technology companies, leaving most other sectors and affiliated individuals missing out. This narrow concentration is part of the reason that the various world central bank actions are not as effective as they could be, and why their actions did not reach down to small businesses and individuals during the 2020 coronavirus crisis. Furthermore, none of them are ready for the unprecedented technological deflation that is soon to arrive from Artificial Intelligence.

The Economics of Artificial Intelligence: The first item in the earlier 'Panoply of Creative Destruction' list was AI, and it is important enough to warrant a full section devoted to it. While this publication will not enter the debate about what meets the increasingly stringent yet strangely fluid definition of AI, there are some crucial factors that most factions in the AI debate have failed to consider. This leaves them and those who follow their guidance unprepared for some of the largest ripple effects of AI.

AI is a field that gets insufficient credit for the advances that it has made. For one thing, each new threshold set for AI capabilities becomes a non-event once met (such as when an AI defeated the top-ranked chess player in 1997). Additionally, each major new AI advance gets reclassified into its own industry (autonomous vehicles, high-frequency trading, intelligent search engines, etc.), and is no longer counted as AI. These factors contribute to a broad underestimation of how pervasive early AI has already become, leading to a doubly-false narrative that AI is both job swallowing and has suddenly appeared out of nowhere.

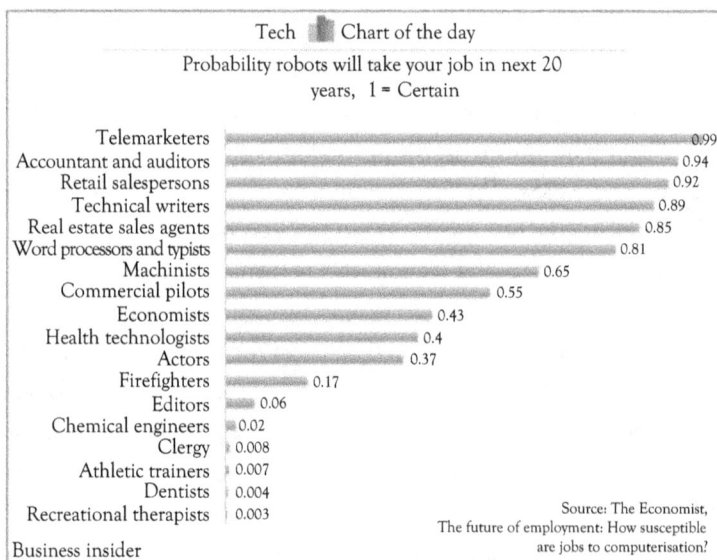

Tech   Chart of the day

Probability robots will take your job in next 20 years, 1 = Certain

Telemarketers	0.99
Accountant and auditors	0.94
Retail salespersons	0.92
Technical writers	0.89
Real estate sales agents	0.85
Word processors and typists	0.81
Machinists	0.65
Commercial pilots	0.55
Economists	0.43
Health technologists	0.4
Actors	0.37
Firefighters	0.17
Editors	0.06
Chemical engineers	0.02
Clergy	0.008
Athletic trainers	0.007
Dentists	0.004
Recreational therapists	0.003

Source: The Economist,
The future of employment: How susceptible
are jobs to computerisation?

Business insider

There has been a recent torrent of articles ranking jobs in relation to their vulnerability to AI replacement (see chart from Business Insider built via

The Economist). This is a very incomplete oversimplification of the topic. Even those who recognize that past technological disruptions have always created an increase in net output and employment somehow worry that this time, the speed of replacement and widening skill mismatch chasm portend to massive dislocation and permanent unemployment. This is not only an incorrect prediction that fails to recognize how much more output will be generated per unit of input, but it distracts the debate from the other side of the coin. The simple fact is that for each job that AI can perform at lower cost than a human employee, an entrepreneur can save that payroll expense relative to a previous cost structure, enabling either widening margins or more hires elsewhere. Hence, job displacement through AI can only increase new business formation by the same or greater proportion. That is, if overt human meddling (whether through government or otherwise) does not unwittingly prevent this process from occurring.

An article in Wired by Kevin Kelly from a few years ago discusses why AI was back in the spotlight at the time after over twenty years of hibernation. Common topics include what various subcategories of AI could be like, and how it may augment human abilities in some areas while be an invisible in others, becoming a utility of sorts within a new status quo. I generally agree with this conclusion, but as far as AI competing with human jobs, these articles overlook the largest factor of all—the AI's borderless and untaxable nature.

Whether an AI performs only the most repetitive work, or has capabilities that surpass that of any human, it can operate from anywhere. The AI can be owned by a corporation located in the most tax-friendly place available, changing its country of domicile in an instant if necessary. The AI does not care about the weather, commute distances, parking spaces, and holidays. The AI is not governed by cost-of-living constraints beyond the minimal costs of running the hardware that hosts the AI. By contrast, human output is taxed at marginal rates that often exceed 50%, and the higher-paying human jobs are concentrated in very expensive areas.

Hence, the primary handicap to human competitiveness in the face of AI is not the raw output of the human, but the taxation of the human's productivity, and the high operating costs that a human incurs. This additionally means that a high tax on higher-income workers are more likely to hasten their marginalization in the face of AI. The state, instead of increasing taxes on productivity, has to figure out a way to move revenue sourcing in the opposite direction. Tax immunity means that AI enables technology to start tightening the screws on government revenue as well, which we will elaborate on in the next chapter. This process will be irreversible long before governments even notice the cumulative revenue erosion.

But as enormous of a factor as unfavorable taxation and megacity living costs may be, they are not the only reasons human workers may be uncompetitive with AI. Human employees demand medical, dental, and vision coverage from their employers. Humans have to interrupt their work several times a day for various aspects of personal maintenance. The AI that can do the work of a thousand humans can reside on hardware that fits in a single room in a remote location and consumes just a few hundred dollars of electricity per month. By contrast, each of those thousand human workers requires a house, a cubicle or office, a car, roads for the car, a food production chain, schools for their children, etc. If that were not enough, human workplaces have recently come under siege by extortionists demanding various politicizations of hiring, even at the cost of company productivity. When taking all these disadvantages into account, it may appear that humans stand no chance whatsoever, and is the basis for many pessimistic statements about the impact of AI, including from Bill Gates and Elon Musk. If even these luminaries of technology are apprehensive about what AI may do to human well-being, is this the beginning of the end?

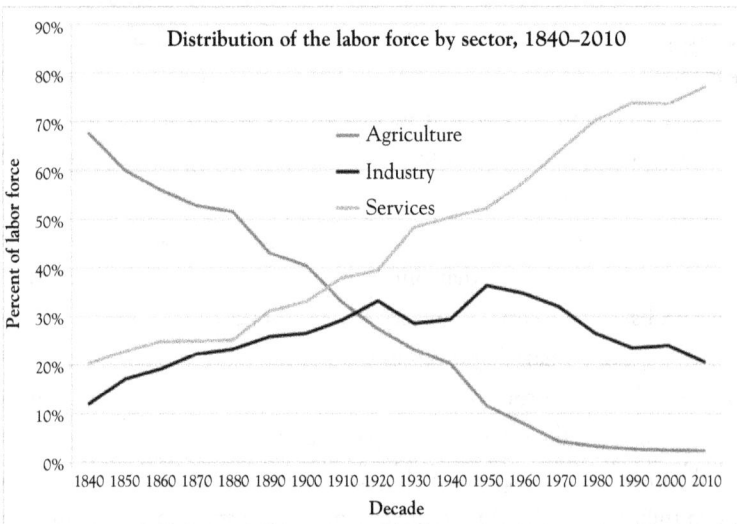

Distribution of the labor force by sector, 1840–2010

One way to approach the concept is to recognize that technological displacement of jobs within the process of productivity improvements has already been underway for centuries. This is enabled by continuous human usage of new technologies as they emerge. There was once a time when 70% of the US population worked in agriculture, but now just 2% of the population work in agriculture. Despite this, there is far higher production of calories per person *and* far greater overall employment in the economy (mostly indoors). This fact reveals how this methodology is somewhat inaccurate as what has occurred is a productivity revolution in agriculture. Job creation in other sectors is a subsequent byproduct of the productivity revolution, which then moved on to manufacturing, services, and knowledge work. Not accounting for productivity creates the misleading impression that the agricultural jobs of the 19th century were just as good as the services jobs of 2020. We know that there are a variety of objective and subjective measures proving this to not be the case.

Real manufacturing output per U.S. worker, 1947 to 2011

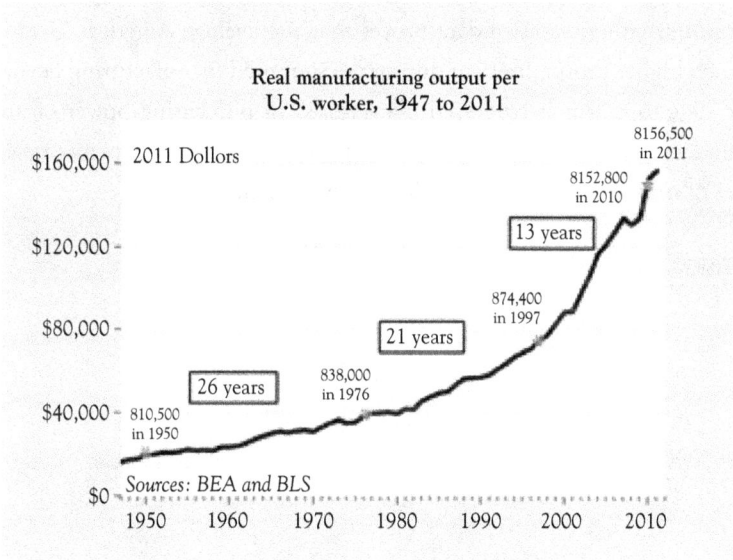

Instead, the most accurate measurement technique is to chart input costs relative to output generated, and observe that human jobs tend to sprout up around this output over time in the process of managing, transacting, and consuming it. Continuing the prior example about agricultural employment and output going in opposite directions, the next sector, manufacturing, has been the subject of countless agonizing over the last 45 years of American economic media coverage. Everyone knows that manufacturing jobs have vanished and some categories of the working class have seen hardship. Yet the overlooked fact remains that US manufacturing output *never stopped rising*, as per this chart from Prof. Perry (that parabolic exponential curve shape appears yet again). Advances in automation have greatly increased output per worker, and shortening time between doublings of output is yet another example of exponential and accelerating productivity. The running joke in these circles is that the continuation of these trends implies an imminent outcome where the US produces $10 Trillion of manufactured goods while employing just one person. Additionally, despite the perception that US manufacturing jobs have moved to China, the reality is that China has lost even more manufacturing jobs than the US, while simultaneously increasing their own output <u>through robotic replacement of human workers</u>. Anecdotes about job loss from manufacturing can easily be used to whip up emotion, but comprehensive data proves that the average American lives in much higher prosperity than during the supposed manufacturing heyday of 1946–69. This is true even if measured in purchasing power of any standard manufactured goods, without even counting how many categories of manufactured products did not exist then.

Ability to automate, % of time spent on activities[1] that can be automated by adapting currently demonstrated technology

O'Net 2014, McKinserv&Co

As the ATOM transformed the agricultural and manufacturing sectors, the service sector was the beneficiary. But the ATOM is now at the service sector's doorstep, and services will undergo an acceleration of the churning process that removes tasks (and some jobs) in the lower rungs to create new tasks and jobs in the higher rungs. This chart from a McKinsey study indicates that it is not a binary outcome of a job surviving or being eliminated, but rather the percentage of tasks per job that can be automated with existing technology. The study estimates that 45% of contemporary tasks can be automated with existing AI, without even waiting for future advancements in AI. This data indicates that there are already many examples of two jobs that can be compressed into one with perhaps a higher salary than either. It additionally indicates that unless you have adopted as much AI as is fully possible for your profession, you are or soon will be a laggard. Fears over 'outsourcing' have been a distraction, since by the time a job can easily be outsourced to a low-cost country, the job is already on the verge of displacement by AI. But most importantly, this chart indicates *which functions an entrepreneur can now have done at a fraction of the previous cost* through use of an AI instead of a human. Indeed, some entrepreneurs may see charts like this, select which functions are the most completely assimilated into AI, and build a business entirely from only the functions AI can perform. Once thousands or even millions of entrepreneurs migrate in this direction, there is far more output generated per human. Within this process, the focus should be on the much higher aggregate output that AI will soon generate.

Fundamentally, if AI can produce the same $10 Trillion of economic output that today takes 100 million workers, then those 100 million people can transition (with varying levels of ease) to produce an additional $10 Trillion of output elsewhere. Hence, a total of $20 Trillion is now generated across the same number of people. Note the difference between 'output generated' and 'jobs created', a distinction that often escapes many participants in this debate, yet will soon be too pronounced to overlook. It will not be uncommon to see new types of small businesses earning $10 Million/year in annual revenue with only three highly-paid human employees. Human + AI teaming will be seen as the obvious end result of AI, with those who predicted massive human unemployment on account of AI being unceremoniously dumped into the dustbin of history, where the languish next to the 'peak oil' and 'QE causes inflation' predictor Hall of Shame.

This effect is certain to broaden the breadth and depth of globalization. What many a globalization pundit gets wrong is the discussion of outsourcing, as if jobs are finite and employers are wrong to seek lower costs. In reality, by the time any job category can be outsourced en masse, it is already very near to replacement by automation. But from the perspective of the employer or entrepreneur, the situation is inverted. If a highly-paid professional in an advanced economy can be replaced by an AI, that same capability is now available in backwater countries that did not even have any such human professionals before. The expertise gap between two economies may narrow in some areas, and widen in others, as the ability to harness AI will be the greatest determinant of competitiveness. Fountains of productivity may erupt in the most unexpected places. As a widening array of tasks can be performed through AI, new business models from agile entrepreneurs will keep emerging.

Not everyone, of course, is built for entrepreneurship or is at a stage in life where it can be entertained on short notice. In addition, our educational system is not structured to teach a child to think like an entrepreneur—quite the opposite, in fact. Therefore, the practical obstacle in this theoretical ascension of AI is the widening skills mismatch across the human workforce, both vertical and horizontal. Humans are not reprogrammable the way computers are, where one program can be uninstalled to make way for another to be installed in mere minutes. As of early 2020, there are over 7 million open positions in the US according to the Bureau of Labor Statistics (BLS), even as several million people remain unemployed, some of them for years. A mid-career accountant or dermatologist cannot simply become a software engineer, let alone an experienced one, after just three months of training. Even when rapid retraining is possible, employers have to adapt correspondingly and accept the retraining as valid, or this will discourage other prospective employees. The subjective cost of stress derived from career uncertainty should not be dismissed. These, along with the aforementioned squeeze that AI will inflict on the tax base of all high-tax locations, are challenges for which I present a solution later in this paper.

Lastly, there is a recurring fear that AI will subjugate or even exterminate humans over resource competition, as depicted in many science fiction works. I believe that this is not a risk, since AI does not consume the same fuels that humans do other than electricity, which itself is becoming cheaper as described earlier. However, there is reason to believe that AI might elect to force humans into more productive/tech-advancing behavior, as determined by the goals of the AI. How this unfolds remains to be seen.

The Tyranny of Insufficient Nominal GDP: A curious thing happened several decades ago, when metrics to measure the output of a nation were being devised. The concepts of Gross National Product (GNP), and later Gross Domestic Product (GDP), measured economic growth by consumption and investment, without particularly high emphasis on productivity. Unfortunately, this meant that high inflation could make many economic statistics appear better than true economic conditions warranted. While some bouts of high inflation were due to one-time demographic factors (such as in the US during the 1970s), others were due to outright mismanagement. Some infamous examples were deliberate actions by corrupt governments.

In reaction to the effect that inflation occasionally had on boosting GDP without true increases in living standards, a mechanism to deduct inflation from raw (Nominal) GDP was devised. This inflation-adjusted GDP was given the credibility-enhancing prefix of 'Real'. Real GDP worked well for a while, as it stripped out inflation, and thus was more closely tied to true gains in productivity and hence living standards. However, economists got carried away with Real GDP, which is only useful if measured over lengthy periods of time. Measuring Real GDP on a quarterly basis has no value outside of academia, yet it is headline news in the financial media each of the three or more times it is released and revised for a given quarter.

At the same time, Nominal GDP is not even reported by the financial media. If someone wants to see an official report on the latest Nominal US GDP, they have to go to a government website and download an Excel file. Hence, the release for NGDP does not show up in Google searches, so the notion of using the data is that much further from occurring to anyone. By training generations of economists, journalists, and financiers to look only at Real GDP, *there is a huge cognitive dissonance about the fact that most other economic indicators are tied to Nominal GDP, as is the performance of every investment vehicle*. Real estate, mutual funds, art, wine, and corporate valuations certainly rise in tandem with NGDP, not 'Real' GDP, and given how most real estate is highly leveraged, this is critically important. Major economic indicators like auto sales, home sales, job growth, and retail sales are similarly tied to more to NGDP than Real GDP. This chart of NGDP represents the trend all the way until the last quarter before the coronavirus pandemic.

US nominal GDP, quarterly

Inflation is similarly viewed through an outdated lens. Trauma from decades-old predicaments gave rise to economic assumptions that are starting to become obsolete. The high inflation of the 1970s created a herd of 'inflation hawks' who continued to overrate the imagined horrors of less-than-terrifying inflation rates of 4%. Intellectually lazy metrics like the 'misery index' emerged (a straight sum of the inflation rate and unemployment rate). Such a metric not only presumes that a 1% rise in the inflation rate causes as much hardship as a 1% rise in the unemployment rate, but implies that non-technological deflation is a good thing. A society with a 5% unemployment rate and 3% inflation rate is seen as no worse than a society with a 9% unemployment rate at –1% inflation rate, when in fact the latter climate is vastly worse for almost every socioeconomic class. A society that has steered a majority of households into acquiring debt to purchase real estate on leverage should be vastly more worried about deflation than inflation, even if 4% inflation were to appear. Sadly, this sort of metric produced by 'egghead' PhD Economists works its way through policy-level thought, with no accounting of the nuances of hardship that average people live under.

This brings us to an extension of the prior discussion about how deflation can be problematic. <u>Some observers have noted that recent economic
recoveries in the US have gotten progressively weaker</u>, and that this has
constrained job growth ('jobless recoveries'). But these observers still focus
on how US Real GDP has fallen from 3% to 2% annual growth rates, over-
looking the far more worrisome shadow trend of NGDP falling from 7% to
4% annual growth rates. <u>There is evidence that insufficient NGDP growth
momentum contributes to financial crises</u>, which are the more common
type of recession in the current era, rather than manufacturing-based production recessions. It was assumed that low inflation did not constrain Real
GDP, but apparently both inflation and Real GDP are trending lower in
tandem, suggesting that the two have become correlated to each other.

Think of sufficient NGDP growth rates as being the speed at which
a bicycle can move forward smoothly, and how insufficient speed makes
the bicycle wobbly. An important component of NGDP is the concept of
the Velocity of Money (VM), or how often the same dollar is transacted
per unit time. Sluggish NGDP growth has greatly slowed VM, which in
turn is a further retardant to future NGDP. This vicious cycle is difficult
to break, for when the economic commentariat fixates exclusively on Real
GDP, there is an underestimation of how much VM has in fact slowed
with the NGDP erosion.

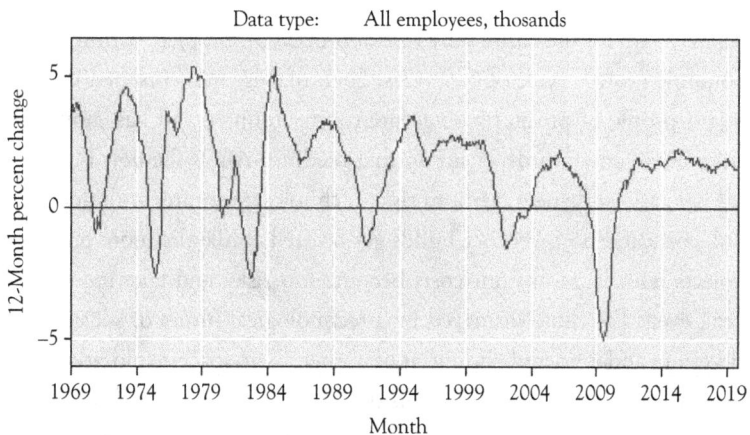

Corporations make decisions on capital expenditure and hiring based
on the expected growth trajectories of revenue and profits, which are a

function of NGDP, not 'Real' GDP. No corporation reports its quarterly results in both nominal and inflation-adjusted terms, so academics are baffled as to why businesses are not hiring or spending just because Real GDP has decelerated slightly from 3% to 2%. As we can see from this BLS chart, percentage job growth is indeed trending lower in tandem with NGDP growth. Paradoxically, Nominal GDP is more 'real' (and certainly more relevant in real-time) than what is termed as Real GDP.

Additionally, insufficient NGDP has greatly constricted the technology industry, and hence technological progress. For one thing, the valuation multiples are not as high as they could be under a higher NGDP economy, as earnings growth rates would be higher. While safer value stocks perhaps saw their forward P/E ratios compress from 12 to 10, high-growth companies saw their forward P/E ratios compress from 60 to 30. This leads to the practice of some corporations (such as Comcast) prioritizing a dividend payout ahead of innovation, since dividends are valuable in a low-inflation climate.

You may think technology startup valuations are high now (most people only notice them at the topmost years of the cycle, not during the other three-fourths of the business cycle). But even these levels are less than what it naturally would be under the more optimal NGDP growth rate. These lower valuation multiples lengthen the duration from inception to liquidity for many tech startups, keeping investor money illiquid for longer. This makes it hard for the entire start-to-exit process to complete within a single economic growth cycle of 6–9 years. Such malaise has worsened the risk/reward profile of prospective venture capital rounds, and has moved the entire curve downwards, ensuring that medium-risk is the new high-risk, and low-risk is the new medium risk. Technology ventures with negligible sunk costs and no inventory builds get favored, while the more profound projects with large upfront costs become too risky and take too long to break even. For those dismayed by a technological future of social media addiction and underwhelming apps rather than space exploration, this is precisely the reason for that. Aside from Elon Musk, Jeff Bezos, and Google, very few entities are willing to risk the upfront costs of ambitious ventures such as private spaceflight and electric cars.

Funding of lower capex 'fluff' at the expense of more serious technology reduces long-term, inflation-offsetting productivity gains. Over time, technological progress slows and gets further and further behind its long-term trendline. At present, my proprietary calculations estimate that after the 2001 technology bust, technological progress has been at only 60–70% of its natural rate, due to insufficient NGDP. This happens to be why many technological predictions made in 1999–2000 for circa 2020, including by Ray Kurzweil, are consistently 6–9 years behind schedule across many seemingly unrelated subsectors of technology. The impedance is holistic and pervasive. There is thus a tremendous opportunity cost involved in this excessive fear of even 3% inflation which has not been seen in two decades, a fear originated from conditions that can no longer arise in a world were technologically-deflating products are prevalent.

Some members of the Federal Reserve have indicated that monetary policy should target NGDP instead of inflation, and that the NGDP target should be 5%. This policy, if formalized, is a huge step in the right direction, but the target NGDP should be 6–7%, for economists will be surprised to see that even such NGDP leads to just 2%/year inflation. Thus, their precious 'Real' GDP will in fact register a superb 4–5% growth rate, or twice what we have seen for most of the 21st century to date. Higher NGDP means more technology which keeps inflation low, even at that higher NGDP, which produces more technology. This virtuous cycle can begin if the current vicious cycle is decisively attacked and broken.

Equity Valuations as Harbingers of Future ATOM Growth: There is a robust and highly visible indicator that is corroborative of the centuries-proven accelerating rate of economic growth, and how that concentrates within technology. That indicator is the percentage of equity market capitalization comprised of companies selling products experiencing rapid technological deflation. How much can it reveal to us about future technological diffusion and resultant growth acceleration?

The S&P 500 is a broad equity index in the US weighted by market capitalization (unlike the Dow Industrials Average, which knowledgeable investors give far less importance to than the S&P 500). The S&P 500 contains about 93–95% of the market cap of the entire US equity market. With almost half of the profits of S&P 500 companies derived from overseas, it is a very comprehensive index. There was a time when companies categorized as part of the technology sector were not selling products that deflated in price so quickly ('high-tech' was just electrical equipment and motor vehicles). But once semiconductors and software started to advance in sophistication and scope, business models built around such rapidly deflating products proliferated and some became incredibly profitable. At first, only one or two such companies became large enough to be included in the S&P 500 index. More followed them as computing began to percolate throughout the economy. Even after the technology bust of 2001–03, technology companies returned to being among the most valuable and highest-earning in the entire market.

As of 2020, the technology sector constitutes about 25% of the market cap, and contributes 22% of the earnings of the S&P 500. The most purely deflating and materially efficient product category of all, software, emerged as the dominant product category sold by the most profitable companies. The other essentials of computing such as semiconductors and storage also feature prominently. Biotechnology is another subsector built around price-deflating products slowly penetrating the healthcare and pharmaceutical fortress. One might think that rapidly deflating product prices would have an adverse impact on revenue, life-cycle management, and inventory, yet the companies producing and selling these products generate 20% of the profits of the entire S&P 500. Within these new business models resides a window into the future of the entire economy, for these economic fundamentals, forged in the crucible of tech companies, are propagating outwards.

Companies established enough to be part of the S&P 500 have a market valuation derived from an expectation of future earnings, with a Net Present Value (NPV) calculation applied to appropriately weight the near future higher than the more distant future. As the P/E ratio of the technology sector is no higher than the broader index despite the higher earnings growth rates of the sector, eventually the price-to-sales ratio of the technology sector may converge to that of the rest of the S&P 500 as well. This could occur from either direction, whether through technology revenue rising greatly, or the price of other sectors rising to synchronize their price-to-sales ratio to that of the technology sector. Remember that some current technology companies may no longer categorized as such in the future, even if their products are of a rapidly deflating nature. The NPV method and standard discount rates estimate this time horizon to be about 10–15 years, for any years further away than that would have too small of a weight under the NPV calculation. We hence have an approximate timeline for this rise in structural valuation, even amidst the booms and busts that will certainly occur along the way.

While this methodology is highly speculative, this coincidentally is along the same timeline where the technological percentage of world GDP is anticipated to reach 10% or higher, and provides independent support to that prediction. This is quite consistent with the exponential, not linear, deflationary trend we are seeing in exponentially rising world QE totals. The trend we have seen in both the computing and economic growth sections of this publication is further supported, and we are indeed very near to the 'knee' of the curve.

Do you remember the earlier mention of nation-state risk to exponential, accelerating economic growth? It is time to elaborate on what that means, and what forward-thinking governments can and must do to manage risk.

CHAPTER 5

Characteristics of the Accelerating TechnOnomic Medium (ATOM)

Tying all of these observations and analyses together, the comprehensive definition of what the Accelerating TechnOnomic Medium, or 'ATOM' is and how it behaves can be summarized as follows, and in the attached Powerpoint:

- Technological change, despite occasional deviations from the trendline, is exponential and accelerating. There is centuries of data to ratify this.
- Economic growth is driven by technology, and has always been exponential and accelerating. Half of all world economic growth that has ever occurred has happened after 1998, and that is even if you use the limited metric of 'Real' GDP. If one uses the more accurate metric of equity indices, half of all world economic growth that has ever happened has been after 2010.
- Technological disruptions generally displace one set of industries and workers, while creating more wealth elsewhere. More wealth is created than destroyed, but often in different places.
- Technology invariably finds a way to displace a commodity, organization, or industry that is resistant to technology or otherwise obstructs the progress of technology, whether directly or very indirectly.
- No industry is immune to technological disruption, and industries that resist this process merely experience a sharper disruption at a later date.

- Technological disruptions tend to be interconnected with each other, and a rapid disruption in one area exerts a strengthening force on other nascent disruptions.
- Artificial Intelligence (AI) will eliminate many jobs, but will also create a vast category of new business models and careers. Media coverage of AI focuses only on the former effect, ignoring the latter.
- Artificial Intelligence always creates more jobs than it eliminates, as long as the government does not make it too hard to be an entrepreneur.
- Technology is inherently deflationary. While this effect was too minor to matter until recently, with technologically-deflating products now comprising 3% of annual world GDP and rising at an exponential rate, this deflation now has significant (and still rising) macroeconomic effects. AI in particular will be exceptionally deflationary.
- An increasingly outdated focus on 'Real' GDP, instead of Nominal GDP, has led to a primary cause of economic sluggishness and weak job creation being overlooked. It is erroneous to assume that low inflation does not correspondingly decrease Real GDP growth.
- The Federal Reserve should aim for an NGDP target, rather than an inflation target. Inflation will still be just 2–3% within a 6–7% NGDP environment.
- The central banks of the world have been generating new money in a pattern that is rising exponentially, contrary to what they expected. This is due to the need to offset technological deflation.
- Despite talk of QE and other expansion programs ending, they cannot end, nor can they even fail to increase the amount of QE each year. The coronavirus crisis jolted central banks into the correct (i.e. higher) trajectory of QE, even if establishment Economists do not understand why.
- World monetary creation by central banks has to rise 16–24% year over year to keep inflation in the 2–3%/yr range.

- March 15, 2020, was effectively the 'Netscape Moment' in Economics, as the US Federal Reserve conceded defeat in their attempts to reverse all prior monetary creation, and instead caught up to where they should have been all along.

The next question becomes how the governments of the world should transition to this new reality. Policy inertia and status quo bias are the default situation for most countries. This has introduced a variety of imminent risks.

CHAPTER 6

Current Government Policy Will Soon Be Ineffective

America will never be destroyed from the outside. If we falter and lose our freedoms, it will be because we destroyed ourselves.

—Abraham Lincoln

Success is a lousy teacher. It seduces smart people into thinking they cannot lose.

—Bill Gates

We are finally in a time where insufficient awareness of the accelerating rates of technological change and economic growth has tangible costs to governments and the citizens under them. The incorrect approach can lead to deflationary crises, while the correct approach can monetize this acceleration to a degree that lifts all boats. Continuing with legacy economic, fiscal, and regulatory policies in an era where the ATOM is now more advanced is analogous to continuing to feed baby food to a person who has long since outgrown it and now requires an adult diet.

Most of the next section is specific to the United States, but other developed countries face most of the same circumstances, and require very similar solutions.

Everything About the Current US Tax Code is Problematic: The current US Federal tax code involves layer upon layer of taxes and exemptions that were each enacted without sufficient holistic assessment of how the new provision fits into the existing tax code, since each was a secret favor purchased through lobbying. The outcome is a labyrinthine morass of esoteric gobbledygook that combines the worst of all worlds, and greatly obstructs the US economy from creating jobs to the extent that it is a miracle jobs are still being created.

First, consider the tortuous filing and collection process. The tax code has layers of contradictory types of taxes, and a vast range of loopholes and legal shelters to avoid each of those types of taxes for those wealthy enough to hire the appropriate tax lawyers. There are so many such loopholes that some have only three attorneys in the entire country specializing in that particular tax structure, each charging five-digit fees or higher to create the structure. Add to that the practice of private rulings, where a particular person can petition the IRS for a specific case interpretation unique to that individual and unusable by anyone else. This reaction to tax complexity is against the grain of uniform laws. As a result, not only has it become impossible to tax the very wealthiest people, but the cost of compliance with such a complex tax code itself wastes billions of hours of productive time each year, amounting to as much as 20% of the tax ultimately collected. This should be the easiest aspect of the tax debate on which to gain consensus, yet it is the least discussed.

But that is just the beginning, for once a person or corporation figures out what they owe, the tax code itself is structured such that the most productive work of all is what precisely falls under the most onerous taxes. The United States has one of the most progressive (i.e. top-heavy) income tax codes in the world, and it has become even more progressive in recent times, with talk of skewing that even further. The tax code is at the point where even slight increases in tax rates invariably crushes productivity by a disproportionate magnitude, particularly when a state or local tax rate rises independent of any assessment of where that fits in relation to the Federal tax obligation. Whatever you tax more, you get less of, and productivity is far too precious to be taxed at the current rates of up to 55% for higher income people in California, New York City, and other higher-tax localities. These locations attracted the highest taxation because they also happen to be the greatest fountains of potential productivity.

Percentage of federal personal income tax paid by earners (1980–2017)

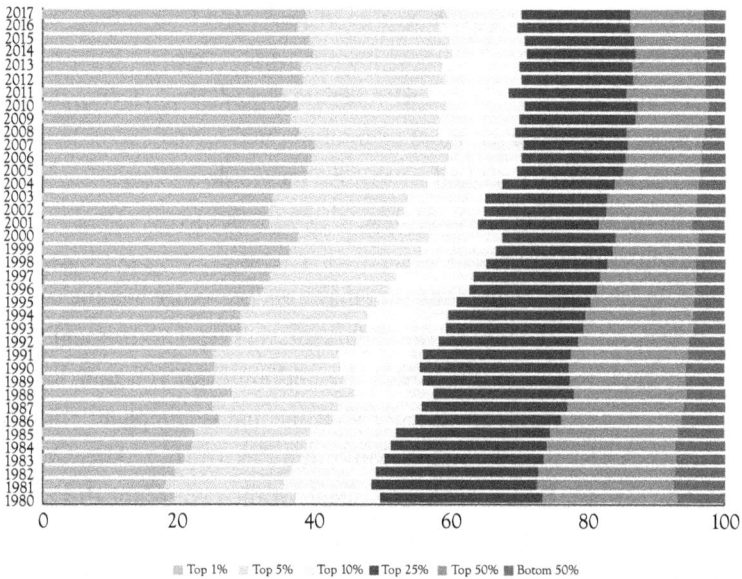

Top 1%   Top 5%   Top 10% ■ Top 25% ■ Top 50% ■ Botom 50%

Once you exclude the 10,000 or so ultra-wealthy households and their custom tax structures, we see that the upper-middle-class and the near-wealthy are the most heavily taxed people in America. The chart on the left reveals how tilted the brackets have become. The top quintile pays the most disproportionate share of taxes, even though many of these households live in those same high-tax states and cities which additionally happen to have expensive housing costs. As explained before, the least-understood aspect of the tax code amidst the debate about 'fair' tax rates is the fact that increasing the tax rate does not capture taxes from the ultra-wealthy (the top 0.01%). The burden instead falls on the upper-middle class, which results in a perverse penalty on some of the most productive workers. Unfortunately, most political posturing does not distinguish between those in the 81st percentile and those in the 99.99th percentile, which leads to tax changes that end up having the opposite effect from what was ostensibly intended. The tax brackets hence are *not* progressive, since the top 0.01% pay the lowest rate of all.

The next problem is the Social Security tax, which unlike the progressive payroll tax, is *regressive*. The employee and employer jointly pay 12.4% of the employee's salary up to a cap of $137,700 in 2020, as an additional tax, split equally between the two. As this is combined with ordinary income tax, it creates a series of peaks and valleys that complicate what each additional dollar of income will be taxed at. If both ordinary income tax and Social Security Tax are flawed, then levying the two of them in tandem is even more counterproductive than either by itself. While the employer pays half of this for an employee (resulting in the salary being accordingly reduced), a self-employed person pays the full tax himself. The fact that this is yet another separate category of taxation, against which some deductions that may apply to other income do not apply, adds even yet more to the nightmare. Lastly, if you thought you were finished, you are really only at the midpoint, for you now have to do an entirely new process to see if your income is compliant with the second tax code, the Alternative Minimum Tax (AMT). After you do both calculations, then you pay the higher of the two. All of this results in a situation where the 'published' tax rate and actual tax rate are widely divergent, and force too many decisions to be based on tax optimization, which in turn become suboptimal decisions for growth.

Finally, lest anyone think their income is not, and will never be, high enough for tax complexity to affect them, remember that employers have to file corporate tax returns, so these costs reduce the number of jobs they can create. It is logical to conclude that an unemployed person with no income bears a huge cost of tax complexity, simply by the hidden viscosity consuming the resources potential employers may have used to hire an employee.

Now, I am going to extend sympathy to a group of people that no one else extends sympathy to—the Internal Revenue Service. What is overlooked by the public is that the IRS has to enforce a tax code that is given to them by the US Congress, which, over time, has become a humanly impossible job.

Congress makes endless modifications to the tax code for purposes ranging from political reciprocity for wealthy donors, to electorally-geared rhetoric designed to court a target demographic. The IRS has very little input into these modifications, yet the IRS nonetheless has to enforce the ever-mutating tax code given to them. The President and Congress may authorize an increase IRS staffing, but even this is deep into the zone of futility, because as the complexity of the code rises, the number of auditors needed does not rise in proportion, but rather as a *square* of the complexity increase. If the code becomes twice as complex, it takes four times as many examiners to audit all returns, ensuring that complexity can eventually surpass any realistic staffing increase or improved training of examiners. Additionally, a tax expert who is extremely well-versed in important parts of the tax code can earn a seven-digit income by working at an elite law firm or as the head of tax strategy and structure for a large, multinational corporation. The IRS has little chance of hiring or retaining the few such experts that exist while bound by government salary grades. AI is not the solution to the processing of tax returns either, as any AI significantly more advanced than TurboTax will keep arriving at the conclusion that the tax code itself is the bottleneck to productivity.

Ultimately, the cumulative frictions of tax complexity and excessive taxation of productivity are a huge burden on all workers and entrepreneurs, yet hard for the public to visualize as there is no window into an alternative universe of simple, light taxation. We may be accustomed to this code, but the effect on the US economy is analogous to forcing a person to breathe with only one lung.

Conventional Wisdom on Monetary Expansion is Flawed: As of 2020, there are two fundamental problems with the way the Federal Reserve has created money over the last decade to offset deflation, the source of which is still not being correctly attributed to technology. The first problem is the belief that each round of QE will be the final one. The second problem is that it is done in a very indirect and convoluted way that disproportionately concentrates the QE money in very few hands. This current approach to expansion leaves the US economy unequipped to deal with the next major recession and financial crisis.

In the US, the Federal Reserve creates money by purchasing treasuries of various maturities, as well as mortgage-backed securities (MBSs), and holding them on the balance sheet. The purchase of treasury debt by the Federal Reserve enables the US Government to lower the interest rate on the debt it issues, so that it can spend more than it collects in taxes.

The belief that the assets will be sold back has induced a selection that only the most credit-worthy buyers would prefer (namely the US, Chinese, and Japanese governments, and the largest banks), hence concentrating purchases in just these assets. Unfortunately, this sort of artificial reduction of yields favors two asset classes—real estate and the equities of the largest corporations through share repurchases financed by issuing corporate debt. If we exclude the effect of international monetary expansion on US assets for the time being, we can see that no other asset type is nearly as equipped to convert Federal Reserve bond buying into price increases. So these two assets rise and fall in price in direct tandem with monetary expansion, while other formerly correlated assets underperform.

Above and beyond the unsustainable distortion that occurs by producing QE money in such a narrowly concentrated manner, monetary expansion with the overt goal of inflating asset prices is itself an ineffective and unsuitable tactic for uplifting the prosperity of average people. In fact, it makes average people much more vulnerable to short-term market volatility than ever before, which creates a long-term milieu of anxiety.

The problem, in a nutshell, is that about 80% of the American population simply does not have the ability to accumulate a substantial net worth (say, several years of living expenses in liquid assets). To accomplish this requires a diverse set of character traits and skills, such as portfolio management, business-cycle awareness, advanced tax code knowledge, deferred gratification, and the utmost importance of having more than one stream of income. It is quite unfair to expect all households to be savvy to these various factors that determine net worth, especially when nothing of this sort is taught in the formal K–12 school system. This toolbox of skills is uncommon, which is why we often see people with high income yet little or no net worth, even if they weren't flamboyant spendthrifts; they just could not sidestep the recession properly.

For this reason, inflating the prices of a few select assets is not the way to improve working class, middle class, and even upper-middle-class prosperity. It does not even benefit all wealthy people, but merely the small fraction of those who happen to be positioned closest to the central bank monetary spigot. This greatly muddles the picture regarding whether a fortune was generated via entrepreneurship or just the connectedness of a crony. While there are sporadic popular protests against entities disproportionately accumulating QE money, this situation is not yet receiving as much populist ire as it soon will. This is because the other asset class being inflated, real estate, has lulled the average household into a stupor of complacency sustained by the vapors of their home equity gains.

The US is in a Real Estate Trap: Conventional wisdom has beatified the status of residential real estate as an absolute must for anyone who can remotely manage to purchase it; an asset class that somehow transcends mere financial properties to become an indicator of a person's self-worth. To question the sacred article of faith that a home always rises in value can get you socially blacklisted, even after the 2008 real estate bust. Some of this stems from the fact that until a century ago, land-owners were citizens with many special privileges (such as voting rights) unavailable to the landless. This made real estate the most visible demarcation of social class, and even the basis of many surnames. Old beliefs are durable, and even people who readily accept that commercial real estate is governed by the same economic fundamentals as other asset classes nonetheless insist that the addition of a kitchen and bathroom(s) somehow exempts the property from the invisible hand of market forces. For this reason, residential homes have become deeply entangled in the politics of economic conditions, and in turn, with the Federal Reserve's monetary actions.

Decades of marketing has manipulated the emotional aspect of home ownership to convince Americans that they 'own' a house even if they have borrowed 80% or more of the price under relatively inclement legal terms. In reality, one only owns the dwelling they occupy if the mortgage payments are completed and 100% of the property is owned by the occupants, for if a mortgaged house misses a couple of payments, the mortgage holder will soon discover how few ownership rights he truly has. Furthermore, most US single-family homes are constructed from materials that deteriorate after about 50 years, a reality reflected in the tax code for commercial real estate depreciation schedules. This precludes the possibility of the structure itself rising in inherent value. In addition, nonpayment of property taxes can lead to liens on the home, and outright forfeiture, even if the amount owed is a small fraction of the home's value. Despite all this, the aura of emotion that surrounds home ownership endures.

But as finance evolved, mortgages have been securitized, and bond yields are being managed by the Federal Reserve. Home prices generally rise and fall with the S&P 500, removing the perceived relative stability that real estate is believed to have, particularly if it is leveraged, as most homes are. This means that real estate no longer represents diversification, as a person's stock portfolio and home decline in value at the same time as when their employment is at higher risk. Both situations are exacerbated by insufficient NGDP, <u>as described earlier</u>.

In the meantime, the Federal Reserve, in lowering mortgage rates through the purchase of long-term Treasuries and mortgage-backed securities (MBSs), is specifically seeking to inflate just one type of asset class and hope that buoys the entire economy. The problem is, any action that increases home *prices simultaneously triggers the construction of new homes, thus increasing supply.* Hence, any government action to boost home prices is like trying to fill a sieve with water.

Now that mortgage rates are have been at historic lows for many years (often under 3% today vs. 8% in the early 1990s), the one-time boost that home prices can get from rate declines is already incorporated. There is very little room for any further price gains from lowering of interest rates. Add to that the fact that property taxes are now as high as mortgage payments in many locations, and the exhaustion of rate-lowering as a technique to inflate home prices becomes even more obvious. Additionally, demographic factors are moving unfavorably towards housing. The imminent retirement of baby boomers and shortage of new first-time buyers (due to a combination of youth unemployment, exploding student loan debt, and a falling marriage rate), means that sellers will outnumber buyers for the first time since data collection began in the late 1940s. Overseas buyers are not numerous enough to affect the total US market, as they concentrate on a handful of specific locations. This is a situation that has never before been seen in the United States since detailed data collection began in 1948.

For these reasons, the current style of monetary policy is near the end of its efficacy. Under current trends, all housing-centric Federal Reserve action accumulates where it is needed the least, namely Silicon Valley and Manhattan, at the expense of the other 95% of the country's homes. No amount of further bond and MBS purchases by the Federal Reserve will be able to manage an orderly unwinding, since those approaches are effectively of a 'fighting the previous war' nature.

The Federal Reserve is Cornered: To review the previously established concepts, the Federal Reserve does not have to overcome just one ideological barrier, but five. The needed paradigm shifts are:

- Monetary expansion has to be permanent and declared as such, instead of one-off programs tied to an assumption that each one is the final round of Quantitative Easing. Actual increases in the Fed Funds rate will be very-short-lived. Ironically, Japan and the EU are already in a mode of de-facto perpetual monetary expansion, even though the US pioneered the idea.
- The Federal Reserve balance sheet can be retired, as the assets held on it will never be resold back into the market, and no such expectation needs to be sustained. The expectation itself has contributed to QE exclusively purchasing US Treasuries and MBSs, rather than riskier assets where the economic effect would have a higher multiplier.
- World money creation has to rise at 16–24% a year, possibly higher, to offset technological deflation and keep the Wu-Xia Shadow Rate in step with the size of the deflationary force.
- It matters relatively little which country's central bank commences a QE-type program, as the liquidity effect quickly flows across the rest of the world if the program is diffuse enough.
- Therefore, despite international monetary action, US programs can no longer be concentrated in just Treasuries and MBSs. They have to be of a more direct, diffuse, and permanent nature.

If that were not enough of a summit to scale, the powers of the Federal Reserve are defined by Congress, and an expansion of Federal Reserve power will surely be a tough sell to the Senate and House at this time. Even if the majority of Congress were amenable to such a broadening, there may be Constitutional Amendments involved. Hence, the debate and legislative drafting process could be lengthy and hostile, and will only be expedited when a crisis is already underway. Barring a political miracle, the Federal Reserve will not be granted the powers to generate money with the versatility and precision to alleviate the next storm.

The Federal Budget No Longer Has a Buffer: The current fiscal and monetary policies have created a distinct if uneven economic recovery, with the job market and S&P 500, as of 2020, both having improved to an extent not seen in decades. Unfortunately, many of the measures taken have only delayed certain inevitabilities. The current pattern of government spending has increased the debt levels to a point where there is no longer the customary buffer to cushion against the next disturbance.

At the peak of the 1990s economic cycle, there was actually a brief budget surplus as high as 2% of GDP from the unexpected surge in tax receipts from the equity boom of the era. The subsequent recession caused the customary revenue crash and hence a deficit. The peak of the next business cycle, in 2007, had a deficit of –1% of GDP. Observers considered this to be acceptable, but at the peak, *there needs to be a surplus*, if only to offset the deficit on the next recession. Sure enough, the crisis of 2008–09 saw huge deficits.

Writing this in early 2020, many of the classical indicators are pointing to us being at or near the cyclical peak. Yet, the deficit is still –4% of GDP. Key figures in the government consider this to be good, just because the deficit has been going down from the extreme depths of 2009. But for the deficit to be –3% during the best years of a business cycle, even after three rounds of QE, is quite alarming. How deep will the deficit be during the next crisis, given that the deficit is already so much higher than it was in 2007? Comparing peak years of each cycle is the only appropriate 'apples-to-apples' comparison, which people will soon be reminded of.

Federal deficit set to reach $1 trillion
The deficit for the current fiscal year will come to $960 billion.
In the next fiscal year, which begins Oct. 1, it will exceed $1 trillion.
Percentage of Gross domestic product

The chart indicates that the Congressional Budget Office (CBO) has projections for the next ten years. Apparently the expectation is that there will be only tightly managed deficits that cling to the long-term average, even though recessions see steep deficit explosions as tax revenue falls. What, exactly, about the last two recessions provides any reason to believe that the next 10 years will be so controlled? If the deficit in the best year of the business cycle is –3% of GDP, there is every reason to think that this is a continuing patterns of lower lows *and* lower highs. A deficit that surges to unanticipated heights has manifold perils, most importantly the reduction of tools available to the government to hasten a recovery.

It is not that the people at the CBO are incompetent—they are just trying to do their job as best they can. The problem is that the primary prerequisite of a recession is the elapsed time since the previous recession. This induces too many people, including government budgetary forecasters, to forget the periodicity of recessions, and become complacent. When that is combined with the other factors we have discussed, such as accelerating technological deflation, inadequate methods and continuity of monetary expansion, and the cornering of real estate as an asset class, the implications are ominous.

Crisis Narrowly Averted Many Times: As Nasim Taleb has explained in his books *The Black Swan* and *AntiFragile*, policies that aim to micromanage the smaller risks in a complex system greatly increase the risks from major events. This is unfortunately the situation that many governments have created today.

All of the aforementioned troubles continue to be postponed by increases in world monetary creation by one of the major central banks. I had originally thought a crisis could start in 2017, but the efforts of readers and myself to send notes to US Federal Reserve caused them to reverse their ill-conceived tightening and resume monetary creation, delaying the problem but not fully doing what is necessary to shift macroeconomics into the ATOM age. It became apparent the only way to avoid an eventual crisis completely *is either a paradigm shift in monetary creation to be more diffuse and exponential, or a massive decrease in regulation and tax complexity, preferably both* Barring this, the potential financial crisis was set to be at least as severe as the previous one (2008–09), and has the added obstacle of being resistant to the type of liquidity actions that worked in the previous instance. To fully illustrate how severe the situation may be, we have to consolidate the looming factors, which in combination are greater than the sum of them individually.

1. The central banks of the world are collectively not creating money in a manner that diffuses broadly, or in a quantity and permanence that keeps inflation and NGDP synchronized with the exponential growth of the ATOM. Hence, world monetary expansion in 2020 is still running at less than half of the estimated $400 Billion/month needed under by that point *just to keep up with the level of technological deflation.* Technological progress always finds a way to revert back towards the long-term trendline. Since the rate of change has been below the trendline for so long, perhaps the reversion necessitates enough technological deflation to force a severe correction in the financial markets. Such a correction will frighten central banks to crank up the monetary presses until deflation is overcome and the ATOM has sufficient fuel.

   While the crisis can be avoided by rapidly changing the style and amount of QE as per the above, remember that central banks are not yet even close to thinking in terms of exponentially-rising money creation, even though this era is already well underway. I cannot overstate how quickly and seemingly without warning an exponential trend can overtake an inadequate linear policy solution.

2. US home prices are reaching a long-term ceiling barring an entirely new stream of wealth creation, given that mortgage rates are so low that property taxes are a larger annual expenditure than mortgage interest. Further Federal Reserve purchases of bonds and MBSs are now past the point of diminishing effect in boosting home prices. Yet policymakers and the real estate industry still do not appear to have any new paradigm that the baton can be passed to, and will be caught unprepared for the end of this era and the complex ripple effects of it. Since home equity has been the sole source of net worth gain for many middle-class people, this stagnation will be problematic for consumer confidence.

3. US National Debt is now over 100% of GDP, and the budget deficit is much higher than it was at previous business cycle peaks in 1999 and 2007. This leaves the US without the fiscal buffer that has mitigated recessionary deficits in the past, ensuring that the upcoming crisis has deeper deficits than the 2008 crisis. Additionally, this makes the US vulnerable to debt downgrades at precisely the time that tax revenue is crashing and sentiment is weakest.

   The US National Debt is not high at all in relation to the present value of future GDP under the accelerating economic growth rate discussed earlier, nor are the annually accumulating budget deficits that created it. Alas, since current fiscal and monetary assumptions do not account for this, the current debt situation is ominous given how institutions and individuals may react to frightening headlines during the upcoming recession.

4. In 2020, the median baby boomer is 65 years old. A person's contribution to GDP is very unevenly distributed across their lifetime, and when baby boomers were at the age of buying homes and starting families during 1982–99, the economy enjoyed that tailwind. Now, the same cohort is older and ramping down their consumption en masse, so a corresponding and proportional economic headwind is emerging, without enough young people to offset it. This additionally means that the number of recipients of Social Security and Medicare is about to rise, while the number of taxpayers is not rising, exacerbating point 3) above. While this effect does not manifest all at the same time, it is a force soon to exert additional downward pressure on the GDP growth trajectory, making the recession deeper.

5. China's Nominal GDP in 2020 is now $15 Trillion, or about 70% of what US GDP is. This will mark the first time in 75 years that there is any other country with an economy that remotely approaches the size of the US economy, with the added certainty of retaining that status permanently. That such a large economy emerged so quickly, is far further along in ATOM-style monetary policy thought, and via a system substantially different from that of any of the G7 economies, will cause the tectonic plates of the world economic order to shift somewhat, as the assumptions underlying many valuations get revised. There is nothing wrong with that, but the process will add

some untimely volatility to markets already convulsing from the first four factors listed above.

These five factors are converging into a dark cloud on the horizon, and while every detail of the crisis cannot be predicted, the general script is emerging. The most unanticipated challenge with the upcoming crisis will be that the levers used to alleviate the pain of the 2008 crisis will be futile this time. Even worse, markets that feel they are at the mercy of politicians rather than economic or technical forces are particularly prone to volatility. While waiting for the political process to catch up, real estate could once again crash, sending millions of homes hurtling into negative equity. This will lead to several million jobs lost, widespread panic, and some violent social unrest.

Coronavirus Pandemic as a Warning Shot: The coronavirus pandemic and resultant quarantine was a version of black swan event that exposed many flaws in the outdating thinking across the Federal Reserve and government. Since the quarantine necessitated the freezing of entire sectors of the economy, the stock market plunged 40% in a matter of three weeks. The Federal Reserve, which was still vastly behind in its understanding of how to keep the economy afloat under such circumstances, reversed their tightening stance and, on the momentous day of March 15, 2020, lowered the Fed Funds rate to from 1.5% to 0%, and embarked on a new wave of QE, as described in Chapter 4. Yet, they still were far too afraid of non-existent inflation to send money directly to people, despite this being the only obvious mechanism to assist people during a mass quarantine.

But the rest of the Federal Government was even less enlightened, and decided to involve large banks and the Small Business Association (SBA) as middlemen between all stimulus and the citizenry. Their 'Paycheck Protection Program' had so many qualifiers and conditions that it was useless for most small companies, plus the program itself did not seem to care about entrepreneurs who are not taking a salary, or unemployed people. The program was obviously devised by people with no concept of what life is like for small businesses, free lancers, or anyone else not employed by the government or large institutions.

As a result, the big banks just granted the stimulus funds to their biggest clients who, by definition, needed the money the least, while small, innovative companies and their employees were left to die. Even worse, the Small Business Association is an agency far too small and insignificant to manage the orderly disbursement of $1 Trillion within a matter of weeks, and the shambolic failure of their execution led to a mass misallocation of funds. By contrast, the IRS program to send $1200 to low-income taxpayers was efficient and painless, with over 50 million payments sent within days of announcement. Congress and the White House made the error of adding a layer of complexity by disqualifying taxpayers with incomes over $80,000, but this was still a far smaller problem than the total failure of the SBA and big banks. Furthermore, the IRS demonstrated an advanced transmission mechanism where money could be sent to virtually all households quickly, and is thus a channel the Federal Reserve could interface with if they wanted to.

When the dust settled, the biggest corporations were making more money than even before the crisis started, the stock market was at all-time highs, while thousands of innovative small companies and millions of freelancers and small-company employees were in dire straits. Aside from the relatively praiseworthy IRS program, every other government action helped exactly who needed it the least. This problem will continue to exacerbate under the current conceptual framework the government and Federal Reserve cling to.

However, much of this can still be avoided if swift implementation of certain comprehensive augmentations is executed. My mission is to present potential solutions, derived from my proprietary research (available to suitable clients), and get as much exposure to these ideas as possible. The summary of the solution detailed in the next few chapters is that the amount of worldwide monetary action needed just to halt deflation will be as high as $800B/month by 2024, and has to rise at 16–24%/year thereafter. Additionally, this money has to be distributed in a diffuse manner, going directly to individuals. The crisis can still be avoided if all of these upgrades are enacted immediately, but the probable failure to do this will precipitate the aforementioned crisis. Over time, this perma-QE can replace many types of government spending, and hence the taxes that fund such spending. For details on how I arrive at this set of recommendations, read on.

While I am under no illusion that policymakers will read, debate, refine, and implement the ideas presented here in time to prevent a new crisis even if there is a lot of grassroots support, the following solutions may nonetheless resemble policies that are fast-tracked in the midst of the turmoil. These solutions may thus become entrenched programs in the era following the crisis.

CHAPTER 7

Government Policies Must Adapt, and Quickly

Three things cannot be long hidden: the sun, the moon, and the truth.
—Gautama Buddha

The problems in the world today cannot be solved by the level of thinking that created them.

—Albert Einstein

The problem in the US and other mature democracies is that new policy ideas do not advance at a faster rate than they did a century ago even though technology has accelerated the speed of many other economic and social forces. Compounding this problem is the reality that government adaptations occur only in reaction to crises that are already fully underway, with the recent coronavirus pandemic as just the latest example. They thus act from a position of panic and duress that leads to overshooting in the other direction.

The American Dream is in trouble, yet neither political party seems able to address why. While even the voters themselves are not demanding that the US government become more dynamic and proactive, there are a number of policy solutions that can pre-empt the calamity if so desired.

The ATOM Political Platform: US political thought has become exceedingly unoriginal, acrimonious, and tribally conformist, with many internal contradictions within both major parties. For example, people who consider themselves proponents of free-market economics generally identify as Republicans or Libertarians (even if Republicans are getting increasingly selective on this front), while people who consider themselves pro-technology generally vote Democrat. Yet, to me, these two things are absolutely inseparable from each other. So many cognitive dissonances have sprouted across US political discourse that the electorate and government will soon find themselves unequipped to interpret or even discuss upcoming challenges. The entire political universe is hamstrung by the two peculiar ideological apertures they are trained to parse information through.

The US political landscape has devolved into a metaphorical checkerboard, where only half of the squares are used for the two sides to wage war against each other, and the other half of the squares are unused and practically invisible. About half of all possible political and economic platforms are not even noticed within mainstream US politics, and people have been conditioned to think only within this box. This is especially true when a person's political bonafides are determined by how completely they remain within a specific box, which itself has ever-sharpening boundaries.

Democrats talk about providing a greater safety net, a 'living wage', and greater 'equality', yet do not see the most effective path to these goals. They do not quantify a threshold that meets the standard of a 'living wage', after which success can be declared. Accordingly, they keep devising new ways of taxing the most productive people, thus reducing their incentives and thus the total productivity of the economy. This strategy is well past the point of maximum tax revenue because tax complexity ensures that any tax increase falls more on upper-middle-class people than the ultra-wealthy and their many avenues of legal tax avoidance that confer immunity to any increases in 'retail' tax rates. An increase in the 'retail' tax rate thus accomplishes little except build a moat around the ultra-wealthy, ensuring that members of the upper-middle-class cannot join their ranks. A cynic might conclude that this is deliberate protectionism for the ultra-wealthy, but I do not believe that was the original objective. Rather, individual loopholes are sold to specific groups by individual legislators in Congress, with no holistic oversight to control spiraling complexity.

Furthermore, while there is some merit to the concept of a guaranteed minimum income even if a person cannot earn that much from their own output, increasing the legally mandated minimum wage is emphatically the wrong way to accomplish that outcome. Such a law merely forces the employer, which is usually a small business or franchise with narrow profit margins and steep competition, to trim any staff that cannot produce enough to justify the new minimum wage. In this age, automation can quickly fill the gap and price out human workers from repetitive, lower-skill jobs, effectively making a minimum wage increase a subsidy for automation. <u>There are other reasons why obstructing the market from determining a minimum wage is misguided and costly</u>. If a guaranteed minimum income is to ever be a reality, it has to be funded from a source that does not have to operate under a tight profit-and-loss reality, and there is only one such entity in existence.

Republicans are equally infected with outdated ideas. The GOP dithers about lower taxes and more favorable policies for small business, but is oblivious to easier methods to accomplish this. While some people are more talented and harder working than others and should not be penalized for their productivity, it is simultaneously true that money created by the Federal Reserve accumulates in very few hands, thus making it very different from wealth creation via entrepreneurship. Furthermore, as discussed before, tax complexity wastes as much as 20% of all tax revenue just in compliance and auditing, without counting the even larger cost of suboptimal business decisions for tax reasons. Yet Republicans are not pushing for tax simplification, even though that would effectively be a larger and deeper supply-side stimulus than the tax cuts they propose.

One faction of Republicans are against QE by the Federal Reserve under the belief that this will someday, somewhere cause inflation that has not yet appeared for over a decade and counting. While that would have been true in the 20th century, it is no longer true in the ATOM age, <u>for reasons discussed earlier.</u> There is still a vocal but shrinking clique of individuals who think hyperinflation is imminent, and a return to the gold standard is necessary. These 'inflation hawks' have predicted about 100 of the last zero bouts of hyperinflation, and don't seem to be interested in reassessing their assumptions. $30T of central bank action over eleven years, with another $300B/month being added to that as of mid-2020 post-coronavirus, has not vindicated this expectation. We can safely declare that the burden of proving that inflation is inevitable is now theirs to bear, and they have yet to provide any evidence to support their blind belief.

If one cannot accept that monetary expansion up to a very high ceiling will no longer cause inflation, and indeed needs to be permanent and ever-rising just to halt techno-deflation, it will never occur to them to gradually fund government spending with central bank money instead of tax revenues. That is a shame, since this is a path towards the goal of vastly reducing and eventually even eliminating all Federal income tax and fostering a huge economic stimulus, specifically favoring entrepreneurship to an unprecedented degree.

But within the respective blind zones of the two parties lies the most magnificent and elegant solution. In reality, we are now in an era where both Democrat and Republican goals can be met and exceeded with ease and simplicity, leaving many difficult tradeoffs behind as relics of the pre-ATOM age. I fully predict that by 2025, this solution will seem obvious in hindsight, despite the reflexive opposition by the ivory tower of the PhD Economists. Allow me to explain.

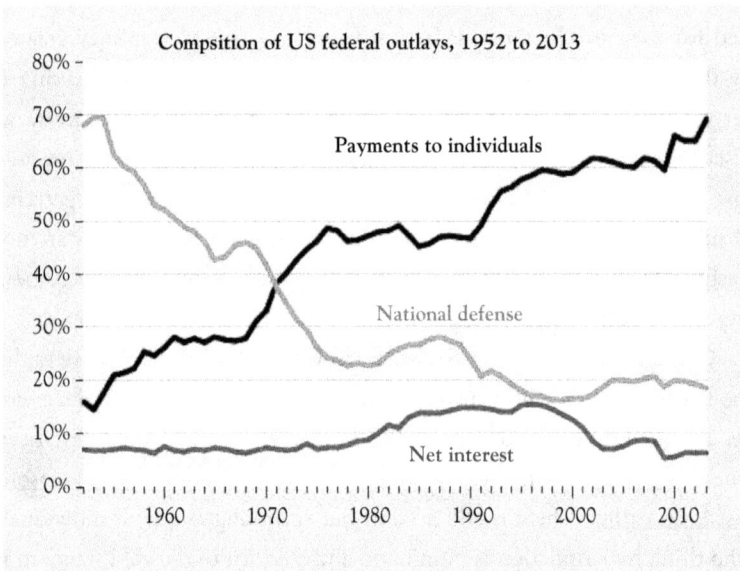

Compsition of US federal outlays, 1952 to 2013

For one thing, the relationship between the American people and the Federal government is not what it used to be. A number of seemingly innocuous changes to the US legislative branch of government in the early 20th century set in motion a mechanism that had large ripple effects over the next century. A succession of tax-and-redistribute programs were created to address current or future poverty, but without holistic oversight, each new program was not sufficiently complementary to existing programs. This led to many contradictory spending outlays, bureaucracies, and incentives. At this stage, 75% of all spending by the US Federal Government comprises of payments to individuals, particularly if politically engineered non-essential jobs of a make-work nature are counted. Unfortunately, even after all the wastage in the tax collection process, there is another gauntlet of rebound wastage within the disbursement process. When you combine this fact with the reality that government spending substantially exceeds tax revenues, the perversity of this situation becomes apparent. The number of voters who are net recipients of these handouts and entitlements is at or near a majority of the electorate, so there is political profit in talking about tax increases, even as it is politically impossible to trim these handouts.

Social security, medicare and other human services area growing share of government spending

Federal government spending as a share of GDP, by function

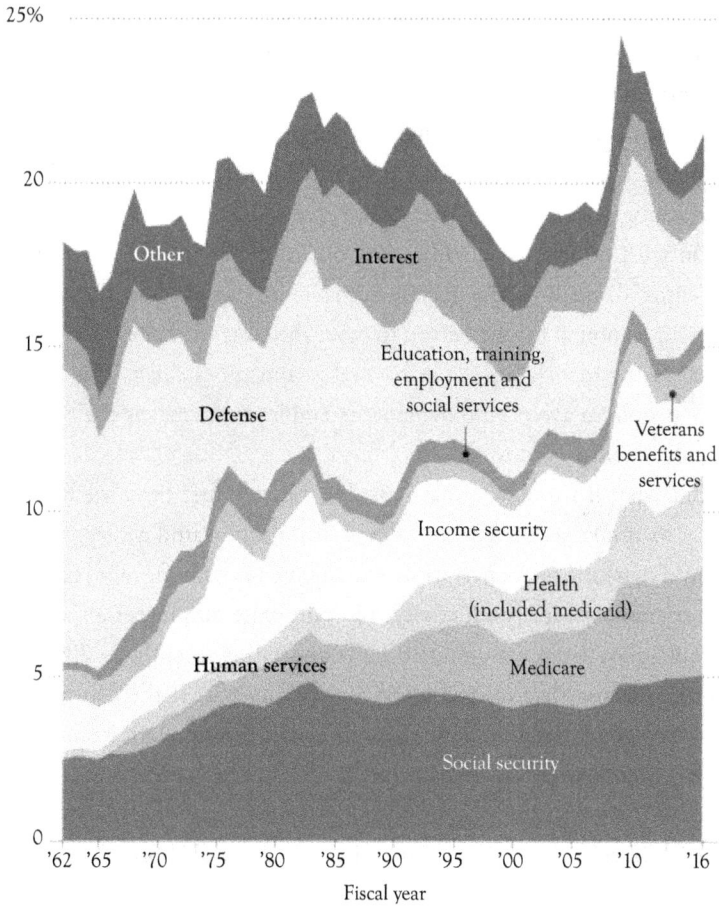

Source: Office of management and budget archives.

Pew research center

<u>In Fiscal 2019, the United States collected $3.5 Trillion in taxes and spent $4.4 Trillion</u>, resulting in a budget deficit of $0.9 Trillion. Remember that this will shoot to as much as $2 Trillion during the depths of the next recession, including the brief coronavirus recession. It is already a moral hazard to spend more than is collected in taxes, but since 75% of this $4.4 Trillion, or $3.3 Trillion (96% of taxes collected), consists merely of transfers of money between individuals, it does not finance any direct governance function. Many of these programs have heavily-staffed departments to administer them, and have complicated formulae and qualification criteria that determine payments. Social Security, Medicare, Medicaid, the ACA, welfare, unemployment compensation, food stamps, housing subsidies, alimony and child support enforcement agencies, etc. are just some of these programs, many of which are contradictory and non-interlocking with each other. As a result, a significant fraction of the funds disbursed are consumed in the processing of applications and payments. Even worse, there is a substantial band of income where non-interlocking policies have entrenched perverse incentives. For example, a person with no income qualifies for Medicare, but income above a certain cutoff disqualifies the person from the benefit without the earnings being high enough for the person to cover the costs by themselves. Hence, by increasing their income, their actual income goes *down*. This induces many people to avoid employment, as employment makes their healthcare affordability go down.

But what if I told you that now, for the very first time, we have the ability to implement a solution that will not only fund a very efficient, fair, and dynamic safety net, while making the tax code far more favorable to entrepreneurship, productivity, and corporate employees all at once? It would have been too good to be true even as recently as 2008, but through the wonders of technology, it no longer is. If the first solution seems 'too good', we even have a second-choice solution that is still a huge improvement over what we have now.

First Choice: The Universal Stipend as a Multi-Solution: Since central bank monetary expansion has to now be permanent, rise at compounded growth rates closer to Moore's Law-type concepts than the 1–2% inflation rates, and can no longer involve buying some asset classes over others, there is really only one solution to this malaise. That is, if the legislatures of the largest economies can untether their central banks to make this possible.

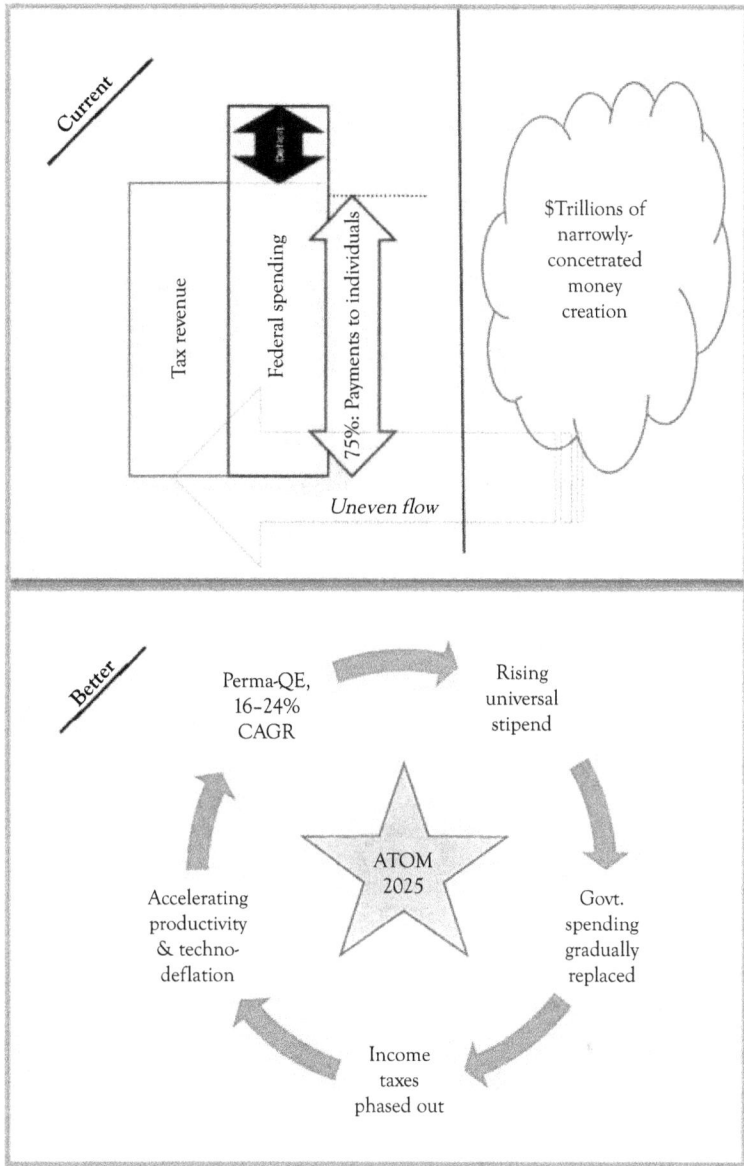

After estimating how much money can be created to keep NGDP in the 6–7% range, simply disburse that new money directly to the people in a uniform, equitable payment. That is the most diffuse and fairest way for central banks to halt inflation and create a broader, smarter safety net, and is the most effective way to offset technological deflation. It is more scalable and confidence-generating ('carrot') than negative interest rates ('stick').

More specifically, we can introduce the Direct Universal Exponential Stipend (DUES), where every US citizen over the age of 18 (230 million people at present) gets an equal share of the Federal Reserve monetary expansion. If such a program were hypothetically implemented in the United States of 2020, my calculations estimate that it would amount to about $5,000 per eligible person for the year. Every US citizen is eligible to receive it, and everyone gets the same amount. Whether rich or poor, young or old, lazy or industrious, male or female, childless or with a large brood, every citizen adult gets the same amount, period. The stipend also has to be exempt from Federal income taxes, and incoming payments cannot be garnished by creditors or bankruptcy courts.

Now, given the rapid and accelerating rate of technological change, consider the possibility that the DUES can rise each year at a speed much faster than the annual increases normally associated with inflation or 'Real' GDP. The steep gradient of increase in worldwide central bank monetary expansion discussed earlier fully demonstrates that the necessary amount to be created in the US itself rises by an estimated 16–24%/year. For this reason, the stipend rises by the same amazing rate, parsed into compounding monthly increments. The Federal Reserve determines the monthly increase by gauging indicators like the MIT BPP, and then publishes the exact increase before the start of the next calendar month.

The stipend can take a couple of months to ramp up to $400/month (say, $100, $200, and $400 in months 1, 2, and 3), so as not to create a small inflation spike from the sudden V.M. jolt. From there, it can then settle into the aforementioned cruising speed of approximately 1.2%–1.8%/month increases (16–24%/year), calculated dynamically in accordance with real-time inflation data. A hypothetical $5,000 in 2020 rises to about $6,000 in 2021, then about $7,200 by 2022, and so forth as the payments compound. As this is money generated by the central bank as cash, it does not need to be recorded on any balance sheet.

We, as a nation, have reached the point where the vast majority of government spending now comprises of payments to individuals, and we recognize that it is politically impossible to reverse this. Simultaneously, the amount of monetary creation needed to halt technological deflation is rising exponentially, and there does not appear to be an easy fix to the fact that technology creates both vertical (skill level) and horizontal (specialization) skill mismatches in the workforce. So why not embrace all of these realities?

The second half of the idea now arrives with a certain inevitability. Since most of this government spending can be replaced with money that has to be generated just to offset deflation, we can proceed to, in a phased and orderly manner, eliminate all types of Federal Income Tax. Yes, you read that correctly. It logically follows that when the primary purpose of income taxes is to make payments to individuals, and the DUES supersedes current payment programs, there is simply too much economic upside to be captured by removing both the filing/compliance burden plus income taxes themselves. Monetization of government spending has been taboo in eras past (see Friedrich Hayek), but that was before technology and the associated deflation was substantial enough that permanent, exponentially-rising easing was needed just to offset it. Like so many worthwhile ideas, it was simply ahead of its time.

This transitional process should be gradual enough to seamlessly let the ATOM advance to a sufficient size, and thus is expected to take about 10 years. As described earlier, the biggest problem with the tax code is not just the tax progressivity, but also the multiple categories that income has been divided into, known as 'character' for tax purposes. As the phase-out is conducted, issues like tax complexity begin to vanish as the concept itself becomes moot.

At this point, we should pause to catch our breath. This solution may seem very sanguine, but the individual components of it appear to be drifting in this direction already, particularly after the coronavirus pandemic forced a huge volume of new monetary creation, that too in a form that is edging towards direct payments to people.

Releasing $1.15 Trillion/year and rising in an economy of $22 Trillion may seem like a bit too much, but that is where the trend of cumulative QE against the deflationary force of technology has already brought us. As explained before, this 6% and rising of GDP in newly generated money, distributed in a method that generates a tornado of VM, will still result in inflation of just 2–3%/year within NGDP of 6–7% a year. It indeed is the minimum needed just to halt technological deflation, especially since central bank money flows across borders quite seamlessly. Eventually, world central banks will have to coordinate with each other to synchronize total monetary generation to world GDP. Note that the phase-out of income taxes will also generate a wave of one-time deflation that has to be offset. Until the MIT BPP annual inflation measurement (or equivalent measurement, if you don't like the official CPI) pierces 3% inflation and threatens to dance with 4%, there is absolutely no reason to fear inflation or worry about the amount of monetary easing being excessive. Even that rate of inflation merely means the next year's rate of increase will be a few percentage points lower, perhaps just 15% instead of 16–24%, but still an increase. The precise number does not need to be very accurate for any one year, for as the self-reinforcing mechanism builds, continual adjustment to economic feedback steers us to the correct numbers over time.

Critics may point out that this is just another 'basic income guarantee' or 'living wage' program. On the contrary, the DUES greatly transcends that, since those other ideas involve impossibly high taxation, whereas the DUES is simultaneous with a removal of income tax. Furthermore, the DUES is not an aid program, but rather a pure win-win through the self-reinforcing feedback loop, without which the payout is not possible in the first place. The fact that the DUES adjusts for inflation and rises exponentially are added elements of difference.

Finally, we can note that the upside of this approach goes well beyond just statistics and fiscal calculations. To truly grasp how many problems are addressed and swept away by the DUES of central bank money and corresponding tax phase-out, we have to delve deeply into the intricate psychology of hardship.

The 'Peace of Mind' Dividend: The curve of human suffering is very non-linear. Deprivation of the most basic necessities is a cause of misery and distraction, and as we saw earlier, only in the last few decades have a significant percentage of humans been elevated above this layer of existence. Yet even in 2020, at least 2 billion people worldwide do not have the very basic necessities, and while this aggregate number continues to drop, the progress remains very uneven.

At the other extreme, if a very wealthy person sees their wealth double, or conversely fall by half, very little about their living standard will change. When leftists see this, they conclude that wealth should be redistributed, since the destitute person's suffering can be greatly alleviated with no real pain to the wealthy, resulting in less net hardship overall. As mentioned earlier, despite the initial appeal of this meme, such redistribution almost never works as intended and ends up shrinking the total economic pie. *Any real attempt to tax the wealthy instead taxes the upper-middle-class that cannot access sophisticated tax-avoidance structures.* This taxation thus has a negative multiplier effect on productivity without collecting much incremental tax revenue.

Another aspect of the poverty discussion is the failure to fully understand the differences, as well as similarities, between the poor-country-poor, and rich-country-poor. This leads to one-size-fits-all approaches that do not help either group. The former suffer from malnutrition, while the latter are more likely to suffer from obesity. The poor in wealthy countries have access to amenities that even the rich in poor countries do not, such as reliable electricity, paved roads, and emergency response services. Yet even those who point out the benefits available to the poor of developed countries fail to recognize the true burden on the human condition. This is an angst common to poor-country-poor, rich-country-poor, and even many people who are not poor at all. We know of this as *hopelessness*.

Hopelessness with one's life and prospects, in a psychological sense, is a state of purgatory where someone truly believes there is nothing to look forward to, nothing that can uplift their current condition, or nothing that can alleviate their despair. It is a terrible scourge on the soul, and is often the reason for depression and suicide (consider that a country as prosperous as the US nonetheless still <u>has over 45,000 suicides per year</u>, a number which has failed to shrink from economic growth). It is also the primary reason that people with seemingly normal lives decide to join fringe hate groups or terrorist organizations.

Hopelessness is a huge weight on the economy, social mood, and individual well-being. Hopelessness is a menace just as familiar to the man in Bangladesh earning just $1000/year who worries about his children's malnutrition as to the working class American earning $50,000/year who can barely accumulate any savings while seeing his industry replace jobs like his with AI. Even people who are wealthy and famous experience hopelessness for any number of reasons (some celebrities loved by millions of fans have committed suicide, after all, and often for reasons related to a bleak and uncertain financial outlook). Furthermore, stress and despair are major contributors to both cancer and heart disease, which are the two most frequent causes of death in developed countries.

While nothing can eradicate every source of human hopelessness fully, implementation of the annual guaranteed stipend will do a great deal to ease the ongoing anxiety of working class people about their employment and their savings. Knowing that the stipend they receive continually rises by 16–24%/year while the price of their essentials does not mitigates the uncertainty factor by providing optimism about their future financial safety net, retirement income, and ability to service debt. This in turn boosts consumer confidence and sparks more entrepreneurial risk-taking. Knowing that the stipend is independent of one's employer is another major relief to one's financial outlook.

Many of the arguments in favor of a minimum guaranteed income and more generous safety net correctly emphasize the savings this may create elsewhere in the economy in terms of lower crime and higher consumer confidence. But all of these ideas involved taxing productive work to a prohibitive degree, and providing money based on some convoluted assessment of neediness that often ends up incentivizing laziness and government dependence. This solution, by contrast, merely takes the large and rising money stream that the Federal Reserve has to perpetually create anyway to halt deflation, and use it to replace the 75% of government spending that is just direct payments to individuals. Since every eligible US citizen over age 18 gets the same amount, it is entirely fair, and the richer a person is, the less this will remove their incentives to produce. Almost all wealthy people continue to work long past the point where their living standards can no longer improve further, and this will not change. Excluding the top 1% of earners from the stipend will only increase the stipend for the other 99% by 1%, making this layer of complexity more trouble than it is worth.

This can be termed as a 'Peace of Mind Dividend'. If this program is implemented, the pervasive boost in economic confidence will be an immense catalyst to the economy, particularly as the stipend rises due to the deflationary effect of the ATOM. While the hypothetical $5,000 payment in 2020 does not seem significant, the estimated 16–24% annual increase in monetary expansion required just to offset deflation means that the stipend could be over $12,000/year by 2025. It will still keep on rising every year after that, from an ever-higher base. Remember that a couple gets two such stipends into their household. If elderly parents live with their married children, then such a household receives four incoming stipends.

Finally, the stipend provides a sense of *participation* in the high-tech economy to all US citizens. Instead of the gains of technological progress seemingly a distant and esoteric concept for the other 80% to 90% of Americans, a stipend that grows quickly for reasons known to be associated with technological progress has subjective ripple effects. It accomplishes a great deal in educating the general public about the accelerating rate of technological change, how productivity flows from technology, and how many fruits are available to them to pick if they know where to look. AI will no longer be seen as a job-swallowing scourge, but rather as the engine that keeps the stipend rising, which in turn reduces the opposition to productivity gains inherent to anti-AI sentiment. The value to the masses of this sort of participatory education and orientation towards welcoming new technologies should not be underestimated.

Allowing the Economy to Breathe from *Both* Lungs, For a Change: Above and beyond this, the gradual elimination of income tax is an incremental and meteoric boost to personal wealth and consumer spending, for people at all income levels. Being inured to tax withholding via their W-2 and then lulled by a direct deposit to their bank account, not many workers have pondered how much more their employer spends on them relative to what they receive in their pockets after all taxes.

Since most well-paying jobs are in states with very high tax rates, the marginal tax on every dollar earned by workers there rapidly crosses 50%. When a person is hired into a job that supposedly pays '$120,000/year plus benefits' in official paperwork, the employer has to spend about $175,000/year for the employee to receive $80,000/year after all taxes, not even counting the time spent by both parties on tax compliance. When you consider this, it is surprising that there are even as many employed people as there are. When income taxes are phased out for individuals and corporations the scenario above will be one where an employer spending $175,000 leads to as much as $150,000 being retained by the employee, inclusive of all benefits. There will be many more jobs created in such a climate as well, since the same example could lead to an employer splitting the position, i.e. spending $175,000 to create two junior jobs where each employee retains $75,000.

It is obvious how much of a boost this would provide to consumer confidence, consumer spending, and debt serviceability. Beyond that, when the marginal output of the most productive workers goes from 50–55% taxation to 0% taxation, their workplace enthusiasm and supererogatory productivity will rise by an astonishing degree. This will have a magnificent cascading effect across every imaginable metric of economic health. The entire culture of work and productivity will change, across all industries and every level of expertise. Complaints about wage growth recede away, while employers have a wider range of tools at their disposal to align compensation with incentives. It is scarcely possible to overstate how much improvement both employers and employees will see across every aspect of corporate culture.

There is considerable evidence that innovators and entrepreneurs flow to where the top marginal tax rate is the lowest. Some will cite Silicon Valley as thriving amidst high taxes and heavily regulated building permits. I counter (with my 25 years in residence) that Silicon Valley's success is *in spite* of the business unfriendliness of the public sector, combined with the fact that the ultrawealthy of Silicon Valley pay almost no income tax due to loopholes available to them that are concealed by tax complexity, as described earlier. Imagine how Silicon Valley could vault higher with lower taxes on startups and individuals, and with the DUES backstopping the living expenses of young entrepreneurs. Countless business models large and small that are unviable under current taxation become viable, and existing businesses will enjoy margin expansion, which in turn leads to more innovation and competition in each space.

Furthermore, the elimination of corporate tax will unshackle the $2 Trillion in cash that US blue chips still have parked overseas in order to indefinitely defer the taxation of those funds, even after the early 2018 reduction in corporate tax rates. It is often written how US job creation would increase if these offshore profits were brought back home, and the removal of the perverse incentive that keeps this money stashed in tax havens will alleviate a huge burden on both corporations and workers. Since all capital expenditure has a quicker payback timeline through the faster compounding of returns without taxation, capex can increase, which means product lifecycles can speed up. This erases the aforementioned problem of low NGDP and the ill-effects that flow downstream from it.

At this point, two common points are invoked by skeptics. The first is the speculation that such a stipend will merely create a leisure class out of the bottom 60–80% of the population, who spend their lives immersed in various types of home entertainment. They may do nothing else with their time and do not set good examples for their children, who then fail to grow into productive innovators that sustain the ATOM. Putting aside the fact that such a concern is mutually exclusive with worries that AI will leave millions permanently unemployed, or that healthcare costs are surpassing affordability, it is unfounded in any event. Since the incentives on productivity, entrepreneurship, and innovation are tremendously higher than ever before, the entire curve of return on investment/labor/risk shifts to a more favorable zone. The absence of income tax will not only lead to much higher pay for the same job, but a greater quantity of jobs than could have come into being under the more oppressive tax code. In addition, customers of each business have more money to spend, generating greater revenue for any business they buy from, and thus more jobs in those companies, some of which generate new technology, expanding and reinforcing the ATOM. The 'sloth class' will in fact be much smaller than it is at present once this virtuous cycle is permitted to manifest. Various dysfunctional subcultures will vanish of their own accord through a form of societal autolysis.

The second group of skeptics consists of those who do a basic calculation to discover that under this rate of increase, the ever-rising stipend will cross $100,000/year by the early 2040s, meaning that every US adult gets for free what few Americans in 2020 can capture post-tax even from full-time work. They contend that this surely cannot be a serious prediction due to the law of large numbers alone, and if nothing else, this will cause inflation. But if you refer back to the <u>earlier charts about exponential and accelerating economic growth</u>, the trendline deposits us at exactly a point where such a stipend and growth rate (now driving the NGDP growth rate itself to that level) is well within the band. The second derivative of the curve cleanly indicates that the next 20 years may see the same multiplier of geometric increase as the previous 80–100 years, making such numbers consistent with the trendline. Remember that AI advances hundreds or thousands of times faster than humans, and will by then be generating tens of trillions of dollars of annual output with very little input; output which humans can consume. Add to that the fact that as per the ATOM diffusion rate established earlier, technologically deflating products may be as much as 8% of world GDP by then. It all combines into a robust yet simple refinement of economic governance with the exponentially rising growth of the ATOM.

This is not to claim, in any way, that recessions and asset price crashes will never happen again after such a complete revamp of economic, fiscal, and monetary realities. To the contrary, the gregarious groupthink of human nature ensures that such dips become inevitable after a certain period of time. What will happen, however, is that the peaks and troughs of each business cycle will be along the much steeper growth trendline. This also means that the old definition of a recession—two consecutive quarters of negative GDP growth, will continue to become more outdated, since even the troughs of the cycle may have positive, albeit below-trend, growth.

Second Choice: The Sovereign Venture Fund: If DUES seems like too drastic an overhaul of the entire fiscal and monetary system, there is another solution for how the central bank monetary creation can be used to uplift an economy without changing fiscal flows. While not as comprehensive and broad in its effect, it still can bring immense improvement to the lives of a country's citizens. This solution is the Sovereign Venture Fund.

This solution is exceptionally simple, as I wrote about in April 2018. It is simply about capturing the rest of the world's technological deflation for domestic benefit, which by definition means that the country that executes the vision first gets all the benefit. Any country with an advanced economy and its own central bank can qualify, and the dollar size of the Venture Fund can be the same no matter how small the country implementing it.

While it is always better to be a prosperous country than an impoverished one, almost every small country (the size of Canada or smaller) is faced with a major vulnerability in the modern economy. Their economy invariably depends on one or two major industries, and is hence vulnerable to a technological disruption that arises from somewhere else in the world. The need to diversify against such external risks is obvious, but most countries are not on the best path to achieve this goal.

These days, everyone I meet from the government of some foreign country seems to have the same goal for their country—to create an ecosystem of local technology startups. This goal is not just extremely difficult to attain, but it is very misguided. Technology is becoming increasingly governed by winner-take-all dynamics and capital concentration, which means even in the US, rival cities are unable to compete with Silicon Valley. Silicon Valley itself has concentrated into a smaller portion of the San Francisco Bay Area than was the case in the late 1990s, with the bulk of new wealth accruing to a group of around just 7000 people within which there is relatively little turnover. Small countries with technology sectors, such as Israel and Singapore, started decades ago and have a number of unique factors in their favor, including a major Silicon Valley diaspora. Hence, a country that thinks it is productive to create a tech startup cluster in their countries will almost certainly create a situation where young people receive training at local expense, only to leave for Silicon Valley. So these initiatives only end up feeding Silicon Valley at the expense of the original country. Even if a few tech startups can be forcibly created in the country, it is extremely unlikely that they will achieve any great size within even 15 years.

Take, for example, a country like New Zealand. It has many favorable characteristics, but certain disadvantages as well in an increasingly globalized economy. It relies on agricultural and dairy exports, as well as the film industry and tourism. It is too remote to easily plug into the well-traveled routes of tech executives (less than 30M people live within 3000 miles of New Zealand) or major supply chains. It is too small to be a significant domestic market for tech (particularly when a functional tech ecosystem has to comprise of startups in multiple areas of tech in order to achieve rudimentary diversification). New Zealand's success in getting Hollywood films shot in New Zealand cannot similarly translate into getting some

Silicon Valley business, as an individual film project has a short duration and distinct ending, with key personnel on site for just a brief period. Technology, by contrast, is inherently endless, and requires interdependency between many firms that have to have co-location. Furthermore, no society is capable of placing more than 1–2% of its population into high-tech professions and still have them be competitive at the international level (most tech innovation is done by people in the top 1% of cognitive ability). For this reason, a tech startup ecosystem does not create broad prosperity (it is no secret that even within Silicon Valley, only a fraction of people are earning almost all the new wealth. Silicon Valley has among the most extreme inequality found in any advanced economy).

As mentioned above, it is difficult for government officials, legislators, and statesmen to undertake the drastic steps of DUES implementation, particularly when the entire Economics profession, as described before, is still mired in outdated thinking about how QE will someday, somehow cause inflation. For this reason, a second, less drastic option is also available for New Zealand. That involves create what I describe as a **Sovereign Venture Fund**, where the <u>New Zealand Central Bank</u> creates a segregated account that is completely partitioned off from the domestic economy, and prints money to place into that account (say, $500 Billion). It is crucial that this money *not circulate domestically at first, as it would cause inflation.* The purpose of this $500B Sovereign Venture Fund is to invest in startups worldwide that might be disrupting New Zealand's domestic industries. This model is extremely effective and flexible, as:

(i) The money was not taken from New Zealand taxpayers, but rather generated for free by the New Zealand Central Bank. Hence, it can invest in speculative start-ups across the world with far more boldness.

(ii) The diversification achieved is immediate, and can always be adjusted with equal immediacy as needed.

(iii) The Fund is leveraging the rest of the world's technological deflation for New Zealand's domestic benefit.

(iv) Tech startups worldwide become extremely vocal advocates for the fund, and even the country itself. It boosts New Zealand's branding (generating even more tourism).

(v) Fund gains can be used to offset government spending by replacement of income tax, or to fund training to enable citizens to modernize their skills. It can also provide a greater social safety net to cushion industries buffeted by disruption, but without taxing those who are still working. This is how to repatriate the money without inflation.

(vi) Even a larger fund of $800B can earn $80B/year from a 10% return, which exceeds the total taxes collected by the country.

The Sovereign Venture Fund is an extremely effective, speedy, and versatile method of economic diversification. It can be customized for any prosperous country (for example, an oil exporter should simply invest in electric vehicle, battery, and photovoltaic technologies to hedge their economic profile). As a huge amount of worldwide QE has to be done just to offset technological deflation, there is no contribution to inflation even worldwide, let alone domestically. As the winds of technological change shift, the Fund can respond almost immediately (unlike a multi-decade process of creating a tech startup ecosystem only to worry if the sectors represented are about to be disrupted).

Since there is a very high and exponentially rising ceiling of how much world QE can be done before world inflation reaches even 3%, there is an immense first-mover advantage that is possible here. The first $1 Trillion is effectively 'free money' for the country that decides to be Spartacus.

New Zealand, in particular, has even more factors that make it a great candidate. The NZ$ is currently too strong, which is crimping New Zealand's exports. This sort of program may create a bit of currency weakening just from the initial reaction. For this additional reason, it is a low-risk, high-return strategy for generating a robust and indeed indestructible safety net for New Zealand's citizens, hedging them from the winds of global technological disruption.

Maintaining the ATOM Economy: For this self-reinforcing feedback cycle to work best, the enabling factors of the ATOM have to be stewarded. While this system is more robust, self-correcting, and decentralized than any existing system, it is not entirely immune to neglect, abuse, or political corruption.

In the political sphere, this new, yet permanent and rising tide of 'free money' will test the principles of even the most frugal of fiscal hawks, because the money is not 'free', but a dividend that continues through the adequate care and feeding of the (worldwide) ATOM. An unrestrained political class may squander this bounty in various shortsighted grabs. Examples include quadrupling military purchases of expensive new weaponry, doubling the number of staffers and aides attending to each high-level official, or making a vote-buying campaign pledge to pay women a larger annual stipend than men. Collective self-control by both the citizenry and leaders in these matters will determine which nation stays competitive relative to others, in the ATOM age.

Excessive and/or outdated regulation quietly suffocates innovation, and the regulatory regime has to upgrade to a new rubric compliant with the speed and effervescence of technological change. When the economic pie grows due to lower taxation and higher velocity-of-money, the most zealous regulators may see the newly created space as an opening for vast increases in regulatory complexity, and the accompanying empire-building. The topic of correcting obese or ill-structured regulation is beyond the scope of this paper, but it is worth mentioning that despite the consolidation of many government programs and departments, the regulatory regime may greatly inhibit the full potential of this system if not subject to independent oversight.

Industries that operate as cartels and monopolies may be the origins of occasional inflation spikes, which provide fuel to critics and can cause lasting damage to the entire philosophical underpinning of the program. While most monopolies will eventually break from the disruptive pressure the ATOM exerts on them, the interim phase can easily be misinterpreted through an anti-technology lens. The regulatory regime must also be wary of not letting the innovators of yesterday become the anti-innovation monopolies of tomorrow, for this impedes the ATOM and reduces the DUES growth rate, or the speed at which the Sovereign Venture Fund can take new central bank capital.

While the stipend itself will automatically generate considerable education about technological change as a matter of course, that alone is not sufficient. Retraining programs to enable workforce transitions have to be far more extensive than they are today, with an associated cultural shift.

It should be expected that at any given time, 10–20% of adults are in some level of retraining even if they currently have jobs, as the churn of creative destruction endlessly remakes the economy. Professions and industries on the brink of disruption have to be identified early in the process, so that the retraining of individuals can happen proactively.

The above maintenance requirements are minimal given how much other complexity is removed in this system. But the human brain is often resistant to change, and has a bias in favor of the status quo, even if inferior. The stipend is the key buffer in the process of cushioning human anxiety while transitioning society to this new age.

CHAPTER 8

The ATOM Transformation by Sector

The whole of science is nothing more than the refinement of everyday thinking.

—Albert Einstein

If these ideas enter mainstream US political debate, the entire landscape will be re-arranged. Many former allies will become adversaries, and vice-versa, in a shattering and reorienting of coalitions. This process will be much faster than the political class is accustomed to, since the speed inherent to the ATOM cannot be kept out of political processes for much longer. Count this as yet another long-overdue disruption that makes way for appropriate modernization.

A robust, entirely fair, and rapidly-rising safety net combined with an eventual income tax rate of zero is what is possible when the afore-mentioned checkerboard analogy is transformed and turned into a chess-board, where *all* squares are used. Society advances when both the left and right are competing to see who has better ideas, and where each side can admit when another had a good idea. I have always been a registered Independent and a 'classical liberal', and hence quite neutral in contemporary American politics, while being a co-blogger on both right and left-leaning blogs. But since it is the left that drives the political agenda in the US and with Republicans only reacting to the space that the left creates, I predict that of the two sides, I will be working with the Democratic Party to move these ideas forward. It is an exciting prospect to bring transformative ideas to the left, making long-sought goals of a guaranteed minimum income and deep safety net possible. This can lead to a return to the optimistic, can-do liberalism of yesteryear. This in turn improves the right as well. It is not an exaggeration to say that the decoupling of a robust, dynamic safety net from taxation may save democracy from itself.

With the general public, many types of petty property crime and financially-driven depression will greatly decrease, not just due to the stipend, but from the knowledge that it increases at a brisk rate each month. This is a significant alteration to the psychology of personal finance, and the relationship that people have with their own future-orientation hence adjusts favorably. While there will always be people who continue to squander all incoming money in addictions or mismanagement, there will be a wider gap between circumstantial and self-inflicted hardship. Simultaneously, about 50% of organized crime will also voluntarily vanish. An astute eye can catch subtle clues from various organized crime themed films and television programs, that most of the incentive for the rank and file criminals is the fact that their earnings are free of income tax (and thus twice as high). This is openly stated in programs like *The Sopranos*. We can conclude that half of all such crime will voluntarily vanish when the 'tax-free' benefit is removed, due to the risk/reward analysis becoming that much less compelling.

High-crime urban communities may get a major makeover with the injection of capital, creating a chance for new local business formation and social cohesion where there previously was none. The stipend creates a strong incentive for young people not to default into gang membership. Why risk an early death or incarceration when your stipend starts from age 18 and rises so quickly each year? This is where the DUES provides a compound solution across both urban ghettoes and withering rural towns with undiversified economies.

The stipend enables an unprecedented degree of economic mobility, evening out some location-chained economic distortions. Some lower-income Americans in expensive coastal cities might elect to relocate to smaller towns in the interior with much lower costs of living, and look for a job after arrival with the stipend bridging the gap in between. There is far too little research into how much an individual benefits from just a slight increase in their economic 'leash', which is what we will see here.

Depopulated locations with excess housing supply will see a new influx of settlers snapping up low-cost properties without an immediate need for employment. As enough of them arrive, their critical mass creates a new local economy to revive the area. Regional supply/demand mismatches of housing will even out, as jobs can emerge *after* the arrivals settle and generate economic activity. Another set of Americans may choose to relocate overseas to a country where the stipend stretches much further. A retiree couple earning two stipends could retire in luxury in Latin America, the Caribbean, or Southeast Asia, *with no worry about outliving their money*. Choices that seemed impossible become entirely attainable with the DUES, and the unnoticed burden of economic bondage is greatly reduced.

The middle class sees a phoenix-like resurgence from an elixir that addresses the poorly understood challenges they face, as the stipend is uncorrelated to their home equity, employment security, and mutual funds, *all of which decline at the same time during a recession*. The DUES, by contrast, keeps rising quickly even through a recession, indeed at an even faster rate than before if the recession features excessive deflation. This buffer reduces the pressure the unemployed face to liquidate their home or other assets at a low price during this period.

Schemes such as the mortgage interest deduction, ostensibly created to help the middle class, are actually detrimental to an unemployed person with no income to write off mortgage interest against. Such a deduction ends up widening the gulf between the employed and unemployed, and the removal of income tax altogether eradicates this hidden vulnerability (and resultant disincentive for entrepreneurship) in the process. Such an independent cushion through the Peace of Mind Dividend addresses the collective blind spot of what truly causes middle class duress in recessions. In accordance with Nasim Taleb's concepts of fragility and anti-fragility, the middle class moves from an existence that is quite fragile in the face of rapid technological change, to considerably higher anti-fragility and true participation in the ATOM.

Immigration to the US will automatically self-select for the highest skill levels since an immigrant, ineligible for the stipend, is at a structural disadvantage relative to US citizens in the job market. This disadvantage is inversely proportional to the skill level of the immigrant, until the immigrant becomes a citizen many years later. This solution thus addresses almost all of the complicated subtopics within the immigration debate at once, from the skill level of immigrants to the competitiveness of domestic workers in relation to recent immigrants, to even the geographic distribution of immigrants within the US. Most illegal immigration will stop of its own accord, since the illegal immigrant is not on a path to receiving a stipend and is uncompetitive in the labor market against stipend-receiving Americans. The stipend hence has ripple effects that repair the seemingly intractable topic of immigration (particularly skilled and legal vs. unskilled and illegal) with nearly perfect precision.

The DUES is particularly helpful to women. For one thing, women live a few years longer than men, so they collect more total funds over the course of their lifetime. Beyond that, there is much discussion about the tradeoffs that mothers incur in taking years off of their careers to have children. The DUES provides exceptional flexibility as a crucial buffer in these circumstances, as does the removal of income taxes, and thus the penalty on the second income that married couples face. There is also the topic of considerable intra-woman hostility from tax-paying career women towards benefit-receiving single mothers, even as individual circumstances vary greatly within both groups. The removal of income tax combined with an identical stipend for all adults irrespective of whether they have children substantially addresses the complicated nuances of fairness in such matters.

Not to be excluded, the wealthy experience a unique and invaluable form of relief from the need to organize their lives around tax efficiency. This frees their minds to focus on what they do best, which is to generate wealth, productivity, and jobs. The shameful yet ever-marketable myth that the wealthy have to lose before anyone else can gain receives a crushing blow when the linkage between taxation and the safety net is broken and the 'make them pay their fair share' bugbear evaporates. Furthermore, the aforementioned effect of improved working-class optimism from the DUES in turn diminishes the menacing threat of pitchfork sentiment directed towards the wealthy. This new climate where their employees retain their full pre-tax compensation and their customers have more spending money infuses all businesses with new energy and profitability. This, in turn, restores the reputation of free markets that the wealthy depend on.

The stipend program requires a negligible staff to administer. This slimming-down of many government bureaucracies and reassignment of staff to better positions provides a benefit to politicians as well, for now they can focus the Federal muscle on grander visions to finally take us to the 21st century we have been waiting for. High-tech infrastructure, a modernized space program, more funding for basic research, more elaborate startup incubators and entrepreneur grants, etc. are all areas that can receive greater focus than before. Some of the redundant employees from the entitlement program departments of government can find more soul-inspiring work in those agencies, as well as in the private sector, which will create far more jobs than the government sheds.

The technology industry, being a source of the ATOM itself, will benefit from the combined effect of multiple catalysts. When an entrepreneur has a guaranteed stipend that enables him to pursue some speculative venture without having to worry about basic necessities, and when the potential payoff is tax free, entrepreneurial activity rises tremendously. Startups will attract more employees for the same reason—more people are available for the uncertainty of startup life. Venture capitalists will fund a greater share of ambitious ventures, since the higher NGDP trajectory moves the risk curve back to what it was in the 1980s and 90s. Liquidity timelines for VC funds shorten from ten years back down to six, and the tax-free nature of all gains improves fund returns. Downstream, the linkage between mass-market demand and product innovation becomes more seamless. The technology paradox, where more technologically deflating devices in one's life entails a rising cost of perpetually upgrading them, is a real imposition. This by definition requires that the wealth generated has to exceed the cost of aggregate upgrades across the majority of the population, for the last thing we need is a belief that the cost of upgrades is making people poorer. Read more about the asphyxiating effect of the 'Upgrade Paradox' over here. The DUES and tax phase-out allow this natural process to manifest, and for the virtuous cycle to proceed apace. All of these factors contribute towards moving the rate of technological progress back to the long-term trendline.

Beyond technology, various distortions in other sectors are ironed out. At present, the US economy has a huge bias in favor of products where the end consumer receives tax subsidies (such as higher education, mortgage interest, and healthcare) relative to those where they do not (such as consumer electronics and unprocessed food). This causes the subsidized industries to be low in innovation, while the unsubsidized ones are forced to be highly innovative. The removal of this bias will lift a considerable disadvantage borne by unsubsidized industries and their employees. Many monopolies and cartels will see an initial burst of profits as consumers simply buy more of what they have always bought, and this is where initial islands of inflation will form. But this widening of margin will attract greater competition and technological disruption, breaking many former fortresses of anti-competition after their initial surge.

Banks benefit from 230 million incoming monthly stipend deposits and the dramatic increase in transactions. Consumer goods companies benefit since they can now improve their revenue projections around the fact that their customers receive a stipend rising 16–24%/year. This larger and more durable market ensures greater dividends on R&D expenditures. More adventurous products can be considered as the path to profitability has shifted, and product cycles are faster. In effect, all companies will be able to adopt some of the favorable economic characteristics of technology companies.

All of these sectors are components of the broader equity index, and the equity market will start to shift into a steeper trajectory, consistent with the accelerating and exponential rise in GDP. The index is further supercharged by the removal of corporate taxes alongside the boost in employee productivity from the removal of individual income taxes. A more steeply rising equity market and the absence of capital gains taxes accelerates the cycle of creative destruction and wealth creation further, tying into the earlier point about venture capital returns and liquidity/viability of new technology startups. Equity volatility, however, will not go down; it will merely seem as though time has moved into fast forward relative to today.

By contrast, the sector of finance that will have to be completely rethought is the bond market. On one hand, the DUES makes it far easier for lower-income but responsible borrowers to service debt, elevating a new cohort of borrowers and driving interest rates lower. On the other hand, the assumption that bond yields are a reflection of inflation has to change, given the 16–24% annual increase in the stipend. The removal of deficit spending will discontinue the issuance of new US Treasuries, which is a huge adjustment to capital markets. International debt markets will see an even greater overhaul, since some countries can start a DUES program sooner than others, creating many peculiar arbitrages. Perhaps the bond market, after serving international finance for so long, will have to shrink to fraction of its prior size and significance with municipal and corporate bonds the only remaining instruments. Bonds may no longer be seen as a hedging counterbalance to equities, due to the advent of the ATOM and the associated deflation. The appropriate yield on municipal and corporate debt per grade will have to arrive at a new equilibrium after accounting for all of these forces.

Overall, a vast range of enterprises, aspirations, and talent utilizations seemingly too unattainable before could now be closer to a threshold that warrants serious pursuit, simply because central bank perma-QE can separate the safety net from tax collection. The battles between taxpayers and recipients that occur in country after country, and that have claimed millions of lives over the centuries, can be greatly reduced, due to this new paradigm of monetary injection. This solution transcends both socialism and capitalism, making the inherent assumptions behind each obsolete. If the Sovereign Venture Fund is implemented instead of ATOM DUES, the economic transformation can be similar, as long as deployment of funds is done algorithmically and transparently, rather than through politicized opacity.

CHAPTER 9

Reframing 'Inequality'

In a country well governed, poverty is something to be ashamed of. In a country badly governed, wealth is something to be ashamed of.
—Confucius

The first lesson of economics is scarcity: There is never enough of anything to satisfy all those who want it. The first lesson of politics is to disregard the first lesson of economics.
—Thomas Sowell

There seems to be an inordinate amount of discussion about 'inequality' in society, even though it focuses only on ratios of financial income between cherrypicked examples. When the social media hordes opine on this subject, there is often a comical inability to distinguish income and net worth. Even worse, when people in positions of power address the topic, there is a fixation on financial inequality, rather than the various other inequalities that exist between people (health and vitality, attractiveness, likeability, physical abilities, cancer susceptibility, communication skills, quality of relationships, the climate where they live, their commute, etc.). Why is the facile metric of financial income ratios between arbitrarily selected strata suddenly a dominant crisis of our age, when by most statistical measures, inequality is far less than it was for the majority of human existence?

The political push behind 'inequality' is mostly because monetary assets are the only possession that can be forcibly transferred from one person to another. If one person is much more attractive than another, amputating the former's nose and grafting it onto the latter's face as a second nose will make both of them much less attractive than they were before the operation, despite the 'redistribution'. Sadly, the process of forcible wealth redistribution destroys wealth and social values with much the same effect. Proponents continually refuse to see the evidence of the failure of this system in country after country.

However, there is a different track of financial inequality that is more valid, and where the focus should migrate to. Now that money-creation by central banks has to become permanent and ever-rising, it is absolutely valid to complain about how QE money accumulates in the hands of extremely few people, who then may or may not spend it in a way that diffuses across the economy. The executives and shareholders of the largest banks, as well as the holders of US Treasuries and Mortgage Backed Securities, are disproportionate recipients of US QE, even ahead of other billionaires in other sectors. This not only is unfair, but after QE1, QE2, and QE3, the finite and diminishing effectiveness of this sort of very narrowly concentrated money creation was becoming more obvious even in 2016, let alone now. Therefore, in addition to being essential that newly created money be given to individuals, the DUES of central bank money addresses a large portion of the inequality debate, because what can be fairer than every US citizen receiving the same share of the required monetary creation?

Inequality is not best addressed by taxing the most productive, or by conflating assets with income, or by assuming that two people of the same income are equally prosperous if they are at very different stages of life and have very different obligations. The real inequality of this era is something quite different.

The Real Inequality: There are many products and services available for little or no cost today, that were inaccessible to even the wealthiest person from a century ago. These examples are more numerous than people realize (such as the ability to research a topic online in a few minutes, vs. spending half a day at the library to mine various books for information). But as good as such examples are, they do not fully explain how different 2020 is relative to just two, five, or seven decades ago. There is a saying that comes up in futurism circles, which is that *"The future is already here, it is just not evenly distributed."* Allow me to present my interpretation of what this statement truly means.

Share of the world population living in absolute poverty, 1820–2015-by Max roser
All incorpes are adjusted for inflation over time and for price differences between countries
(1985-PPP before 1970: 2011-PPP after 1970).

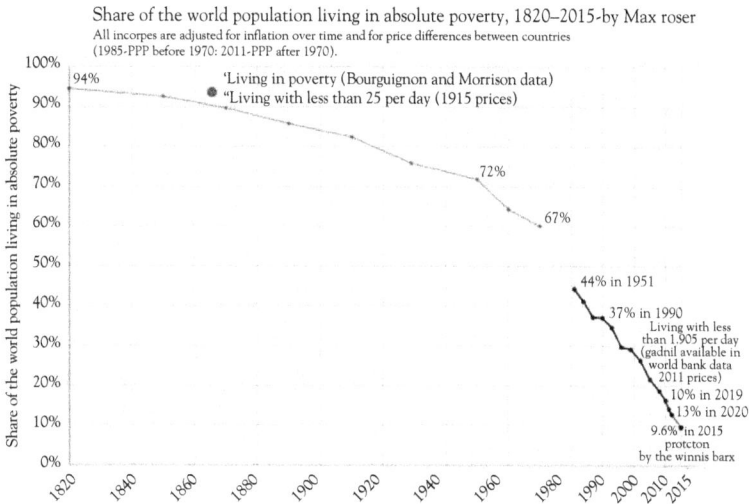

This chart from Max Roser is a byproduct of the earlier exponential GDP growth charts. For most of human existence, the only occupations available to the bottom 99.9% of people were handicrafts, agriculture, construction labor, or military service (usually not by choice). Ordinary people often had to partake in very dangerous work just to earn basic food and clothing, while today the same necessities can be earned in an hour of work within a safe environment. Most individuals with very high IQs, deep musical or artistic talent, or exceptional innovative capacity never got a chance to see if they could earn a living from such aptitudes, if those attributes were even considered valuable at all. This is still true for the billion plus people who earn less than $2/day in the most destitute countries, and their condition is a window to what almost all humans lived like before modern times. Very few people have ever lived in a time and place where they had any chance to monetize their more exclusive, specialized talents.

Starting at the very top, we see that today, there are a select few people who earn over $10 Million per year in careers that could not have existed just a generation ago. Would Oprah Winfrey be a billionaire in any other time, or in most other countries, considering how many enabling factors of hers are exclusively contemporary? Would professional athletes not only earn millions from their sport, but additional millions by 'endorsing' products that they themselves may not use? Would musicians be earning millions in royalties for decades after their best songs are released, even from countries they have never been to? We can see that some people are extraordinarily fortunate to be born in the right time and right countries for their talents to be actualized, but what about the rest of us?

You may not be quite as supreme an extractor of modern opportunities as an A-list celebrity or self-made tech billionaire, and fame will always be finite in a way that wealth is not, but lest you think this concept is applicable only to those at the apex, take an inventory of your own career. Is your profession one that either did not exist a century ago, or otherwise pays much more than it used to, due to productivity-enhancing technologies? If you think the answer is no, consider how many of your tasks involve the use of MS Word, Excel, or Powerpoint (or equivalent non-Microsoft programs). Think about how often you communicate with a colleague who might be hundreds or thousands of miles away, via a medium that carries little or no cost of communication. Think about how often you travel, for business, to a country that your home country was at war with less than a century ago.

Now, think back to what professions your grandparents did, both your grandfathers and grandmothers. If you happen to have a grandfather who was an illustrious success, he is just one of the four, and is not representative of the dataset. If you don't know what some of your grandparents did, they were almost certainly not in a profession that would be considered impressive today. Once you list out what all four did as their primary occupation (most of your grandmothers were housewives), consider how fortunate you are to be born just two generations later, where someone of the same genetics has such a better suite of career choices available to them. To broaden the dataset even further, consider all of your cousins who are common to these grandparents, and assess the professions they are in and their general prosperity levels. You will find an overwhelming rise in the variety as well as quality of professions between the two groups, over just two generations of genetically similar people.

Thus, the real inequality is not one of present income or some other short-sighted metric, but rather one of era. Until recently, only a few skills could be monetized and rarely were they the person's 'dream'. In the modern age, a much higher portion of the workforce is able to utilize a wider range of their talents at higher compensation and with great safety. This, more than anything else, indicates how fortunate the vast majority of people in all but the poorest countries are, compared to their ancestors just two or more generations earlier.

Yet, it gets even better, as we circle back to the favorite subplot of this piece, that of exponentially rising prosperity. There are many products, services, and conveniences that are almost free today, but were inaccessible to even the wealthiest people of 40 years ago. Returning to the celebrated smartphone, the device that serves as your telephone is now wireless, and further serves as your camera, music player, calculator, geo-locator, alarm clock, and much more. The peasants earning just $4000/year in emerging countries now have a smartphone that is better than what anyone could have purchased in 2006, with the ongoing rate of improvement continuing to amaze. The same goes for many other types of electronic devices.

At this point, a critic will emerge who utters a memorized line like "people don't eat computers and smartphones, so this progress is overrated". This conclusion is incorrect, as the processes that create low-tech consumer staple products continue to become more efficient from the implementation of technological stardust. A few graphs from Prof. Perry's blog depict the trend of price declines in some products that by themselves are low-tech consumer staples. Everything from <u>food</u>, to <u>clothing</u>, to <u>housing square footage</u>, to <u>energy bills</u>, to the cost to travel by either <u>airplane</u> or <u>automobile</u>, has been dropping relative to average household income. Even if the end product is apparently low-tech, the processes that go into producing, delivering, and improving them continue to adopt the latest productivity-enhancing technology, becoming part of the ATOM.

Spending on; Food (At and array from home), cars, clothing, household furnishing, housing and utilities, and gasoline as a share of total personal consumption expenditures, 1929–2016

Average and median square feet for new single-family US houses vs. Average US household size, 1973 to 2015

Average US domestic air fares, 1995:Q1 to 2019:Q3

Consumer spwnding on energy as a share of total consumption expenditures, 1920 to 2016 (through Nov.)

In the first half of 2016, spending on "life's basics" leas the lowest ever as a share of consumer spending (42.3%)

Average US arrares (inflation-adjusted) fell to an historical low of $345 in Q3 2019

Source: SEA

Source: Census bureau

Source: Bureau of transportat on statistics

Source: Bureau of economic analysis

Average house size (left scale)
Median house size (left scale)
Average household size (right scale)

Battery energy density Watt-hours per litre

Avg. 0.4%

Anyone of a certain age remembers when airline travel was only for the wealthy, cars broke down often and left oil slicks in parking spots, clothes deteriorated more quickly than today, and almonds and cashews were considered expensive for the average household. Most complaints about the inflation seen in basic necessities are either very selective or outright inaccurate, for in reality the price of most staples continues to decline. The only exceptions are invariably from products derived from industries that have concocted a deep entanglement with government to willfully obstruct market forces.

If all of this is not enough to demonstrate that a later a person is born, the more blessed they are with resources, luxuries, and branches in their life script, consider one particularly profound frontier of research— anti-aging and longevity. While this is still a very distant prospect, serious observers agree that there is at least some chance for a longevity miracle treatment to emerge. People spend most of their lives coming to terms with the grim reality of their own finite lifespan, yet now there is the slim possibility that people born late enough might be able to readily reach ages of 100 or higher. Before long, we will see examples of older billionaires pledging most of their wealth towards longevity research in a desperate bid to turn back the clock. Meanwhile, a younger person with no money can simply wait until the treatment is mainstream and inexpensive, with little risk of cutting it too close. An extended lifespan may ultimately be no more than the random luck of having been born before 1970 vs. after 2000, with those in between on the fence. That, dear readers, is the ultimate inequality. Consider the misfortune of those who die just a year before some breakthrough longevity treatment.

Hence, the real inequality, affecting the greatest percentage of people, is one of era. The message here is not to depress those who were born a bit too early to have a realistic shot at living until the age of 100. Rather, that many discussions about inequality today are misguided, incomplete, and seem to be built around an agenda to forcibly transfer wealth. This is, in the age of the ATOM, an obsolete ideology. Under the hypothetical ATOM transition, when the DUES eventually crosses $50,000/year or more by the 2030s, the distribution of net worth will still not be very different than it is today, nor should it be, given the differences in effort, talent, and enterprise among individuals. Nonetheless, the greatest fortunes will be more tightly tied to entrepreneurship and innovation rather than embedded cronyism, while ordinary people operate from a much higher floor, with a wider range of choice and options than ever before.

This juncture is where the future starts to become more evenly distributed. We are at the point where early adoption of ATOM economics begins to transition to mass-market adoption, if governments reorient accordingly.

CHAPTER 10

Implementation of the ATOM Age for Nations

If a man is proud of his wealth, he should not be praised until it is known how he employs it.

—Socrates

Given how recently the world economy has entered this situation of accelerating technological deflation, only the most prosperous and technology-dense countries currently have the ability to generate central bank money in a perpetual and rising stream, and in turn divert it to fund their government spending. Sometimes, a country is closer or further from this threshold than countries of similar prosperity.

While the transformation is a continuum, in general, a nation has to cross a threshold where technological products are approximately 3% of its GDP, which the US has recently surpassed. At the 3% threshold, there is a sufficient buffer against inflation upticks in the early incubatory period, where critics still have followers. For example, the nations of Northwestern Europe could embark on this restructuring right away, but the nations of Southern and Eastern Europe are not quite there yet. The EU cannot easily blend the varying ATOM levels of different countries into one and expect ECB monetary expansion to diffuse evenly. Similarly, while China as of 2020 has a similar prosperity as Latin America, the technological depth of China's economy makes China fewer years away from this transformation than Mexico and Brazil are.

There was a time when vast reserves of natural resources (such as oil) were seen as the most fortuitous stroke of luck for a nation to have. In this age, the tables are turned, where having significant ATOM density is an even more profitable resource, and unlike oil, is self-reinforcing and ever-expanding. Ironically, the countries that were the most deprived of natural resources (such as Japan and South Korea) had to rely heavily on technology to further their economies, which has now made them among the most ready for the marriage of the ATOM with central bank monetary creation.

While the US has reached a point where it can implement this only at this stage at $65,000 per capita GDP, China could implement this upon reaching a mere $20,000 per capita in the mid-2020s. This is simply due to the percentage of Chinese GDP that will be composed of ATOM-derived deflationary products approaching 3%, despite being merely at a similar level of prosperity as the US was in the 1970s. Even impoverished, low-tech India can implement this by the 2030s, despite still being much poorer at that point than the US is in 2020, due to the same 3% threshold.

Each country has to do an ATOM assessment to determine if their central bank can generate money without generating inflation, and if not, how many years away they might be from such a capability. I have detailed data and algorithms that can help each country estimate where it is on the progression towards the ATOM threshold, but for the purposes of this publication, I will discuss a few select countries and their specific characteristics, starting with the United States.

How the US Can Inaugurate the ATOM Age: I repeat that there is virtually no chance that these topics will be researched, the ideological barriers overcome, the Federal Reserve's powers expanded, and an ATOM-ready DUES program implemented before it is done by a number of smaller countries first. I am also relatively certain that the US will not be the first, second, or even fourth country to implement such a revamp of its monetary and fiscal paradigms (more on those other countries later). But if the US were to hypothetically start this program by 2020, one attractive avenue (as an alternative to starting with the flat $5000/year to all US citizen adults) to ease into it is through that venerable old program, Social Security.

As of 2019, Social Security (SS) collected about $1.2 Trillion in taxes, and distributed roughly the same $1.2 Trillion sum out to recipients. The tax is 12.4% of the employee's income, up to $137,700 of income, after which there is no tax. While there is an illusion that this 12.4% is split between the employee and employer, this is obviously money that would otherwise land in the pocket of either if not for the tax, and is certainly a contributor to angst about the 'lack of wage growth'. The SS payout formula calculates payments with some correlation to how much a worker paid into the system, but the correlation is not exact. There are other complicated calculations for spouses of workers, immigrants who were in America for a period but never became US citizens, and so on, all of which are often gamed and exploited. There is the additional cost incurred by the fact that millions of households would not need to file tax returns at all if not for SS, which adds volume to the already-bursting IRS processing system.

There is a great deal of apprehension about the future of the SS program, since US demographics are far less favorable than they were in the first 70 years of SS. The age at which a person can receive benefits was set when US life expectancy was itself around 65, and now, the powerful senior lobby prevents the government from indexing the eligibility age to rising life expectancy. This means that the average duration of receivership has increased from 2–3 years to 12–15 years, or roughly six times longer, even though the duration of working-age payments into the system has not increased. The ratio of intake to payouts has thus been very adversely affected by what should be celebrated—rising life expectancy. This in turn leads to a rather peculiar and morbid opposition to rising lifespans in some quarters, as if the fear of updating a government program from another era is more important than the single most comprehensive indicator of societal well-being.

Instead, since we know that the central banks of the world will soon have to permanently generate well above $4 Trillion/year, it would be appropriate to directly fund all SS obligations with that very monetary influx, making good use of this established distribution channel. Simultaneously, the regressive SS tax can be the first income tax to be eliminated. The recipients see no change in their payment amount, but gain the eventual benefit of their SS money now being exempt from income tax (unlike today) due to the commencement of the income tax phaseout. Note that the monthly increases in the ATOM stipend are far more granular than the annual SS increases, to facilitate dynamic responses to inflation changes.

Meanwhile, working-age people and their employers immediately get more money in their hands to the tune of 12.4% of their paychecks up to the first $137,700, which creates a huge surge in consumer spending and job creation. Debt servicing becomes easier for individuals, and since all other types of income tax are still in effect, those tax collections rise as a ripple effect. The US enjoys a win-win all around, all because the Federal Reserve has to produce that much money anyway to offset technological deflation.

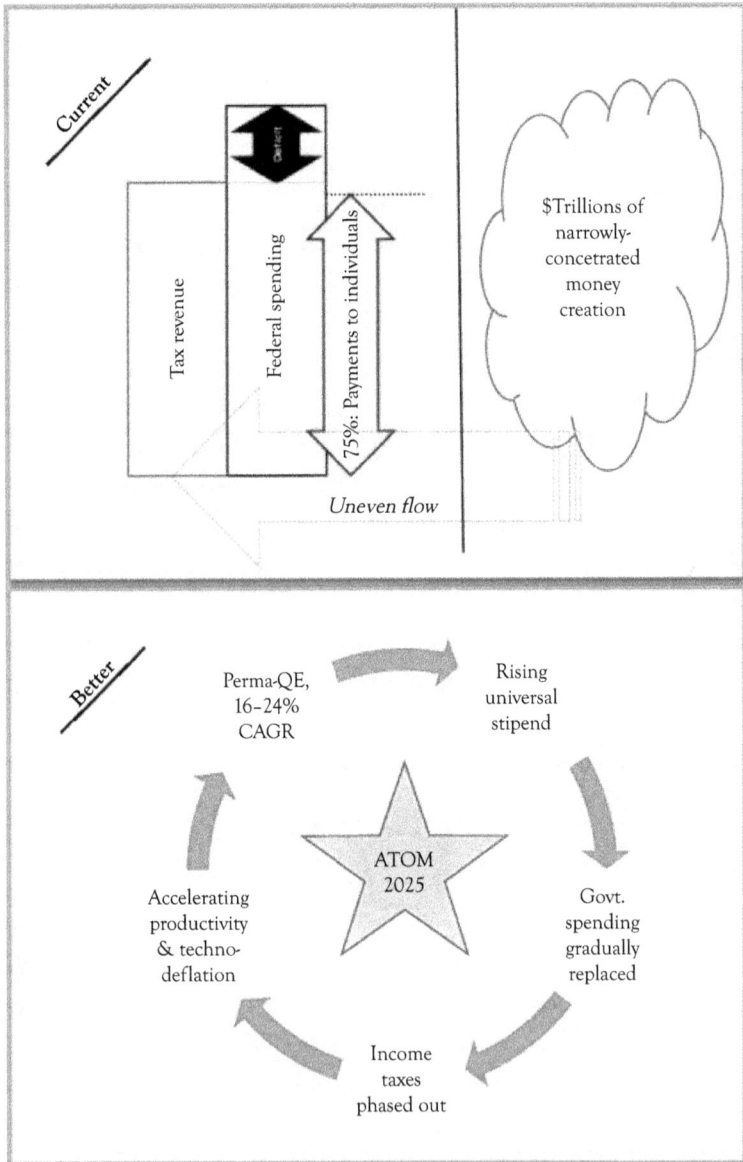

After the inaugural year of funding a government spending program with Federal Reserve QE proves that neither the inflation rate nor fiscal budget was destroyed in the process, it is time to increase this disbursement by the annual 16–24% to match the higher degree of technological penetration in the economy. This should be done by merely extending the payout down the age brackets to people younger than the SS recipients, one age cohort at a time. By 2020, every US citizen over the age of 18 is receiving their payout, while the Federal Reserve is now dispensing over $2.3 Trillion per year ($10,000+/year/person), with broad recognition that Federal Reserve QE has to permanently rise at 16–24%/year. Inflation is no longer a serious concern, since the expansion is within the aegis of the ATOM.

As the DUES is extended to all US citizens, other government wealth transfer programs should be steadily and proportionally phased out. The order in which this is done has to be decided by policy researchers, but over the 3–5 years that it takes to extend the stipend all the way down to age 18, every Federal payment program from Medicare to the Pell Grant to food stamps should commence the retirement process. This achieves the goal of replacing the 75% of US government spending comprised of payments to individuals with the vastly more efficient and fair DUES. The stipend will rapidly become large enough where it can allow anyone to purchase private health insurance of varying coverage. This retires the system of the government paying healthcare providers directly, thereby distorting prices, reducing efficiency, and throttling innovation.

Simultaneously, the rest of the income tax code can follow the SS tax into the pages of history. This is best achieved by sequentially eliminating each category of tax one by one, based on how similar to a payment program it already is. After the SS tax, perhaps the Medicare tax can be next, followed by the AMT, the capital gains tax, the corporate income tax, and finally, the ordinary/individual income tax. Note that as each tax is eliminated, the collections from each remaining type of tax balloon from the economic stimulus created by the absence of the previous tax. This cushion should not give pause to the plan of systematically phasing out every one of these taxes, since humans are already handicapped relative to the untaxable and borderless output of AI.

State and local governments do not have their own central banks and cannot run budget deficits, so will have to continue to fund themselves with existing methods of taxation, which vary greatly by location. Some states, like Texas, Florida, and Nevada have no income tax, while others like California have top bracket rates as high as 13.3%. Some cities have no income tax, and property taxes also vary greatly. High-tax states might see the vacancy created by the absence of Federal income tax as an excuse to greatly increase state income tax, but this would be a blunder, as the absence of Federal income tax will greatly widen the spread between states with unequal business friendliness. Furthermore, states with income tax rely on the Federal 1040 for a verification of taxable income, but once the Federal 1040 is gone, states will have to do their own auditing and verification. The competition between states and cities will become more direct, which, in a way, was the original intention of the Founding Fathers over two centuries ago.

The remaining 25% (and shrinking) of US Federal spending not in the form of payments to individuals can also be funded with money originated by the Federal Reserve. Just as with state and local governments, the real test with this component of government spending is whether the voters and officials can keep these expenditures contained, or succumb to the urge to overspend. Maintenance of the ATOM economy, as described earlier, will be a key determinant of competitiveness between nations, with societies that fail to maintain this resource swiftly incurring the penalty of seeing others surpass them.

Lest there be any confusion about the speed at which such a transition could be managed, I emphasize that the full expenditures of the US Federal government *cannot* hypothetically be funded as soon as 2020 by central bank action alone, as the ATOM is just not broad and deep enough yet to produce enough deflation. Rather, the transition has to be structured to intercept the ATOM at a point a decade away, and staged accordingly. By around 2025, unless another country moves first to capture the entire world's ATOM dividend for itself, the previous calculations predict that the ATOM will be advanced enough to metabolize a level of perma-QE where every US citizen over age 18 gets a stipend that by then has grown to $12,000/year in current dollars and keeps rising each year, pushing 'Real' GDP growth rates higher despite low inflation. The Federal income tax, now entirely phased out, is recognized as a relic of a bygone age.

A vision of this theoretical 2025 America presents itself. The economic climate at all levels of American society is fundamentally transformed. Careers are plentiful and compensation is more closely aligned with productivity than before. Entrepreneurship has become more widespread and lucrative, and is now the largest occupation, with clusters of tech startups sprouting in all cities. Inflation is minor, and many products cost the same or less than they did in 2020, particularly when adjusting for ATOM impact on product quality. Debates about living wages, minimum wages, federal tax hikes, and two-income traps have vanished into the dustbin of history. Even if state, local, sales, and property taxes still exist, the burden seems minor, and governance in most state and city governments has improved, partly due to a reduction in some categories of crime, and the government resources freed up through this.

At the highest macroeconomic level, the US National Debt, which has recently crossed the psychologically significant threshold of 100% of GDP for the first time in a non-war economy, ceases to grow since government spending no longer generates a deficit funded by US Treasury debt. The $23 Trillion of existing Treasury bills, notes, and bonds will shrink as each individual debt contract matures and expires without being replaced with new debt contracts from a new deficit. This eventually makes the entire debt, which is going to be a major factor in exacerbating the pain of the next eventual recession as previously described, gradually shrink and disappear. Thus, the supposedly ominous National Debt and budget deficits become a non-factors in future fiscal policy structuring under this model.

Not every problem dwindles away, of course. If America of 2020 has proven anything, it is that some people just cannot handle prosperity. When serious problems recede away, they devote their lives towards inventing new ones, as the endlessly mutating victim-chic culture demonstrates. Some people will always concoct new grievances as a cloak through which they resentfully harass others, and most of the tired old shibboleths will continue. What may be different is that AI may greatly empower the efforts of factseekers, enabling them to obstruct the grievance extortionists more effectively than is possible now.

This is where the second-choice program, the Sovereign Venture Fund (SVF), becomes an alternative. Since the first-mover country is effectively capturing the entire world's ATOM deflation for domestic benefit, it should have its central bank generate a full $1 Trillion (possible $2 Trillion), and keep *it in a segregated account and out of the domestic economy*, as this actually would cause inflation if it circulated. Then, before another country becomes aware of this, deploy it into overseas allocations (equities, real estate, etc.) as quickly as possible. Hence, these are positions now owned by the SVF, and can then be more precisely deployed into projects or technologies that specifically hedge domestic risk. This can make far more speculative bets than a Sovereign Wealth Fund, which was built through decades of taxpayer money and understandably wants to be more risk averse.

As I have stressed, no country will even begin to implement this plan in the immediate future, and even then, the US will definitely not be the first to embark on this path. But there are four countries with unique attributes that enable them to be the first to reap the benefits of this approach to fiscal and monetary governance. These four countries, which happen to be four of the best-managed economies in the world, consist of two single-party Pacific Rim city-states, Hong Kong and Singapore, and two Western democracies, Canada and Switzerland.

Hong Kong and Singapore: Hong Kong and Singapore have shared origins that led them to become city-state tax havens with small, efficient governments. Both have per-capita GDPs that are manifold higher than the countries they were separated from (China and Malaysia, respectively), and their economies have high ATOM densities. Both are routinely ranked within the top four financial centers in the world, despite having been quite poor as recently as the 1970s.

Each of these city-states has a government budget of about $60 Billion/year. As small nations with very high interconnectedness to much larger economies, they could each fund their governments with central bank money, waive all of their already-low taxes, and still be just a rounding error in the world monetary and inflation data. In fact, the inflation rate of Hong Kong and Singapore is more determined by whatever monetary expansion is done by the big central banks of China, Japan, and the US. As a result, both Hong Kong and Singapore can proceed with the full knowledge that their money creation will not cause any significant local inflation or currency devaluation. Once they fund their existing government budgets, they can proceed on their own program to phase out taxes and disburse a DUES, which itself can rise at a faster rate than a larger country could manage.

Hong Kong and Singapore are not democracies, so their political process does not double as an entertainment genre. Hence, the sequence of decisions involved in this sort of restructuring can be made and executed quickly. Due to currency pegs, a currency flight is not a risk. The stipend may have to start small, but can rapidly scale up at speeds a large country could not manage. The stipend could reach $50,000/year within five years, without triggering any domestic inflation. They could, similarly, implement the SVF immediately, at a size of $1 Trillion or more.

Decades of low-tax, business-friendly policies have cultivated a culture of governance that makes them among the least likely governments to get carried away in a frenzy of 'free money' gluttony. Whatever approvals Hong Kong needs from China are unlikely to be a problem given China's own massive and innovative monetary practices, and inclination to observe how well the Hong Kong experiment works. Success in Hong Kong and Singapore can clarify a roadmap for other countries in the region that could already implement the strategy (Taiwan, South Korea, and Japan), and eventually, the largest practitioner of ATOM monetization in the future (China).

Canada and Switzerland: Among Western democracies, there are two very different countries that share the distinction of being the best positioned to transition to the ATOM paradigm of fiscal and monetary governance. Traditional disadvantages can now be converted to advantages, in a historic turning of tables.

Canada is in the unique situation of having a sole geographical neighbor with an economy ten times larger, with which Canada conducts most of its trade. Given the high ATOM density of both nations, the inflation rate in Canada can never deviate significantly from that of the United States. At first, it may seem troubling that a major aspect of the Canadian economy is predominantly pegged to how America performs on the same measure. But from what we have seen about the potential re-direction of central bank monetary easing, Canada is superbly well-positioned.

Most Americans are not aware that Canada's federal government does not typically run a budget deficit. The Canadian government, as of 2019, collects about $340 Billion in tax revenue, and spends a slightly higher $355 Billion in an impressive demonstration of political restraint. The national debt of Canada is only about the third the proportional size of the US debt, a trajectory quite the opposite of the one the US is currently on.

If the Canadian Parliament were to authorize the Canadian central bank to merely create the entire $355 Billion of federal expenditures and waive all federal income taxes, the amount of monetary expansion is negligible relative to the broader US money supply. This ensures that there is no possibility of any Canada-specific inflation. It really is that simple, amidst Canada's favorable conditions (Canada also happens to have a more skill-based immigration policy and better regulatory philosophy than the US at present, all of which strengthen the ATOM levels in the country).

Canadian provinces have taxes and budgets of their own, of course, but the entire federal government is already well within the zone where taxation of Canadian citizens is no longer necessary. Due to this, a DUES program can be constructed in short order without generating any discernible inflation in either Canada or the US. For any Canadian reading this, perhaps you should send this reading material to your elected representatives and start urging them to examine these ideas.

Switzerland, by contrast, has arrived at this juncture along a very different path than Canada. Few countries have done more things correctly for as many centuries as Switzerland, which built an economy entirely around high-margin industries and is synonymous with an elite image of wealth and sophistication. Switzerland is not part of the Eurozone currency block, but is completely surrounded by it. The Eurozone economy is about 16 times larger than the Swiss economy, and most of the Eurozone's GDP is generated within 300 kilometers of the Swiss border, representing a huge ATOM-deflationary sink. This guarantees the Swiss central bank's ability to generate an almost unlimited amount of money without causing any domestic inflation.

Above and beyond the extremely suitable geographical location, Switzerland has already considered experimenting with the idea of a universal stipend (as has Finland). The only missing piece is to have the stipend paid with money created by the Swiss central bank, rather than by the large tax increase they were considering. As the stream of money increases, the rest of the government budget can draw from this source, while all Swiss income taxes can be gradually eliminated.

Excellent governance, high technology density, their own central banks, and proximity to vastly larger economies with low inflation will hopefully lead Canada and Switzerland to become the first to undergo the legislative and political process of implementing this solution, setting an example for the larger Western democracies to follow. Similar to the example of New Zealand provided in Chapter 7, Canada or Switzerland could also implement a $1 Trillion SVF in the same way, provided one of them moves first. The US and Eurozone will only implement such programs when they already see it succeeding in a smaller Western nation, and that too after the first-mover advantage is no longer available.

CHAPTER 11

Implementation of the ATOM Age for Individuals

Live as if you were to die tomorrow. Learn as if you were to live forever.

—Mahatma Gandhi

Ability will never catch up with the demand for it.

—Confucius

Building upon the meme presented in the previous section on how the future is not evenly distributed, it is now time to take steps to get more of the future distributed in your favor. As an individual, there a myriad of resources and capabilities at your fingertips, that can make you healthy, wealthy, and wise with a speed and efficiency that was previously impossible.

How to Think Like Part of the ATOM: You are not merely a hapless creature being swept along by the ATOM, you are a part of it. Whether a person is interested in the subject matter discussed here or not, the ATOM is interested in them. Every aspect of life is being woven into the ATOM as existing hierarchies and power structures are being toppled and re-arranged at accelerating speeds. Therein lies tremendous opportunity, and thus opportunity cost for those who fail to become sufficiently astute. Just consider a few of the examples that come to mind:

- Never before has it been easier to research a career, or to contact someone who is in a position you wish to attain in the future. A skilled and determined user of LinkedIn can replace much of the networking utility of an MBA degree from all but the top few institutions, saving considerable time and expense. The ability to keep track of the career progression of dozens of peers, and identify common elements of success among them, is often underestimated.

- An amateur filmmaker now has access to high-definition cameras, editing software, terabytes of storage, and sound synthesizers that would have been prohibitively expensive just a decade ago. A film project can be financed through a crowd-funding site, the work and reputation of potential collaborators can be researched easily through their web presence, and trailers can be marketed through YouTube. Such a project has at least six components that did not exist at the start of the century.

- Before Yelp and other review aggregators, there was considerable uncertainly when patronizing a new restaurant. Now, not only are user reviews easy to find, but pictures of many menu items are posted on Yelp itself. This information arms the diner with much more awareness of the menu, and enables the restaurant to avoid being castigated due to a misinformed order by the diner. The same applies to checking the reviews of a new film or theater production beforehand, greatly reducing the chance of a negative surprise after the sunk cost of tickets. Dentists, auto mechanics, photographers, hairdressers, etc. can be similarly vetted from a computer screen. This new convenience to the consumer experience is not recorded favorably in GDP calculations, even though millions of instances of dissatisfaction and lost time have been avoided.

- Automobile commuters with good jobs but lengthy commutes have joined Uber-type platforms to take a rider along with them on *the commute they have to undertake anyway*. The driver earns an extra $200–$400/week (against which an appropriate portion of car and smartphone costs can be applied as deductions) with no incremental input time or cost. Meanwhile, other commuters enjoy having one less car on the road for each such dynamically generated carpooling pair. The key is that a dead commute is now monetized even by corporate-class people, increasing passengers per car and reducing traffic congestion, while replacing dedicated taxicabs. For the macroeconomy, it also creates new VM where none existed before.

- A trifecta of new technologies has enabled small manufacturers to experience a phoenix-like resurgence in the US. Fracking has toppled the price of US natural gas to a sixth of what it was in 2007, bestowing any gas-intensive manufacturer with a major cost advantage over non-US rivals. Low-cost 3D Printing has lowered scale as a barrier to entry for many types of manufacturing and prototyping. Manufacturing robots can perform many tasks better than human workers, 24/7/365, at a cost as low as $1/hour, while being continuously augmented with new software updates. The rise of the solo advanced manufacturer is now upon us, with individuals operating out of a small space producing and selling millions of dollars of high-margin goods.

Have you done enough aggregate Internet searching and forum commenting to capture all the low-hanging fruits available to you for your personal advancement and risk management? If you answer that question in the affirmative, I am here to tell you that you have not come even close to realizing what is possible. Even heavily committed people barely access 10% of the information that could greatly improve their careers, finances, health, and relationships, and I don't think there is anyone in the world, no matter how successful, who has implemented more than 50% of what is available to them. I myself am nowhere near this level.

Recall the earlier point about how it is now possible to research in minutes what used to take half a day in the public library (that too if you were fortunate enough to be in a country that even had public libraries at the time). Add to that the ability to get your questions answered in forums like Yahoo Answers, Quora, etc. Then combine that with connections between different memes, factoids, and tangents that would not have been visible in the glacial pace of information accrual and exchange before Internet search and forums. Integrating all this, you can see how your ability to access and implement valuable information can take a great leap forward, and how almost everyone can participate in the creation of knowledge.

Case Studies of the Personal ATOM: Sometimes, a story can better illustrate the ways a person savvy to the disruptive and augmentative nature of new technologies can rapidly upgrade one or more aspects of their life. There is more fluidity and mobility across classes and strata than was possible before, and the ATOM is now the land of opportunity. The following are four examples of how someone might adapt and thrive within the new realities of the ATOM.

1. Lisa wanted to become an exceptionally good amateur chef, but back in 1998, she found the available instructional materials to be limited and uninspiring. Every cooking show on TV required the viewer to be interested in the item being presented in that specific episode, with no way for the viewer to search for their own preferences. Cookbooks were not a good solution either, for each ingredient listed in a recipe required that item to be purchased in a larger quantity, leaving remainder quantities of each item in the refrigerator and pantry. Lisa wondered for years *why none of these cookbooks had a matrix in the back of the book, linking ingredients across recipes, to make the shopping process for the layperson more efficient and less wasteful.* Lisa found this oversight among the sum total of published cookbooks to be quite ridiculous. She knew that there was major overlap in the basics of cooking, but this was not easy for an amateur to discover without taking an expensive cooking class.

   By around 2004, however, something began to change. Lisa found that many of the premier French, Italian, and Indian chefs were posting knowledge online. The common theme among them began to emerge. Great chefs think not in terms of compliance to a fixed recipe, but rather see what ingredients are available, and create a production from them. Cooking has to be bottom-up, not top-down. The 'eureka' moment for Lisa was that she could simply type ingredients into Google, and recipes that utilize those ingredients would come up. This was vastly more efficient than a cookbook, and allowed Lisa to get past the learning bottleneck holding her and others back. She could also now buy certain perishables without worrying about exactly what she will make from them as the clock ticks. The arrival of YouTube was another godsend, where, unlike a regularly scheduled cooking show, the user can merely search for whatever recipe she wants. A video is far easier to emulate than a text recipe, and further expanded upon the list of perishable ingredients she can now purchase in a shopping trip.

After years of stagnation, Lisa's skills improved rapidly after these revelations, and she even posted some of her own cooking videos to YouTube. Comment feedback from like-minded viewers led to additional improvements. Lisa eventually reached a level of expertise where she was able to produce cuisine that met or exceeded what was available at fine restaurants, with her YouTube channel accruing over 1,000,000 subscribers, elevating her hobby to a full-time, commute-free career.

2. Fred always had a keen financial mind, and wanted to do better with generating a return in his IRA and his brokerage account, for he knew that this is just as important as his paycheck from his day job. He did not believe in individual stocks, for he knew he was unlikely to ever close the information disadvantage he had relative to institutions and those very close to the companies. He also found mutual funds to be uninspiring due to their high fees, and the inability to short them or write options on them.

The advent of Yahoo Finance in the late 1990s made a wealth of information available for free, but most of the information was still about individual stocks, which was not Fred's target. In the process of mining Yahoo Finance, he found a great deal of information on options, as well as daily quotes that were previously unavailable so freely. It was exceedingly difficult for a layperson to research, let alone trade options before the late 1990s, with truly abundant information only appearing around 2005 or so. The discovery process made Fred knowledgeable about options, and eventually futures. As computing and data transmission became cheaper, brokerage firms were able to lower their trading commissions. Fred began to create algorithms to generate returns strictly from options and futures of broadly traded commodities, such as oil, gold, natural gas, and

^vix volatility. Despite some early setbacks, he eventually was able to generate 30–50% annual compounded returns from his algorithms, built around the principle of capturing the various time decays (option decay, futures contango, leverage decay) inherent to those instruments.

As these returns became routine for Fred, his day job became optional, and he gave some thought to managing client money full-time and establishing a hedge fund. Fortunately, in the Internet age, it was easy for him to locate attorneys, auditors, and other service providers. By shopping around, he found that the Internet had increased competition amongst these providers, and thus the fixed costs associated with operating a hedge fund have fallen from about $500,000/year to just $30,000/year, greatly reducing the minimum assets needed for the hedge fund to be viable. Fred's hedge fund became sustainable with just $10 Million in assets, a threshold unheard of in the past, and he joined the new layer of hedge funds with under $20 Million in assets under management returning over 30%/year. The ability to run his fund from anywhere enabled him to relocate to a preferred destination.

This story is not to say that the percentage of people who become good at generating returns has increased, but rather accessibility is now far more democratic, permitting talented people from outside the establishment to make use of skills that may have gone to waste in the past. On this front, we are still only at the beginning.

3. James is an accountant, and has been employed at a large multinational corporation for over 15 years. As a top performer, he enjoys higher job security than his peers, but is nonetheless apprehensive about the speed at which his colleagues are vanishing and being subsumed by AI. After reading a number of frightening articles in the media, James was deeply worried about how long he could stay ahead of the machines.

Then, one fine day, James came across this publication, and began to see AI in a different light. It dawned on him that what he was observing was not the utter disappearance of accounting jobs into thin air, but that an accounting department with ten accountants at a payroll cost of $2M/yr could now generate the same services for a mere $100,000/yr (and falling) in AI costs and a sole human manager. James started to ponder the implications of starting his own accounting firm, where the work that could bring in $2M/yr in fees could be performed just by him and this new AI capability. His deep knowledge of accounting and reputation in his field meant he could accommodate a large portion of his former employer's accounting work into his own private practice, on top of acquiring additional clients. One man and his AI was now doing the work of ten, and could earn the income formerly earned by those ten. Until now, most solo practitioner accountants only handled smaller individual clients, and it was unheard of that a single-person firm could presume to undertake the enormity of work generated by an entire corporate department. James was one of the revolutionaries changing this, even though he never thought he would become an entrepreneur.

As happens whenever a new business model becomes highly profitable, James' success attracted competitors and pricing pressures began to manifest. At the same time, this competition created many additional jobs in sales, marketing, and support. Next, the market itself grew from the entry of smaller firms that could now avail themselves of elite accounting services previously beyond their reach. The ecosystem began to mature, but James continued to earn several times more than he did as a corporate employee, simply by continuing to refine the implementation of AI in his practice.

Lastly, what of the other accountants who saw their positions eliminated, and are not as talented as James? Well, some were able to get jobs in accounting working alongside AI, while others had to transition to different careers. This illustrates why the cushioning effect of the universal minimum stipend supplied by central bank monetary expansion is so essential, as it ensures that everyone gets some return from pervasive and accelerating forces of technological disruption while conducting their own transitions.

4. The legendary 'Delta Team' is a team of three video game creators who had produced a sequence of extremely successful games. The team was widely acclaimed in their field, and there were able to do almost aspect of game development for a top-flight game by

themselves, but in the past, were dependent on working within large game companies for the brand, corporate-class resources, and distribution channel.

As the Delta Team's successes accumulated, even the brand of the large company became secondary to their own, but the distribution channel kept them chained. Video games in 2006 sold as boxed products, and while one could buy it online, most sales were still through brick and mortar stores. The boxed product in the form of CDs or DVDs did not have a large fixed cost per unit (unlike the cartridges that caused an infamous inventory bust in 1983), but still required capital outlay, production time, packaging, and shipping. After that, the retailer margin consumed 30% of the retail price, even stocking a retail channel had onerous requirements of inventory, and had to be done again and again for each country, often with translation requirements for retail packaging, leading to complicated supply/demand mismatches that were tedious to rectify. This led to each boxed game selling for a retail price of $50. Hence, over 20,000 boxed copies had to be produced for a rudimentary launch, and that too only for the US, UK, and Australia.

But as the ATOM progressed, the convergence of broadband, anti-piracy technologies, price declines of advanced tools, and more, it became possible for the Delta Team to produce games entirely by themselves. Their YouTube livestreams of gameplay during development created a direct connection between the developers and their customers and enabled feedback to be incorporated into the game itself. Furthermore, they were now able to sell games exclusively through a website via unique downloads, thereby removing dependency on the big corporate umbrella and large retailers that require upfront inventory, as well as country-by-country permits and retail localization. Suddenly, forecasting sales was no longer an important part of the equation, as long as revenue met a minimum threshold for a certain game to be justified on the production roadmap.

The Delta Team could now operate as their own independent company for the first time ever. In this age, they could sell games for $30 instead of the previous $50, while earning about the same per unit sale. Customers countries that would have been too cumbersome to stock with retail inventory in 2006 were instantly available. Best of all, the situation of boxed games needing to be destocked from brick and mortar retail because a certain retail chain required at least 300 units/week in sales no longer existed, as residual sales for successful games continued for years after this point, which could be serviced by the download purchase model. The Delta Team agreed to relocate to a tax haven and produce games on their own. They churned out game after game that sold 100,000 units or more, or $3 Million in revenue each. Hence, all three members of the Delta Team achieved a great combination of success and independence.

These are just four examples of how someone might view the advent of accelerating technological disruption as an endless stream of opportunity, no matter what field someone works in. I have detailed maps for how specific professions, such as engineering, marketing, product management, investment banking, management consulting, medicine, and law could each supercharge their careers with greater ATOM awareness. The savvy and observant individual has a galaxy of avenues from which to choose from, ensuring that more of the future is distributed towards them. Everyone is surrounded by dozens of such avenues to pursue, no matter what your technical expertise, age, or station in life.

CHAPTER 12

The ATOM's Effect on the Final Frontier

Astronomy compels the soul to look upwards and leads us from this world to another.

—Plato

Ultimately, the endgame of any treatise on future visions invariably marches toward one particular topic. We earlier examined how the ATOM was creating commercial activity in space for the first time, such as private spaceflight, asteroid mining, and zero-gravity 3D Printing. As sophisticated as this may seem, these are still just stepping stones to how the ATOM links our civilization to space.

When the space race was underway in the 1957–77 period and mankind made seemingly giant leaps, many enthusiasts extrapolated that rate of progress forward and predicted a substantial human presence in space by 2020. That has not happened, for there are presently only an exiguous number of people in space (on average about one human out of every billion, at any given time). No humans have been more than a few hundred miles above the Earth's surface in decades.

Unfortunately, assessments now veer towards the opposite extreme, with proclamations such as "Human civilization peaked in 1969–72 because we haven't been on the Moon since then!" dominating the discourse. Quite to the contrary, the ATOM has enabled great strides in space exploration. This becomes apparent once one realizes that humans setting foot on an extraterrestrial surface is far from the only measure of progress. This is even despite the fact that landing a man on the Moon would cost far less, as a percentage of US GDP, than it did in 1969–72. The following content is a continuation of my article from 2009, SETI and the Singularity.

Space is For the Robots: For all the popular culture imagery around humans in space, such missions will never be as economical or efficient as sending advanced AI into the heavens. The overwhelming difference in space suitability between humans and AI can scarcely be exaggerated.

An AI does not require air or water, and can survive across a much wider range of temperatures, pressures, gravity, and radiation than a fragile human. An AI can load into a body or bodies (becoming a robot) as needed, or be stored in a tiny volume that is orders of magnitude smaller than what a human crew would require during space travel. The cost divergence begins at the time of launch itself, as it consumes far less fuel to launch a 100 kilogram piece of AI-installed hardware into space than a human-suitable spacecraft that may be 1 million times more massive. This hardware itself continues to shrink for each generation of Moore's Law, while a ship designed to transport humans does not. Furthermore, if the spacecraft is destroyed in an accident, only the hardware has to be replaced, with the AI software loaded onto it. The tragic deaths and resultant delays associated with failed human missions become a non-issue.

The chasm widens further when one sees how few celestial destinations can host human life. In the entire Solar System there is no world aside from Earth where a human can remotely survive without an elaborate spacesuit, that too for just a short time. By contrast, every single solid world other than Mercury and Venus can host a suitable robotic lander or rover for years. Probes have even landed on comets despite their low gravity. Even with Mercury and Venus, orbital probes with sophisticated AI can operate for decades, and never have to be brought back to Earth. The AI can be endlessly upgraded from Earth via wireless transmission of software updates. Add all of these factors up, and the indisputable advantages in cost, durability, and versatility ensure that most scientific exploration of space will be done with AI housed in relatively small hardware. Each such probe or rover can transmit data back to Earth as well as to other AIs in other locations in space, creating an interplanetary network effect. A few humans may be sent up by their governments for political purposes, and brief recreational space trips for the ultra-wealthy may become a viable business, but that is about the extent of human space travel to occur over the medium term. The uncanny suitability of AI for space leads one to contemplate whether this is some pre-ordained grand design of which we are merely facilitators.

Instead, for the rest of the human population, the celestial will become the virtual. Images and videos beamed back to Earth by the AI will be incorporated into VR experiences, enabling humans to 'walk' on the surfaces of Mars, Europa, Callisto, and Titan from their own homes, or even 'fly' between worlds faster than the speed of light. More people will be able to experience space with considerable realism, even as real exploration advances without human presence in space.

Exponential Exploration and Discovery: If humans are to be Earth-bound for a long time to come, that does not mean we miss the chance to revel in the growing wave of discoveries. Space exploration, particularly telescope power and data crunching, is being pulled into the ATOM, with the expected rate of exponential progress that entails.

No matter what, the greatest question of all is whether we are alone in the universe, and if we are not, what form has that other life taken. As our technology has advanced, some of the assumptions around this question have begun to shift. This is a vast subject and cannot be done full justice here, but one trend that stands out is the rising power and precision of telescopic methods and their merger with big data and supercomputing. Back in 2006, I estimated that telescopic power is rising at a compounded rate of 26%/year (the square root of Moore's Law, as pixel count increases as a square of the shrinkage of the side dimension). This has, among other discoveries, resulted in the detection of planets outside of our solar system, known as exoplanets.

Most stars are too inherently dim to be seen from Earth, unless they are very near (the nearest star, Proxima Centauri, is nonetheless far below the brightness threshold where it might be seen with the naked eye). Since many of the dimmer, cooler stars have planets, and planets only reflect some miniscule fraction of the light they receive from their primary star, a planet within a star system several light years away is vanishingly faint when viewed from Earth. Such planets were impossible to detect until new methods independent of luminosity emerged, such as observing radial velocity and transits of the planet in front of its primary star. Astronomers have continued to refine these methods, and with the technological improvement of their instruments both on the ground and in space, the rate of exoplanet discovery is rising exponentially.

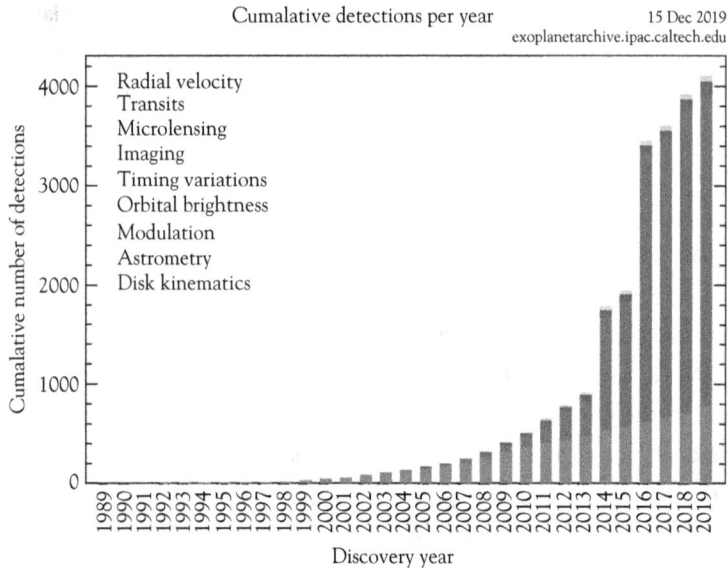

Cumalative detections per year   15 Dec 2019

exoplanetarchive.ipac.caltech.edu

As recently as 1995, there were hardly any exoplanets identified, but as the chart of annual discoveries shows us, we are now discovering an increasing number of them, in a curve that fits the familiar parabolic trajectory. There are now over 4000 planets confirmed, and the next 4000 will naturally take far less time than the first 4000. Note that newer methods are now generating the most detections (chart from Wikipedia).

The majority of early detections were larger, Jupiter-sized planets, and the discovery of Earth-sized planets has only begun more recently. Whether other forms of life require conditions similar to ours remains to be seen, but it is probable that any biological life forms may be just as unsuitable for space as we are. Nonetheless, if a small fraction of worlds with life have reached the threshold of creating their own artificial intelligence, their intelligence is similarly freed of conditional restrictions as ours would be, and then they might be easier to detect or even meet.

However, the paradox of this means that under the accelerating rate of change, it is very hard for a civilization even slightly more advanced than us to avoid detection, due to the much greater presence and detectability it would have. This may explain the Fermi Paradox, and increase the chances that we are one of very few advanced civilizations, or at least one of the earliest, and at least in our own galaxy. Over time, the exponentially

rising rate of discovery will enable us to narrow down the range of prob-
abilities of extra-terrestrial life and intelligence, and there will be orders
of magnitude more candidate planets as soon as the 2020s. For a detailed
article about how the ATOM affects SETI and the Drake Equation, and
how there is a good chance that we are the most advanced civilization in
at least this portion of the galaxy, see my 2009 article.

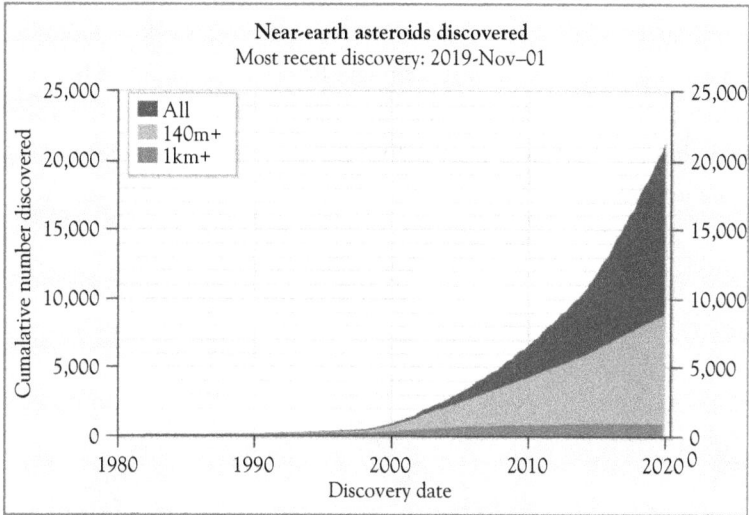

The second major benefit of telescopic progress is in the detection of asteroid impact threats. While there was a real risk of a surprise impact before
2000 (recall the films made in the 1990s about exactly this sort of disaster) the expansion of telescopic power has since identified almost all risky
Near Earth Objects (NEOs) to date, revealing which are an impact risk
at what point in time. Almost all objects large enough to be a problem
have been mapped, and none are expected to strike the Earth in the next
20 years, by which time our technologies for detection, deflection, and
even capturing of asteroids will be far more advanced. Notice the same
exponential chart appear here yet again, further proving that telescopic
power is yet another crucial technology that went from low-tech to high-
tech once the ATOM got to it. Just like 'Peak Oil' before it, the ATOM
has made a previous, seemingly insurmountable problem all but vanish
through sheer force of technological progress. Even better, the ATOM
will convert this into a business opportunity, as these asteroids contain

billions of tons of useful metals and hydrocarbons. There are a number of 'precious' metals on Earth that are in fact far more abundant in asteroids, and the supply of these metals could rise dramatically, sending the price lower and contributing further to ATOM-derived deflation.

As we can see, the majority of future space activity does not involve manned space missions. In contrast, with the ATOM converging discovery technologies into a rapid rate of improvement, astronomical research has become an information technology. This dichotomy does not fit into old assumptions about how space might be explored, but there has never been a better time to be a space enthusiast, whether scientific, industrial, or philosophical. This is a statement that can only become increasingly true each passing year.

CHAPTER 13

Conclusion

We can easily forgive a child who is afraid of the dark; the real tragedy of life is when men are afraid of the light.

—Plato

When a wise man points to the stars, an imbecile criticizes the finger.

—Confucius (modified)

This book is the culmination of years of observations in combination with some proprietary research across different fields. The process of shaping these ideas involved deep immersion on both ends of the political spectrum, as well as in many alternative ideologies across fragmented parts of the Internet. I have had to adopt various online personas and wade through swamps of fanatics and mentally ill people, pretending for years to have views that I actually do not hold in real life, to find the occasional genius who delivers one profound sentence after another. Then the same had to be done in the opposing ideological camp. The process of creating transformative new knowledge is a messy one, full of many dead ends, distractions, and dances with lunatics. From this process, I hope this research has given rise to material that starts a trickle that grows into a stream, and later into a mighty river.

I do not claim to have all of the answers, but if some of these ideas are refined and implemented, we will make it easier for trends to return to established trajectories. This may permit us to enter a new age of abundance and upliftment and avoid at least one massive fiscal crisis and deflationary depression. A lot of material has been covered and it may be a challenge to retain the holistic case in the first read, but if I were to summarize the most crucial themes and ideas into a condensed list, it would be:

- The accelerating rate of technological change, while previously a topic of interest only to futurists and related technophiles, is now at a stage where insufficient awareness has tangible costs to individuals.
- Economic growth, which has always been closely pegged to technological progress, has similarly been accelerating through centuries of data, and we are now entering a steep trajectory for the trendline, indeed the 'knee of the curve'.
- The world economy has been underperforming for years, with growth rates continuing to register well below the aforementioned trendline rates. This is due to the silent suppressive effect of some outdated policies and macroeconomic assumptions.
- Technological deflation, while easily accepted when one is a shopper for a new computer, is almost entirely ignored by macroeconomists, even as effects of this deflation on economic data are pervasive and rising.
- Technological disruptions across disparate areas are all interconnected with each other, and mutually reinforcing. There is a fixed but rising amount of aggregate disruption that is underway at any given time, in accordance with the accelerating rate of technological change. These first five bullet points effectively describe what we define as the 'ATOM'.
- Monetary expansion by central banks has served to merely offset the accelerating deflation that technology is generating across the economy. This deflation is international in nature, and so is most monetary expansion, no matter which country originates a particular expansion program.
- Artificial Intelligence (AI) will be able to move many types of productive output into tax-free locations, eroding the tax base of high-tax locations. The borderless and untaxable nature of AI will effectively tighten the screws on nations and jurisdictions that tax productive output excessively.

- Excessive fear of inflation, and assuming that even 3% inflation is high, has led to a chronic decline in the growth rate of Nominal GDP. This is a source of many types of malaise in the economies of wealthy countries that 'Real' GDP will not detect, and is constricting the rate of technological progress and productivity gains.

- The ATOM will react to ensure technological progress reverts to the trendline rate, bypassing or toppling obstacles such as inadequate fiscal, monetary, and regulatory policies in the process. This will begin to happen in the 2020s, and may accelerate after that point at a speed far too rapid for many governments to react to.

- Barring the preemptive adoption of the technology-friendly monetary policies recommended here, another major financial crisis and deep recession remains an ongoing risk. Existing methods of monetary expansion will prove ineffective due to saturation of the inefficient methods used by central banks to date. In reality, the solution to the problem is elegant, simple, and ushers in a new era of rapid growth.

- Central bank monetary expansion has to be made permanent as a policy, and openly declared as such. There can no longer be one-off programs tied to an assumption that each one is the final round of Quantitative Easing. Assets stored on central bank balance sheets can never be sold back into the market, so the balance sheets themselves are moot.

- Western central bankers have been taught very outdated principles regarding the risk of inflation from monetary creation, rendering them virtually incapable of seeing these truths, even as they are evident to the technology industry, small business owners, and more. Hence, the fact that $23 Trillion of cumulative monetary creation since 2009 has not caused inflation is still a complete mystery to Economists with formal credentials.

- Monetary expansion has to be of a direct, diffuse nature. Current methods of bond-buying used by the US Federal Reserve are well into the point of diminishing returns, and end up concentrating the QE in very few hands. The only real discussion and analysis should be about the rate of annual increases. The US Federal Reserve has not yet been granted this power by the US Congress, which restricts the Fed's ability to do what is necessary.

- Monetary expansion has to rise at a compounded rate of 16–24% a year, possibly higher, to offset technological deflation and keep the Wu-Xia Shadow Rate in step with the size of the deflationary force. Current patterns of monetary expansion and the absence of inflation already supply the data to support this conclusion.

- Since most government spending in the US and similarly advanced nations constitutes direct payments to individuals, these payments can and should be consolidated and formalized into a Direct Universal Exponential Stipend (DUES) that is paid equally to all citizens, and is funded by this central bank monetary expansion.

- This DUES constitutes a dynamic and rapidly strengthening safety net, as well as a catalyst for entrepreneurship. Unlike negative interest rates, this does not punish savers, and is more scalable in accordance with accelerating technological deflation.

- Federal income taxes can be phased out gradually and systematically, with all Federal government spending covered by monetary expansion, which itself is mostly the DUES.

- This sort of reform taking current levels of technological progress and the associated deflation into account to create tax, monetary, and regulatory policies far more favorable to entrepreneurship transcends both socialism and capitalism. It is also the only way to harness disruptive technologies, such as AI, into a vehicle of broadly increased human prosperity.

- Barring the first-choice avenue of ATOM DUES, the second-choice avenue of the Sovereign Venture Fund (SVF) is easier to implement politically, and still a huge improvement over the current status quo. The SVF carries a tremendous first-mover advantage, since a country can capture the entire world's technological deflation for domestic benefit as long as it is the first country to do so. The size of the SVF can be the same even if done by a relatively small country, hence delivering very high assets per capita.

- The US is not going to be the first nation to transition to such a new policy era, and certainly not before the next crisis. Hong Kong, Singapore, Canada, and Switzerland are more suitable candidates to be the first countries to reform in favor of 21st century economic forces.

- Few individuals, even if they work in the technology industry, have trained themselves to think like an active part of the ATOM. This mindset can be very profitable once adopted, and will become one of the core skillsets that an adult needs to have in order to prosper.

If you read this entire publication, I thank you, and if some points are unclear, I urge you to read the text and view the associated video again. It is not easy to make what is essentially an economics textbook into something interesting. Given the urgent importance of getting these ideas to the people in power, I chose to post it online for free and add videos, rather than expand this to the length of a full book (or thrice again that length, like Thomas Piketty's 700-page book) and market it as such.

I intend to devote a significant campaign towards bringing more exposure and debate to the ideas contained in this publication. I am embarking on this journey because I believe these concepts and policy recommendations can eventually benefit billions of people. When someone has the opportunity to make that sort of difference, it is their duty to devote a portion of their lives to such an endeavor. If you feel that some of these ideas have merit and should get in front of the right people, I invite you to join me and bring your talents to this campaign. Our civilization has to upgrade to the next era. It is time.

CHAPTER 14

The Campaign to Make This a Reality

There is no great genius without a mixture of madness.

—Aristotle

All great truths begin as blasphemies.

—George Bernard Shaw

Take up one idea. Make that one idea your life—think of it, dream of it, live on that idea. Let the brain, muscles, nerves, every part of your body, be full of that idea, and just leave every other idea alone. This is the way to success.

—Swami Vivekananda

I fully recognize that in 2020, much of this will still be dismissed as too radical, despite the greater acceptance since the first version published in 2016. Terms like 'crazy' and 'economically ignorant' will intrude as mosquitoes of disapproval, and I am prepared to withstand that phase. Soon, opposition will start to erode as the recession begins to manifest and deflation starts to exceed even seemingly high levels of monetary expansion. By 2021, there will be even less resistance to these ideas once '#Another$TrillionQE' is no longer an unusual recommendation, and so on. Eventually, it is my goal to have the Overton Window move to a point that these concepts receive serious debate. If we are very fortunate, at least some of these ideas may be seen as prescient by the 2020s.

I am just one man, without any 'establishment' backing, posting this ebook on a blog. I have run solo, multi-year, volunteer-sustained charities in the past, such as The Uplift Prize, but this endeavor is much greater in scope. Since the greatest things ever accomplished have been accomplished by teams, and if you like some of the ideas presented here, I would like to recruit your help. As a grassroots campaign, some of the avenues we can begin with are:

- Send this to people you know who may be interested in the subject matter , and persuade them to digest the material. Especially if they are outside of the US.
- Viral marketing through social media. Whether Facebook, LinkedIn, Twitter, or anywhere else, post this wherever you feel it may be appropriate (such as retweeting my 'ATOM Award of the Week').
- Help me build exposure by connecting with, and present this material to, key figures in the mainstream media, who can then bring this to a broader audience.
- Following some media exposure, the next step is to present to central banks, elected officials, and thought leaders. If you have a suitable contact, help arrange a meeting or phonecall where I can present these ideas to them.
- Help this set of ideas become part of the discourse for the 2024 US election and other elections worldwide. Refer back to the 'ATOM Political Platform' section.
- If you are good at getting sponsors, the right type of sponsorship is very valuable here.
- Help me organize and execute an ATOM video contest, where entrants produce a video that evangelizes and simplifies the concepts and ideas for a mass audience, for a prize of ~$20,000 or so.
- Help me appear at venues such as TED to deliver a presentation on some or all of the subject matter here. Smaller conferences are also valuable, provided the talk is videotaped and posted online.

Think about <u>what is it that you do exceptionally well</u>, and we will try to incorporate your talents into this campaign. Keep reminding yourself how great it will be for your Federal income taxes to evaporate away, and how your stipend keeps rising exponentially. Each action you take, however small it may seem at the time, assists the campaign of making this a reality. Getting these ideas to the decision-makers may take time, and the skepticism and debate may take even more time. But always remember that every grain of sand we deposit in the ocean makes the level of the ocean rise a tiny bit, so each action edges us towards the grand goal.

If you are enthusiastic about these ideas, join with me in this campaign, and start working on some of the bullet points above, as well as ideas of your own. Contact me on LinkedIn.

FAQs

This section of FAQs compiles the answers to these questions that are already in other chapters, into a resource for quick reference. More questions and answers will be added as patterns of repetition emerge.

What qualifies you to come up with an idea that the established experts have not come up with?
Some would say 25 years of career experience across technology and finance is a sufficient qualification by itself, but I do not, for there are thousands of people worldwide with comparable resumes. Instead, my 14 years of successful predictions at The Futurist, and proprietary research into this subject is where the intricate connections between seemingly unrelated topics began to emerge.

One truth of the ATOM age is that a 'credentialed' person is no longer the authority on his subject, as the Internet always contains more knowledge than any one person can have. Furthermore, orthodoxy creates blindspots, within which a disruptor can operate unnoticed until the disruption is already underway.

Refer to every prior instance of a major disruption to an established order. The disruption always originated from the outside, and from someone who was not shackled by existing assumptions of 'what cannot be done', particularly when what may have been impossible at a certain technological level often does become possible with further technological improvements.

Most great innovations have been by outsiders undeterred by the 'conventional wisdom' of that particular moment. I am quite certain that policies similar to my ideas will be the norm in some major nations by 2025.

Hasn't money-printing caused a lot of inflation in other countries in the past?
While there have been examples of money-printing causing high inflation, those instances were in a time where the percentage of world GDP comprised of technology was far lower than now. Even in 2008,

the technological component of the economy was too small to offset monetary creation. This is the primary reason formal economists are opposed to the ATOM set of ideas, because they have studied these past examples, but do not understand the technological component as a new factor. Furthermore, the ATOM-DUES program calculates the appropriate amount of monetary creation on a monthly basis, rapidly adjusting for any ebbs and flows in inflation or deflation.

Many PhD Economists have studied past examples of how money-printing caused inflation in poor, low-tech countries (such as Weimar Germany and contemporary Venezuela), and so are trained to overlook the much more recent examples of high-tech economies with technology-derived deflation. All the examples they cite are from long before high technology was even 0.5% of the economy, let alone the solid 3% that it is in 2020. Remember that PhD Economists have predicted about 100 of the last zero bouts of inflation in the last 35 years.

Why are formal Economists (with PhDs) hostile to this idea? Surely they know the most because of their credentials.
If incumbents with a vested interest in the status quo were the ones who could originate paradigm-changing ideas, then Uber would have been founded by someone who ran the taxi medallion commission for the New York City municipal government, and Tesla would have been founded in Saudi Arabia. The truth is, the establishment in any industry or field has a vested interest in perpetuating the status quo, and little reason to innovate or even listen to any ideas outside of their miniscule echo chamber.

But there is another barrier in addition to the above. The Economics profession is almost entirely immersed in academia and closely associated organizations. Hence, it is exclusively populated by those who could excel within the narrow skillset required from academia (thereby earning a PhD), and thus has no inputs from people who make decisions of consequence in the real economy. Consider the following fact: innovative companies that produce a value-added product that sells in the free market have been started by Engineers, Doctors, Lawyers, Salespeople, ex-Military Officers, Finance professionals, college dropouts, and more, but *never* by someone with a PhD in Economics. Even if we restrict the criterion to financial services or FinTech companies, this group has contributed no entrepreneurial value. This damning indictment is exceptionally revealing, and indicates that Economics has a more extreme 'egghead' component than any other field of consequence, and thus there is no field where the establishment is more out of touch with the effect of technology on their subject matter. Their utter lack of curiosity about why their predictions continue to be wrong compounds the problem.

Furthermore, the Federal Reserve has a vast phalanx of 600 Economics PhDs on its staff, yet was exposed as recently as mid-2019 for deciding that the *only* determinant they use on whether to tighten or loosen liquidity is the unemployment rate. No other metric, such as the CPI or yield curve, was even used. Even worse, they actually say things like *"too many people have jobs"*. Who speaks like that? Why do the taxpayers have to pay for 600 PhDs to tell them this sort of thing? Also, they brag about how they send four highly-paid PhDs to a pizza parlor to 'study' the effects of a $15/hr minimum wage law on their business. The owner of the pizza parlor told them that it was forcing him to raise the price of pizzas and pricing him out of the market. Hence, the four PhDs concluded their three-month study, with a finding that anyone who has ever run a pizza parlor, coffee shop, or barbershop could tell them. To have PhDs in Economics running a Central Bank is no better than expecting a business school professor with no corporate P&L experience to step into a CEO role at a Fortune 500 company. As a further example, consider that most PhD Economists were full believers in 'peak oil', all the way until the price started to crash in 2014, but never admitted their error. They also never evaluated the reasons for their extreme inaccuracy in make predictions, and thus still make similar predictions about other shortages. Having predicted 100 of the last zero bouts of hyperinflation in the last 35 years, they have led us down a strange, winding path to a dark, ugly place, and still insist that they know what they are doing.

Therefore, if the Federal Reserve decided monetary policy based on 100 small business owners who just cast their votes once a week (i.e. none of them are full time on the taxpayer trough), we would have a far more durable and productive economy than with a Federal Reserve staffed by 600 full-time PhDs on the taxpayer payroll who just reinforce each others' outdated assumptions. Your own net worth could be twice what it is now.

Why are productivity gains so sluggish? Is that not evidence of slowing technological change?

Chapter 4 addresses this in detail. Technology leads to productivity gains, but with Nominal GDP (NGDP) so low, there is not enough of a tailwind in economic growth for technology startups to receive valuations as high as they might. Valuations for ambitious technology ventures are heavily dependent on the trajectory of the stock market, which depends on earnings growth, which is a function of NGDP, not 'Real' GDP. Hence, low NGDP indeed leads to less technological progress and thus lower productivity gains.

Technological progress may return to the trendline rate by forcing central banks to increase NGDP through more monetary creation, which may be forced via a major stock market correction and deep recession. To avert this crisis, policymakers must focus on elevating NGDP in the US from the current 3% back up to the 6-7% seen prior to 2006. The increase will not merely be comprised of inflation, but rather a rise in 'Real' GDP as well simply due to a restoration of the trendline rate of technological progress.

Isn't inflation always bad, and thus deflation always good?

Economics is far more nuanced that that. First of all, if you have debt (such as a mortgage), inflation is your greatest friend, and deflation your greatest terror. If your income keeps up with inflation, then inflation is not a problem. But if you have no income and live on savings, then deflation is better for you.

Countries like the US have forced too many people into too many types of debt (mortgage, student loan, auto). Each debt payment may be fixed, which means the borrower's ability to service it with increasing ease depends on a rising income. Hence, inflation of 2-3% is better for the US economy than inflation of 0% or less.

Why was March 15, 2020 the 'Netscape Moment' for Economics?

In the midst of the stock market crash triggered by the Covid-19 pandemic, the S&P 500 declined over 40% in a matter of days. In past recessions, peak-to-trough durations were 30 months in 2000-02 and 18 months in 2007-09 respectively. Over here, it happened in mere days, forcing the Federal Reserve to abandon their outdated dogma about 'high inflation' that never seems to arise. They were forced to lower the Fed Funds rate from 1.5% to 0%, and authorize over $2 Trillion of new monetary creation. They simultaneously abandoned the practice of only buying Treasuries and MBSs, and moved closer towards a more diffuse, granular type of monetary transmission (albeit stopping short of the true necessity—sending money directly to people and in equal amounts irrespective of their past or present income). March 15, 2020 was the exact day on which most of these major actions were taken, and the European Central Bank joined in with $820 Billion of their own. These are actions that the hundreds of PhDs at the Federal Reserve would never have imagined they would undertake, just two weeks prior.

If you recall the first Internet boom, the Initial Public Offering of Netscape on August 9, 1995 was not just highly successful on its first day, but it triggered a cascade effect of new Internet companies and an Internet boom 4.5 years long. Even after the boom ended, the speed of everything was faster due to the permanently higher trajectory the Internet placed the economy on. Hence, that was the original Netscape Moment.

March 15, 2020 was a comparable day, for it was the exact day where outdated economic thinking was unceremoniously swept aside and replaced with the ATOM age. 'Egghead' Economists in their ivory towers still don't realize it, but now the eventual normalization of ATOM principles and policy retooling across the world is not merely inevitable, but it is not very far off. Hence, what the Internet did for commerce and communication shifted into a higher gear on August 9, 1995, and the same is about to happen for economics, specifically the economics of technology, through an analogous historical event.

Economic growth may have grown exponentially, but what if we have reached some fundamental limit at this point?
Bottlenecks to economic progress are often attributed to factors such as finite natural resources, human intelligence limits, and political will. The first two of these three are not going to be obstructions, because of the rise of Artificial Intelligence.

Artificial Intelligence is quickly subsuming many laborious tasks that humans used to do, generating the same output for far lower input.

Furthermore, the rate at which AI improves is much faster than human learning, so that continues the matching acceleration of economic growth rates.

Regarding the third factor, that of political will, the Direct, Universal, Exponential Stipend (DUES) combined with an elimination of all income tax (and associated processing and disbursement wastage) will re-align incentive structures towards productivity and entrepreneurship, allowing technology to return to its trendline rate of progress, bringing economic growth with it.

It is possible, however, that once AI can advance entirely without any human assistance, technologies that increase human living standards may plateau. This is unlikely to happen before mid-century, and is a topic beyond the scope of this publication.

How do technological disruptions in one area increase the strength of disruptions in other areas?

Technology is about lowering costs of something that was too expensive, either through replacing or bypassing the existing obstacle. When technology succeeds in one area (such as lowering oil prices), the money saved by those who paid too much for oil instead creates new demand elsewhere, enlarging a previous market and attract more competition, and hence innovation to it. This is explained in Chapter 3.

It may appear that there is no connection between oil and natural gas fracking innovations in the central US, and an e-commerce revolution in India that modernized banking, retail supply chains, and high-speed Internet access, but the former was absolutely what accelerated the latter.

Of the two ideas presented, is ATOM DUES better or is the Sovereign Venture Fund better?

Both are vastly better than our current mid-20th century fiscal and monetary framework and pre-software assumptions. However, ATOM DUES is both the far more broad-based prosperity enhancer, as well as the one that will encounter the most resistance within policy circles, since it involves reworking the entire taxation and spending system. For this reason, the Sovereign Venture Fund, which can be done completely detached from taxes and spending, is the one more likely to be implemented first. Alas, the Sovereign Venture Fund is less able to deliver a permanent structural improvement to working-class people than ATOM DUES.

How on Earth can income taxes be gradually phased out under ATOM DUES?

Consider the following three points.

1. 75% of all US Federal government spending (if you exclude deficit spending, it is 96% of all income taxes collected) comprises of payments to individuals.
2. Federal Reserve QE has to be permanent and rise exponentially.
3. The only way for this QE to be fully effective and enable technology to have enough fuel to progress at the trendline rate, is for these funds to be given directly to people.

When these three points are combined, replacement of current spending with QE money becomes natural, and with it, the gradual cessation of income taxes to fund this government spending. The phase-out of taxes will provide an immense boost to economic growth, even though the safety net is far more robust than existing programs. Read Chapter 7 for full details.

Isn't the DUES just another ill-conceived 'Universal Basic Income' or 'living wage' scheme?

The DUES greatly transcends those schemes and removes the primary negatives of those schemes. First of all, those programs rely on increased taxes on productive work. By contrast, for the DUES to work, it has to be simultaneous with a phase-out of all income tax, so technology can generate enough productivity to allow a certain level of central bank money creation without inflation. Anyone who calls this 'socialism' has to explain how the ATOM program can require 0% income taxes (and no increases in consumption/sales taxes), and still be 'socialism'.

Secondly, those schemes do not provide for rapid annual increases in their payouts, whereas the DUES is fused with the ATOM and enables annual increases of an estimated 16-24%/year. Other such programs have no provision for rapid annual increases.

Thirdly, those schemes are still seen as a form of welfare or anti-poverty program, whereas the DUES is a complete win-win for all levels of society, since it continues to reinforce the same technological progress that enables an increase in the DUES.

How is this different from Modern Monetary Theory (MMT)?
The ATOM is vastly more advanced than MMT, since MMT is not really a new idea at all. The problems with MMT are two-fold. First, MMT does not account for technological deflation, so it cannot see that monetary creation by central banks will not cause inflation. Second, MMT does not include an awareness of the Accelerating Rate of Change, which leaves MMT ill-equipped to take advantage of the exponential progress of technology and its ever-rising proportion of the economy. Hence, MMT still comprises of just tinkering around the edges, and does not provide a substantial improvement to the human condition.

Won't the DUES program merely create a massive leisure class, with no incentive to produce?
Definitely not, as explained in Chapter 7. The reasons for this are :

1. The Federal income tax rate will be gradually reduced to 0%. This creates a huge increase in incentives relative to what exists today. The return on productivity is twice as much under a 0% tax rate as under a 50% tax rate. Many people will be thrilled to work harder than they are now.
2. The removal of the tax filing burden and a large portion of regulatory complexity creates a far more favorable climate for entrepreneurship.
3. A worry about a large leisure class is mutually exclusive with a worry about technological elimination of jobs, and with a worry about rising healthcare costs. For someone to worry the former implies they are no longer worried about the latter.
4. The range of professions that exist, and of talents that can be monetized, is ever-rising, as discussed in Chapter 9.
5. Moving from a dreary or humiliating job in an expensive area to a life of leisure in a low-cost area is hardly a bad thing, including for peripheral people.

I don't pay much in income taxes, so why should I be interested in a tax phase-out for the rich?

You may not pay a lot in income taxes, but your first, second, and third level bosses certainly do, and this is money that instead might go towards giving you a raise. Your customers also pay income taxes, which prevents them from buying more of what you sell, instead of being mandated to 'buy' what the government sells. Plus, the hassle of filing and calculating one's tax prevents employers from creating new jobs, as described in Chapter 6. If you are unemployed, and people who might hire you instead have to worry about taxes, then they are specifically sending to the government the funds that instead should be used to hire you.

Some argue that 'trickle-down' economics has not worked, but the truth is :

1. 'Tax cuts' are reductions in published rates, which do not affect the ultra-wealthy, as they have the means to avoid reporting income on their 1040s to begin with. An increase in income tax rates hits the upper middle class, not the ultrawealthy, as explained in Chapter 6.
2. Tax complexity remains the same after a reduction in a tax rate, and tax complexity is the biggest drag on this stimulus effect.
3. Nonetheless, when tax rates were lowered (such as in the early 1980s, in 2003, and in 2019), there was a sudden boost in economic activity.

Why is an extremely complicated tax code bad, if I have Turbotax anyway?

A complicated tax code has four primary problems:

1. It is complex specifically to hide various loopholes designed to enable the ultrawealthy to avoid paying income tax or estate tax. There are so many loopholes that even tax lawyers don't know about all of them, but rather each specializes in just a small fraction of them. Many legislators can thus be bribed into creating a loophole for just one big donor. Add up over 100 loopholes, and the tax code becomes incomprehensible, contradictory, and impossible for the IRS to enforce fairly.

2. The cost of tax complexity costs over 20% of tax collected, and that is even before accounting for the even larger cost of suboptimal business decisions driven by tax reasons.

3. The loophole-utilization industry enriches a few elite tax lawyers and tax-haven countries. When you realize that there are over two dozen small countries that exist for the express purpose of capturing a cut of the net savings gained by an individual or corporation through the avoidance of US income tax, you realize how much in the way of time and resources are wasted in this bizarre process of pretending the entity pays more tax than it does.

4. Unfortunately, the ultrawealthy will never agree to paying income or estate tax, and the street-level socialist activists make no distinction between a surgeon and a billionaire in terms of the reviled 'wealthy' that they want to tax, and thus cannot grasp that raising the 'retail' tax rate does nothing to separate the ultrawealthy from their money, and in fact ensconces them deeper by chopping down the mere millionaires who might have been their competition.

See Chapter 6 for more details.

Does this program correct the US National Debt?

Yes, it does. Under the ATOM DUES program, we could hypothetically get to the point by as soon as 2025 where income tax has been phased out and all government spending is funded with Federal Reserve QE instead of taxation (most of it consolidated into a DUES). Hence, there is no spending in excess of taxes, which is where the annual budget deficit and resultant issuance of debt (US Treasuries) arises. For this reason, there is no new addition to the existing National Debt.

From here, we move on to the matter of the existing National Debt, which currently stands at about $23 Trillion and will continue to grow by the time the full transition to the ATOM DUES is phased in. As the existing Treasuries mature and expire, they will, for the first time, not be replaced by newly issued Treasuries since the US government is no longer issuing debt to finance a deficit. Hence, the existing pile of Treasuries will continually expire without replacement, ensuring that the existing bond holders see the debt instrument end after the expected duration even as the debt gradually shrinks. If there is full DUES implementation by 2025, the existing National Debt will shrink to a negligible portion of US GDP by 2035.

What is the Upgrade Paradox?

See the article here. The technology industry is effectively a victim of its own success. There are too many products the average household now has to upgrade frequently, as the number of exponentially improving nodes per household is now in the dozens (see Chapter 3). Since people are expected to spend more and more to upgrade their entire family's PCs, smartphones, tablets, television screens, and even cars, but are not receiving any significant share of the gains made through technology, it is becoming too expensive to keep upgrading. This means that the speed of technology diffusion ironically slows. This is why a more direct and democratized monetization of diffuse technological progress is crucial, and ATOM-DUES enables technology to return to the long-term trend-line of progress it has failed to keep up with.

I am not a technology expert. How do I begin to improve my life and career through the ATOM?

One does not need to be tech-savvy at all to become an expert 'lifehacker' through targeted Internet research. A number of people have already figured out the solution(s) to most of your challenges, and have posted the material online.

The best way to start is to think about all the challenges you have in life, and all the examples of how someone else managed to obtain what you want. Then, begin the metamorphosis into a search demon who reads as much as possible about how others achieved your goal. You will become better at searching once you practice search engine optimization, algorithmic AI, and speed reading. With more practice, you will know how to identify the right blogs, and the right people at message boards who have valuable information, and with your own rising ability to contribute information of value to others, some knowledge will find itself pulled towards you. The more of this you do, the better you become.

The other key component is confidence. Don't assume that a highly credentialed doctor, lawyer, or financial advisor will always know more than you can mine from the web. See them as components of a solution; beacons to help point you in the right direction of discovery. In this age, knowledge is highly decentralized with ever-lowering barriers to access. This, not coincidentally, is why knowledge is expanding faster than before.

What asset classes should one keep their money in, if they believe in the ATOM thesis?

Historically, people have assumed that gold is a hedge against inflation. While this may have been true prior to the modern era, today, that is one of the worst allocations a person can make. To believe that gold is going to be the beneficiary of permanent monetary creation is to have no understanding of technology. For one thing, technology will rapidly increase the supply of gold if the price rises to a point where this is economical (as happened with oil). Secondly, gold is an inert commodity that has little practical, essential use in the economy (people need oil to get to and from work, but there is almost no one who cannot survive for four days without gold).

By contrast, technology equities are the biggest beneficiaries of the ATOM. A simple observation of the price change in gold vs. in the Nasdaq 100, since QE began, reveals the essence of ATOM truths. Even in just the five years before the v2.0 release of this publication (i.e. from May 31, 2015 to May 31, 2020), the huge divergence in the trajectory of gold relative to the Nasdaq 100 is evident. This divergence will continue, as per the foundational ATOM principles. Note that this refers to a broad index of technology companies, such as the Nasdaq 100, not any individual company's stock.

ATOM Awards of the Month

This chapter is a dossier of all the ATOM Awards of the Month granted since version 1.0 of this publication, in reverse chronological order. This will enable the reader to see actual examples of ATOM effects in action. Not every month has an awardee.

ATOM Award of the Month, June 2020

The pandemic has ratified and accelerated a whole host of ATOM principles, so I have to update parts of the entire publication. Suffice it to say, a number of pent-up ATOM predictions just got fast forwarded, with a seminal day in the history of economics having been forced into manifestation. We can divide the events into two parts: technological and monetary.

Among technological disruptions, there are three that qualify as having been overdue for a long time, that got tipped over by this catalyst:

1. **Video Conferencing:** This was something that Cisco expected to take off 14 long years ago, but expensive proprietary hardware and the inertia of old habits prevented it from attaining the critical mass necessary for entrenchment. Cisco lost at least $6 Billion on this endeavor. Now, however, as people are forced to work from home, a critical mass of users have to adapt to this usage, which in turn attracts more innovation and capital to the technology. While none of the companies advancing videoconferencing in 2009 are the same ones as the ones winning now, this is common in the technology sector (recall the search engine wars). The cascade of disruptions I listed in 2009 still apply. Among other things, if cubicle-style workplaces can agree that all on-premise meetings are restricted to three days a week (M-W, or Tu-Th, or whatever), then the distance that an employee can commute effectively doubles, and the housing availability for them thus increases 4X. The current status quo of certain real estate being vastly more expensive than equivalent real estate 30 miles further from the jobs cluster may finally correct. This is a form of standard-of-living increase that is poorly captured in GDP statistics.

2. **Educational Institutions**: The extraordinarily distorted cost/value equation of both higher and lower educational institutions (which should not be conflated with the concept of 'education') already crossed the point of no return in 2015. But, as with videoconferencing, too few people were willing to be 'Spartacus' and make use

of alternative solutions that were in fact lower risk. This applies to both students and employers, for employers declaring that they will hire based on on-site testing and online certifications, rather than degrees that bear little to predictive value of employee performance, is the catalyst that would have induced more students to bypass the universities-as-gatekeeper oligopoly. The fact that universities want to charge the same tuition for online classes (and are being sued by students disputing this), when comparable online classes are available for orders of magnitude lower prices, is going to reduce US university enrollment permanently. To cope, there is no reason that US universities cannot be forced to return to a 1980s-era cost structure.

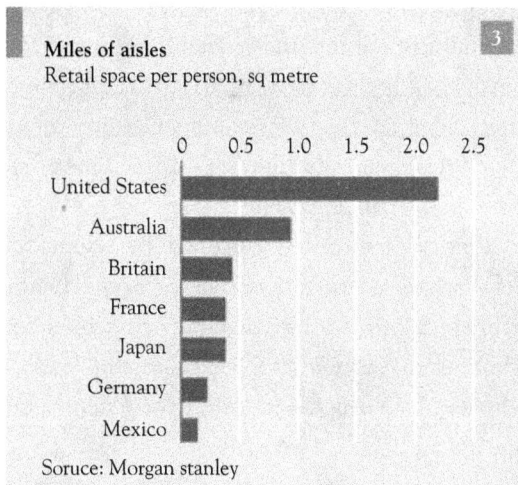

Miles of aisles
Retail space per person, sq metre

Soruce: Morgan stanley

3. **Retail Real Estate Re-Purposement**: Overlooked among the technological and economic effects of this black swan is the fact that the "retail apocalypse" and shift to e-commerce has fast-forwarded to such an extent that millions of acres of US retail land (including parking lots) will never return to previous levels of usage. This was partially mentioned in the ATOM AotM for August 2017, and is often brought up in comments. E-commerce was still just 12% of all retail sales before the pandemic, but if that 12% were to shift

to 15%, or effectively jump two years ahead of the previous trend, that alone is a vast acceleration with visible results for the suburban landscape.

In fact, when you combine the permanently lower demand for premium office space from the greater usage of videoconferencing, and the mass closure of retail real estate (at least in the US, where six times as much land is allocated to retail relative to most advanced countries), the correction and pressure to reallocate could be extreme. In places like California, the extreme restrictions on new residential construction will be exposed even more visibly as office space joins retail in a permanent glut.

But the bigger event was not even these technological accelerants. Instead, the complete and supreme validation of all ATOM conclusions was manifested fully. Recall that the Federal Reserve was actually reversing QE and increasing interest rates in 2019. It had begun to pause and correct that misguided reversal process, but still at too timid of a rate of net increase to even keep up with the ATOM trendline of monetary creation required to halt technological deflation.

However, this crisis forced the Federal Reserve to do the right thing, even if they still don't understand the new economics of technology. March 15, 2020, is a day that can fairly be described as the "Netscape Moment in Economics." For those who recall the original "Netscape Moment," on August 9, 1995, the Internet browser company Netscape did an IPO that exceeded its anticipated price by a huge margin, and triggered a boom in Internet company formation for the next 4.5 years. Even after the bust, the economy was permanently into the Internet age. Similarly, March 15, 2020 is the day where the Federal Reserve, in one fell swoop, lowered the Fed Funds rate to 0% (where it should have been all along) and signaled permanent QE. In the following 10 weeks, over $3 trillion of new QE was done, and the entire trajectory is starting to look more like the exponential parabolas that we are accustomed to seeing wherever the accelerating rate of change and exponential technology emerge. As of May 31, here are two charts to depict the total QE effect (source : Yardeni):

Figure 2.

Major central banks: Total assets
(Trillion dollars, nsa)

Total of
Fed, ECB, BOJ, & PBOC (25.2)

Total assets of major central banks

Figure 3.

Major central banks: Total assets of FED, ECB, BOJ, & PBOC
(yearly percent change)

Latest (28.8)

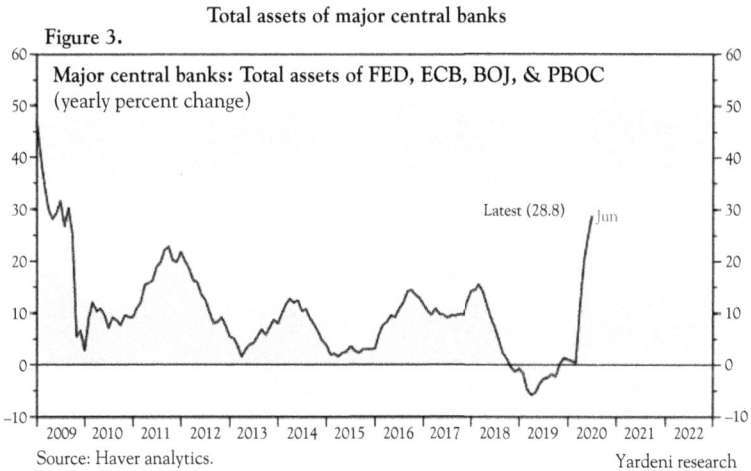

Source: Haver analytics.

Yardeni research

The first chart indicates the cumulative rise in the sum of the four major central banks. Note the feeble attempt to reduce the balance sheets in 2018–19, only the forced to return to the trendine. The second chart is the YoY percentage increase. I have always said that the ATOM requires 16–24%/yr as an annual rate of increase to offset deflation and maintain optimal (2–3%) inflation. The increase is now probing the upper limit of even my range, and it will be interesting to see if inflation emerges even then, or if the ceiling is even higher than I estimated (meaning that technological progress is now even faster and broader than before, and monetary creation could be higher than before).

I said elsewhere that the decade of the 2010s had $23 trillion of cumulative QE worldwide. The PhD Economists of the world, who have predicted 100 of the last zero bouts of hyperinflation, still believe QE is an aberration and assume that the cumulative QE will be reversed (i.e., that the 2020s will have −$23 trillion of cumulative QE). I claim the opposite, which is that under both ATOM principles and the Accelerating Rate of Change, the 2020s will see about $100 trillion of QE, *and* that this will move toward sending cash directly to people (rather than the esoteric bond-buying that comprises of QE today, which inevitably concentrates the benefit of this monetary creation in very few hands).

Mark my words. The entire profession of economics, full of PhDs who have never had any contact with entrepreneurs and real-time economic decisions, will be wrong by an epic margin.

ATOM Award of the Month, February 2020

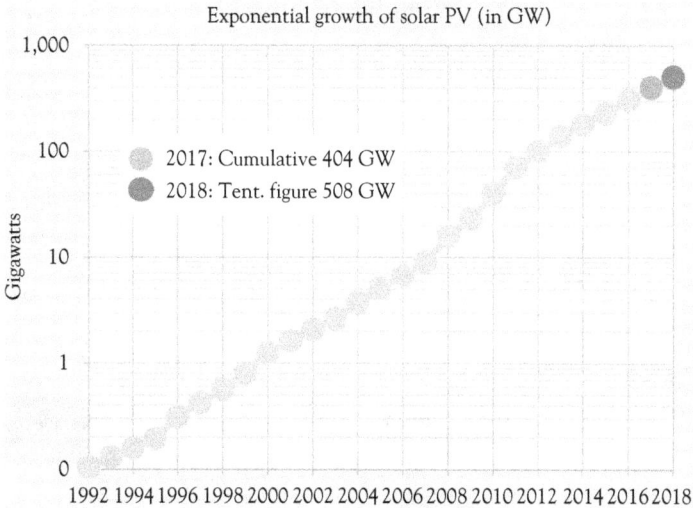

Exponential growth of solar PV (in GW)

It is time to award a new ATOM AotM, and the first one some-what coincident with the newly published version 2.0 of the ATOM publication. This one has been discussed elsewhere on this website, but at the moment, it is perhaps the single biggest disruption in the global economy.

First, a small story. Photovoltaics (PV) is actually my first exponential technology, and what made be aware of the concept in a time when even "Moore's Law" was not a household term and Intel was a very small company. When I was 10 years old, I wrote a 5th grade paper (about 800 words) on exponential improvement of solar cells of about 5% a year. It predicted cost-effectiveness in the "early 21st century." The paper was a hit and was submitted to a contest that all the elementary schools submitted papers to, and I was taken, along with a number of other 5th graders from the Cleveland area to an event where the Mayor of Cleveland at the time (George Voinovich) meets the children and does a photo-op. We didn't understand any of that, but each child got a framed certificate.

Solar PV prices vs. cumalative capacity, 1976 to 2016
Solar photovoltaic (PV) module prices (measured in 2016 US$ per watt-peak) versus cumulative installed
(measured in megawatts-peak, MWp). This represents the 'learning curve' for solar PV and approximates a
22% reduction in price for every doubling of cumulative capacity.

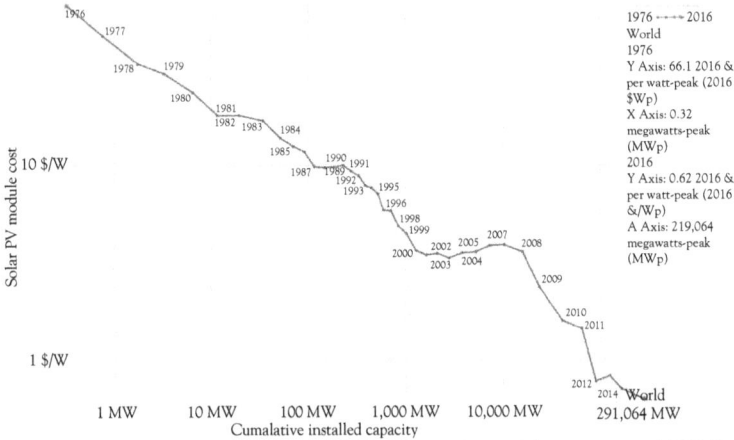

Source: Lafond et al. (2017); IRENA; Solarserver   Ourworldindata.org/energy-production-and-changing-energy-sources/ CC BY-SA

Sure enough, as the decades passed, PV did become cost-effective in
the early 21st century. It has been a subject on this website for a long time,
and while we often point out how many technologies have failed to meet
industry-derived projections, as you can see from this old 2007 article, a
US DoE chart thought PV installations in the US would be merely 15 to
30 GWs. In reality, the 2020 number is about thrice the upper bound of
that projection, at 80–90 GWs, with over 3% of US electricity generated
through PV. Even better, the world average is higher than the US average,
and the world total continues to grow in excess of 25% a year. Remember that this ATOM advancement is tied to the advancement of electric
vehicles, as not merely is crude oil being replaced with electricity. For
many countries, the oil was imported, while the photovoltaic electricity is
generated domestically. This is a victory against OPEC, as imports from
OPEC are being replaced with domestic energy.

Matthias loster, 2006

0   50   100   150   200   250   300   350 W/m² $\Sigma \bullet$ = 18 TWe

As we recall Swanson's Law, the 40-year trend is consistent (note that both axes are logarithmic). While it took decades to get up to 3% of world electricity consumption being through PV, the jump from 3% to 12%+ will not take longer than a few years. The inflection point is here, and the dollar impact is among the biggest of any ATOM transformations currently underway. Even more than the dollar impact, it is the multiplier effect of these specific dollars given where the shift is being generated.

(Images from Wikipedia and Our World in Data. Click to enlarge).

The best part about solar, which is not true of wind power, is that the poorest countries in the world are in fact the ones with the greatest solar intensity, and are thus the most suitable for solar. Much has been written about why cold-weather cultures have done better than hot-weather cultures on average, but now the very resource that was not being monetized can be monetized. By contrast, wind power, while good, is both slower-advancing and most applicable in countries that are already wealthy, and so does not have quite the same multiplier effect. This map of solar intensity indicates where the greatest utility of photovoltaics can reside.

The absolute lowest-prosperity countries are still too disorganized to take advantage of this, but even the third quartile is well-prepared to rapidly increase PV installations and move away from oil imports. In the near future, it will seem quite absurd that people were importing their energy from thousands of miles away.

ATOM Award of the Month, November 2019

It is time for another ATOM AotM. This month's award has a major overlap with the November 2017 award, where we identified that telescopic power has been computerized, and as a result was rising at 26%/ yr. This itself was a finding from a much older article from all the way back in September 2006, where I first identified that telescopic power was improving at that rate.

But how do better telescopes improve your life? Learning about exoplanets and better images of stars are fun, but have no immediate relevance to our individual daily challenges. If you are not interested in astronomy, why should you care? Well, there is one area where this advancement has already improved millions and possibly billions of lives : we have now mapped nearly all of the Near Earth Objects (NEOs) that might be large enough to cause a major disaster if any of them strike the Earth. Remember that this is an object with a mass that may be billions of tons, traveling at about 30 km/sec (image from sciencenews.org), of which there are many thousands that have already orbited the sun over 4 billion times each.

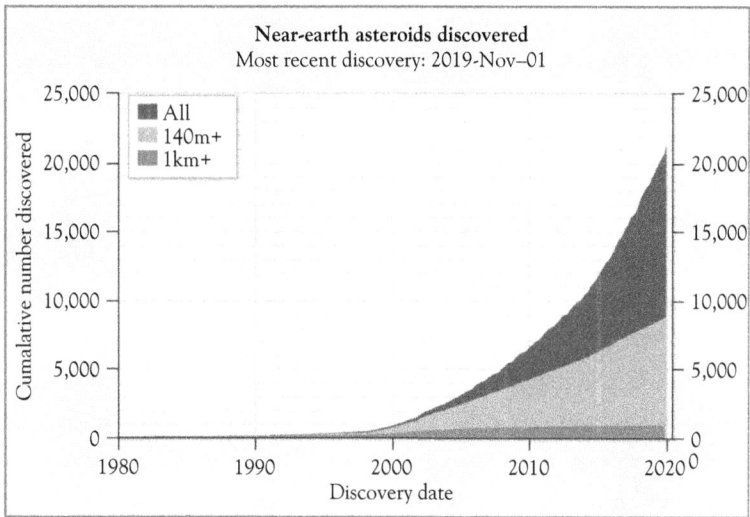

Near-earth asteroids discovered
Most recent discovery: 2019-Nov–01

All of us recall how, in the 1990s, there were a number of films portraying how such a disaster might manifest. Well, in the 1990s, we had little awareness of which objects were nearby at what time, and so there really was a risk that a large asteroid could hit us with little or no warning. However, as telescopes improved, 26%/yr (the square root of Moore's Law, since pixel numbers increase as a square of linear dimension shrinkage) got to work on this problem. Now, as of today, all asteroids larger than 1 km are mapped, and almost all of the thousands that are larger than 140 m (the size above which it would actually hit the surface, rather than burn up in the atmosphere) are mapped as well (chart from Wikipedia). We have identified which object might be an impact risk in what year. In case you are wondering, there is a 370m asteroid that will get very near (but not hit the Earth) in 2036. Of course, by 2036, we will have mapped everything with far more precision, at this rate of improvement. In other words, don't worry about an asteroid impact in the near future, as none of significance are anticipated in the next 17 years, and probably not for much longer than that. Comets are a different matter, as we have not mapped most of them (and cannot, as of yet), but large ones impact too infrequently to worry about.

Hence, the risk of an impact event, and mitigation thereof, is no longer a technological problem. It is merely a political one. Will the governments of the world work to divert asteroids before one hits, or will they only react after one hits in order to prevent the next impact? These questions are complicated, as this problem is completely borderless. Why should the United States pay the majority of the expense for a borderless problem, particularly one that has a 71% chance of hitting an ocean? At any rate, this is another problem that went from deadly to merely one of fiscal prioritization, on account of ATOM progress.

More interestingly, within this problem is another major business opportunity that we have discussed here in the past. Asteroid mining is a potential industry that is simultaneous with asteroid diversion, as asteroid pulverization may waste some precious metals that can be captured. Many asteroids have a much greater proportion of precious metals than the Earth's surface does, since "precious" metals are heavy and most of the quantity sunk to the center of the Earth while the Earth was forming, while an asteroid with much lower gravity has its precious metals more evenly distributed throughout its structure. There are already asteroids identified that have hundreds of tons of gold and platinum in them. Accessing these asteroids will, of course, crush the prices of these metals as traded on Earth (another ATOM effect we have seen elsewhere in other commodities), and may reduce gold to an industrial metal that is used in much the way copper is. This, of course, may enable new applications that are not cost-effective at the current prices of gold, platinum, palladium, etc. But that is a topic for another time.

ATOM Award of the Month, April 2019

For this month's <u>ATOM AotM</u>, we return to the familiar, but in the process, we want to recognize an <u>ATOM</u> trend that has not gotten as much credit as it has deserved.

We all know what Moore's Law is, and what has been enabled by it. But what has always been amazing to me is how little recognition a similar law has received. Storage capacity has risen at a rate equal to (or slightly higher than) Moore's Law. It is not a technological byproduct of Moore's Law, as it has always been worked on by different people in different companies with different technical talents.

If storage capacity were not improving at the same rate as Moore's Law, most computer-type products would not have continued to produce decades of viable new iterations. From PCs to Smartphones to Video Game consoles, all have a storage requirement that has to match up to the size and number of files downloaded and processed. Correspondingly, data transfer speeds have also had to rise (USB 1.0 to 2.0 to 3.0, Ethernet to Fast Ethernet to Gigabit Ethernet, etc.). A 2019-era PC could not have a 2006-era hard drive and be very useful.

Hard drive cost per gigabyte (USD)

Like Moore's Law, the exponential doubling has spanned a sequence of technologies that all sustain the underlying megatrend, from internal spinning hard drives, to flash storage, to storage in the cloud. Greater density has been matched by shrinking weight per unit storage and less power consumption. This also means that has computing decouples from Moore's Law and moves into different (and probably faster) forms of exponential growth, storage will almost certainly also follow suit. DNA-based storage is a prospective technology that has many attributes comparable to expected future computing technologies such as Quantum Computing.

Unlike Moore's Law, storage has not always advanced at a steady rate. There are times when it advanced much faster than Moore's Law, and times when it advanced much slower (such as in recent years). The 40-year average, however, does appear to match Moore's Law's doubling rate rather closely, and hence what one dollar purchases today is the same as what one billion dollars could purchase then, which itself would have been the size of a house.

Also unlike Moore's Law, there is not a universally accepted name associated with this trend. Mark Kryder is sometimes given this attribute, but he did not put forth a prediction early enough for it to be a prediction by any measure (Kryder officially spoke of this in 2005 whereas Moore made his prediction in 1965), his name is not mentioned in any of Ray Kurzweil's writings or other publications, and since he was not the founder of a major storage company, he is not analogous to Gordon Moore.

As rising storage efficiency is crucial towards the productization of any other form of computing product (including Smartphones), it deserves recognition for its contribution to the technological age, despite often being overlooked in favor of Moore's Law.

ATOM Award of the Month, February 2019

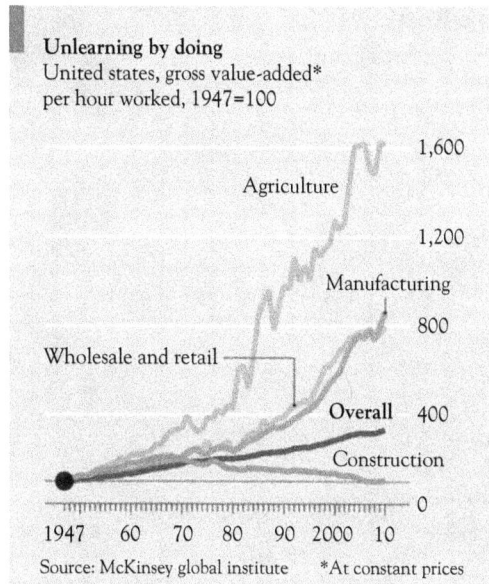

For this month's <u>ATOM AotM</u>, we examine something that even the rest of the technology industry has virtually no awareness of, and the US public is entirely oblivious of, even though we have a President from the construction industry.

The US construction industry has had no net productivity gain in the last 70 years. Even worse, it declined by 50% over the last 50 years. Construction should be seen as a type of manufacturing, as most construction is not devoted to anything highly customized or unusually complex. Yet, manufacturing itself has risen in productivity by 800% over the same period that construction has not risen at all. A combination of organized crime, government graft, and an anti-productivity ethos have contributed to this epic failure.

Given that construction is about 7% of the US economy, this is troubling. Imagine if that 7% was 16x more productive (i.e. merely keeping up with manufacturing). Americans, particularly urban Americans, don't realize that they could have thrice the square footage for the same price if this sector merely kept up with manufacturing. There would also be several hundred thousand more jobs in construction, and much broader home ownership.

Means of production

Construction, productivity levels against growth rate

● Construction productivity growth exceeds total economy growth

1,000 — Size indicates construction investment 2015, $bn

500

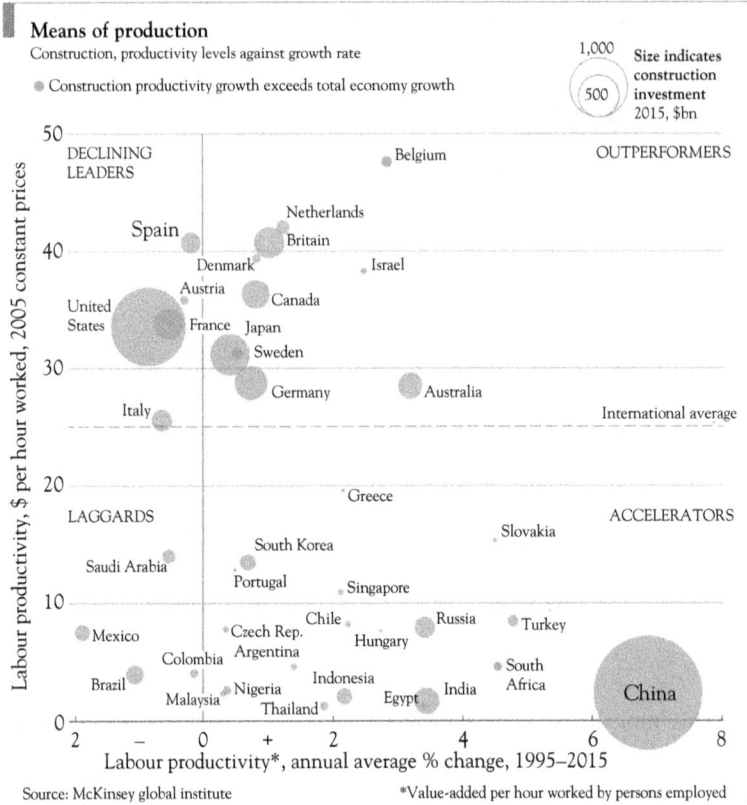

Labour productivity, $ per hour worked, 2005 constant prices (y-axis)

50 — DECLINING LEADERS / OUTPERFORMERS
- Belgium
- Netherlands
40 — Spain / Britain
- Denmark / Israel
- Austria
- United States / Canada
- France / Japan
30 — Sweden
- Germany / Australia
- Italy / International average
20 —
- Greece
LAGGARDS / ACCELERATORS
- Slovakia
- South Korea
- Saudi Arabia / Portugal / Singapore
10 —
- Chile / Russia / Turkey
- Mexico / Czech Rep. / Hungary
- Colombia / Argentina
- Brazil / Nigeria / Indonesia / South Africa / China
- Malaysia / Thailand / Egypt / India
0 —

Labour productivity*, annual average % change, 1995–2015 (x-axis: −2, 0, +2, 4, 6, 8)

Source: McKinsey global institute   *Value-added per hour worked by persons employed

Meanwhile, outside of the many biases of the Western media, there is an amazing example of supreme construction efficiency. China has grown at 7% a year over the last 20 years, even as the United States has shrunk at −1% a year (click image to enlarge). The productivity of China has greatly enlarged the size of its construction sector, to the extent that it is 20% of China's economy vs. just 7% in the United States. While the two countries are a different stages of growth and China is still at a much lower absolute level, the differential is still immense.

Normally, in any industry, such an immense productivity differential leads to the productive country exporting products to the less productive country, swiftly driving local unproductive businesses to their deserved demise. Construction, however, produces a product that is not transportable, so a productivity normalization has not happened. At least not yet. But this high of a differential eventually finds a way to engineer a normalization. Modular construction is one method where parts are manufactured, and then assembled on site. China could start exporting this to the rest of the world.

Here is a Spire Research report on the advances in China's construction technology.

The Western media, in its hubris, is quite willing to criticize China for building entire cities 10 years before they are needed. How often have we seen stories about empty cities in China that take a few years to fill up? By contrast, the United States (and California in particular) does something much worse, which is to build structures 20 years *after* they are needed. Given the choice between these two schedule misalignments, China's approach is vastly preferable.

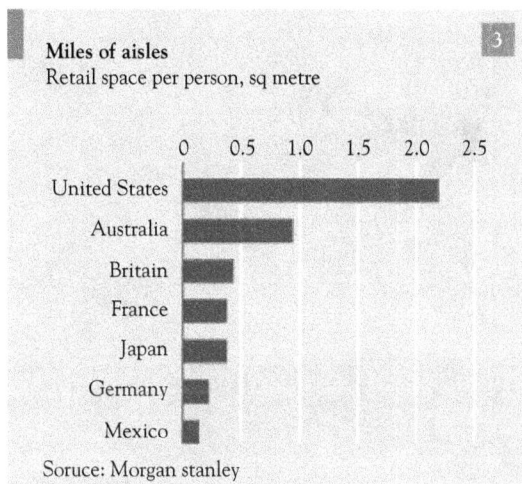

Miles of aisles
Retail space per person, sq metre

| | 0 | 0.5 | 1.0 | 1.5 | 2.0 | 2.5 |
United States
Australia
Britain
France
Japan
Germany
Mexico

Soruce: Morgan stanley

Beyond this, the costs of US ineptitude are about to become more problematic. The e-commerce revolution is exposing the massive misallocation of land toward retail space, that is a uniquely American distortion. Part of this is due to a peculiar depreciation schedule in the tax code originating in 1954. The abundant land in the US interior led to the same lopsided usage of land in California, leading to the grotesque situation we have today where ultra-expensive housing resides next to vast, empty parking lots. High California housing prices are the product of extreme artificial supply restriction, aided by low construction productivity that ensures an apartment complex takes three years to complete, where the same in China takes under one year.

Dramatic photos of dead malls can easily evoke emotions in the average American, who has been trained to think this sort of retail experience is normal. But charts that reveal the unique extent of US profligacy with regards to retail land reveals a much more logical sequence of impending events. As e-commerce continues to shutter brick-and-mortar retail, there will be a rising groundswell of pressure to repurpose this land for a more contemporary use. Unfortunately, the inadequate level of US construction productivity threatens to greatly delay this conversion, severely damaging our national competitiveness relative to China.

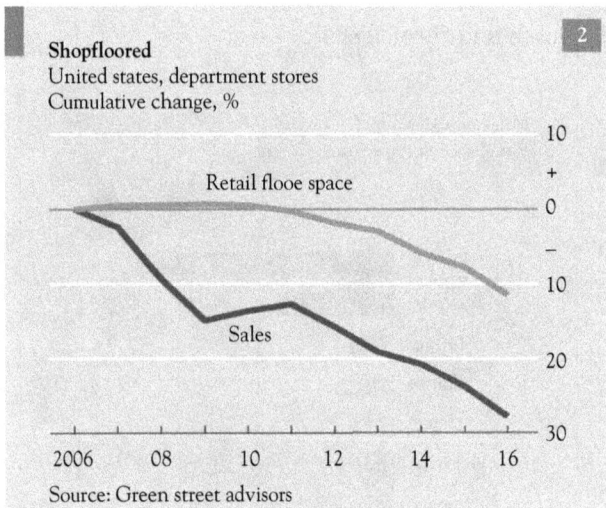

Shopfloored
United states, department stores
Cumulative change, %

Retail flooe space

Sales

2006   08   10   12   14   16

Source: Green street advisors

On the subject of where the United States may see China catch up, most of the focus is on Artificial Intelligence, Quantum Computing, and other high-concept technologies. Yet the construction productivity differential alone represents the single biggest sectoral deficit from the point of view of the United States and many other countries. China is well-positioned to dominate the entire construction industry worldwide once it can more easily win international contracts and transplant its productivity practices abroad. If the US blocks Chinese construction imports, other countries across the world will happily partake in these high-quality end products. This should be welcomed by anyone with a free-market bent.

For this reason, China's construction sector, in breaking the low-productivity pattern seen in almost the entire rest of the world, is the recipient of the February 2019 ATOM AotM.

ATOM Award of the Month, December 2018

It is time for another ATOM AotM. This month, we return to the energy sector, for it is where the greatest size and scale of ATOM disruptions are currently underway.

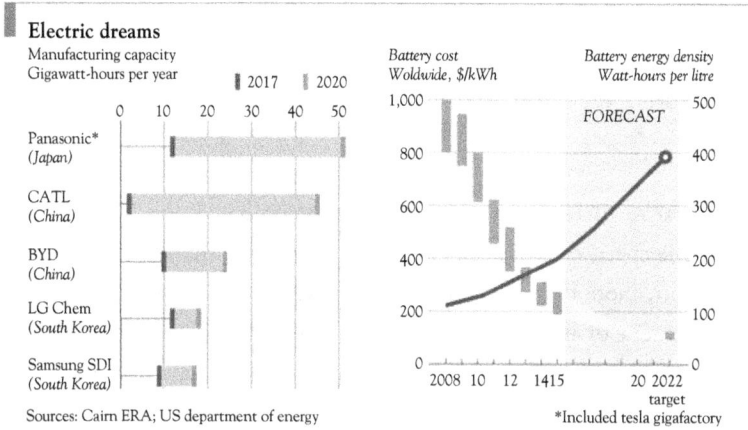

Electric dreams

Manufacturing capacity
Gigawatt-hours per year   ▮ 2017   ▮ 2020

Battery cost
Woldwide, $/kWh

Battery energy density
Watt-hours per litre

Sources: Cairn ERA; US department of energy

*Included tesla gigafactory

We visited batteries briefly in <u>August 2017's ATOM AotM</u>. There are two exponentials here, battery cost per unit of energy, and battery energy density per unit volume. Hence, despite 40 years of apparent stagnation interspersed with angst about how electric vehicles failed to arrive in response to 1973 and 1981 oil spikes, the exponential trend quietly progressed toward the inflection point that we have arrived at. True to the exponential nature of technology, more progress happened in 2011–20 than 1970–2010, and we now have viable electric vehicles that are selling rapidly and are set to displace gasoline consumption in a matter of just a few short years. Electric vehicles are now 2% of all new vehicle sales in the United States, and 3% worldwide, with a high annual growth rate. Due to the rapid cost improvements in EVs expected in the next three years, a substantial tipping point is perhaps no more than three years away.

This rapid rise is in the face of two major headwinds: the low price of oil (<u>due to another ATOM disruption</u>), and the high price of EVs (the top-seller in units is a $50,000 vehicle). It is now a certainty that once a high-quality EV becomes available at the $30,000 price point, the speed of displacement will be startling.

U.S. Plug-in car sales

A tracker that records monthly sales at both US and WW levels is here. The speed of advancement merits monthly visits to this tracker, at this point. Note that over time, the United States is actually where total displacement of ICEs by EVs will be the slowest, since other countries are more suited for EVs than the United States (they have higher gasoline prices, and often 220V electrical outlets that lead to faster charging). In fact, a suddenly popular home upgrade in the United States is, ironically, the installation of 220V outlets in the garage, specifically for EV charging.

As an example of a true ATOM disruption, the transformation will be multi-layered. From oil import/export balances, to gasoline refinement and distribution networks, to the reduction of near-slave labor from the Subcontinent forced to find work in Gulf petrostates, to mechanics dependent on ICE vehicle malfunctions, to surplus used ICEs unable to sell and thus forced to slash prices, to power management and pricing by electric utilities, to prime land occupied by gas stations, a variety of status quos will end.

Don't underestimate how soon the domino effect will take place. Once EVs are sufficiently mainstreamed in the luxury car market (which is set to happen in 2019), then the entire range of urban commercial/government vehicles will swiftly transition to electric. The United States has 800,000 police cars, 210,000 USPS vans, and a variety of other government vehicles. On top of that, private enterprises include 110,000 UPS vehicles, 60,000 FedEx vehicles, and perhaps over 300,000 pizza delivery vehicles. As these transition, observe how many gasoline stations shutter.

The much greater lifespan of EVs relative to ICEs will be one of the four factors that lead to the majority of automobile use migrating to an on-demand, autonomous vehicle model by 2032, as discussed before.

ATOM Award of the Month, October 2018

For this month's ATOM AotM, we visit the medical industry, and examine a technology that seems quite intuitive, but on account of patents and other obstacles, has seen rapid improvement greatly delayed until now.

Surgery seems as though robotics would be ideally suited for it, since it combines complexity and precision with a great deal of repetition of well-established steps. The value of smaller incisions, fewer instances of bones being sawed, etc. is indisputable, from qualitative measures such as healing pain, to tangible economic metrics such as hospital stay duration post-surgery.

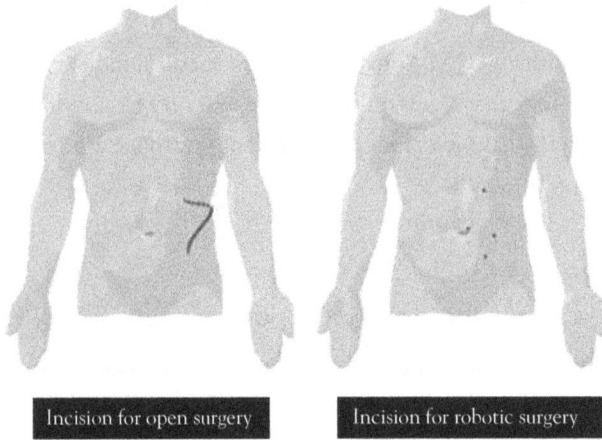

Incision for open surgery   Incision for robotic surgery

Intuitive Surgical released its Da Vinci robot to the market in 2001, but on account of Intuitive's patents, they sustained a monopoly and did not improve the product much over the subsequent 17 years. Under ATOM principles, this is a highly objectionable practice, even if technically they can still earn a high profit margin without any product redesigns. As a result, only 4,000 such robots are currently in use, mostly in the United States. Intuitive has achieved a market capitalization of over $60 billion, so it has succeeded as a business, but this may soon change. Now that Intuitive's patents are finally close to expiry, a number of competitors are ready to introduce ATOM-consistent exponential improvements into the competitive landscape.

The Economist has a detailed article about the new entrants into this market, and the innovations they have created. In addition to mere cost-reduction due to smaller electronics, one obvious extension of the robotic surgery model is for each robot to be connected to the cloud, where the record of each surgery trains an Artificial Intelligence to ensure ever-improving automation for several steps of the surgery. With AI, greater usage makes it improve, and when thousands of surgeries around the world are all recorded, that makes *each* machine simultaneously better. As costs lower and unit volume increases, the volume of data generated rises. As the accumulation of data rises, the valuation of companies capturing this data also rises, as we have seen in most other areas of technology.

This level of data combined with greater circuitry within the robot itself can also increase the speed of surgery. When more of it is automated, and the surgeon is doing less of the direct manipulation, then what is to prevent surgeries from being done at twice or thrice the speed? This enables a much shorter duration of anesthesia, and hence fewer complications from it.

ATOM Award of the Month, May 2018

For the May 2018 ATOM AotM, we will visit a technology that is not a distinct product or company, but rather is a feature of consumer commerce that we would now find impossible to live without. This humble yet indispensable characteristic of multiple websites has saved an incalculable amount of frustration and productivity loss. I am, of course, referring to Web-based reviews.

Lest you think this is a relatively minor technology to award an ATOM AotM to, think again, for a core principle of technological progress is that a technology is most successful when it is barely even noticed despite a ubiquitous presence.

Part of what has enabled e-commerce to siphon away an ever-rising portion of brick-and-mortar retail's revenue is the presence of reviews on sites like Amazon. Beyond e-commerce, sites like Yelp have greatly increased the information access of consumers seeking to patronize a low-tech business, while media sites permit a consumer to quickly decide which films and video games are worthwhile without risking a blind purchase. While false reviews were a feature of the early Internet for over a decade, now there is considerable ability to filter those out.

I recall a frustrating episode that a friend and I experienced in 1999. We wanted to rent a film from Blockbuster videos, but did not know which one. We found one that had familiar actors, but the movie was extremely subpar, resulting in a sunk cost of the rental fee, transportation costs, and time spent on the film and two-way transit. When returning to Blockbuster to discharge the VHS Cassette of the film, we selected another, based on the same criteria. It was even worse. We had rented two separate films over two separate round trips to Blockbuster, only to be extremely unsatisfied. Movie review sites like IMDB did exist at the time, but my friend did not have home Internet access (as his Internet activities were restricted to his workplace, as was common at the time).

Now, in this anecdote, just list the number of <u>ATOM</u> disruptions that have transpired since :

1. There is no longer a "Blockbuster Video" that rents VHS Cassettes, as films are rented online or available through a Netflix subscription.
2. Everyone has home Internet access and can see a film's reviews before ever leaving home.

Hence, it is no longer possible to waste hours of time and several dollars on a bad film. The same goes for restaurants, and in this case, both the consumer and the business are shielded from an information mismatch on the part of the consumer. I have always felt that it was unfair for a patron to judge a restaurant negatively if they themselves did not order what they might have liked. Now, with Yelp, in addition to reviews, there are pictures, enabling a vastly more informed decision.

Even higher-stakes decisions, such as the selection of a dentist or auto-mechanic, has slashed the uncertainty that people lived under just 12 years ago. The better vendors attract more business, while substandard (or worse, unethical) vendors have been exposed to the light of day. This is a more powerful form of quality control than has ever existed before.

Now, to see where the real ATOM effects are found, consider the value of the data being aggregated. This drives better product design and better marketing. This also expands the roadmaps of accessory products or complementary products. The data itself begins to fuel artificial intelligence, for remember that any pile of data of sufficient size tends to attract artificial intelligence to it. This leads to a lot of valuable analytics and automation.

If one were to rank the primary successful Internet use cases to date, the ability to see reviews of products and services would rank very high on the list. For this reason, this receives the May 2018 ATOM AotM.

ATOM Award of the Month, February 2018

For this month's ATOM AotM, we will address the sector that any thought leader in technological disruption recognizes as the primary obstruction to real progress. When we see that sectors that are overdue for disruption, such as medicine, education, and construction all happen to be sectors with high government involvement, the logical progression leads us to question why government itself cannot deliver basic services at comparable costs to private sector equivalents.

As just one example out of hundreds, in California and other high-tax states, the annual license plate registration can cost $400/year. What does the taxpayer truly receive? The ability to trace license plates to driver's licenses and insurance. Why should such a simple system cost so much? It seems that it should only cost $2/year under 2018 technological levels. By contrast, note how much value you receive from a $96/year Netflix subscription. By all accounts, many basic government services could easily implement cost reductions of 98–99%.

While the subject of government inefficiency vs. the ATOM is perhaps the primary topic of this website and the ATOM publication, just one small example across the world demonstrates what a modernized government looks like. The tiny country of Estonia contains just 1.3 million people. A desire to catch up from decades of being part of the Soviet Union perhaps spurred them into a unique desire to modernize and digitize government services into a state that Americans would scarcely believe could exist. Here are some articles by publication about Estonia's successful digitization, where you can read about specific details:

The New Yorker

The Atlantic

Fortune

Estonia has also taken early steps toward certain ATOM realities. While it does have high consumption taxes, income tax is a flat 21%, thereby saving immense costs in complexity and processing (which cost the United States over $700 billion/yr). If only it figures out the ATOM principles around monetization of technological deflation, it could reduce income taxes to zero.

Now, for the unfortunate part. When a country manages to produce a product or service that the rest of the world wants and cannot produce at the same quality and price themselves, the first country can export the product to the outside world. From Taiwanese chipsets to South Korean smartphones and television sets to Italian cheeses, the extension of sales to exports is straightforward. Yet in the governance sector, despite being a third of the world economy, Estonia has no market where it can sell its services to hasten the digitization of other governments. Whether at the Federal, State, City, or County level, the United States has hundreds of governments that could simply hire Estonian consultants and implementation staff to rapidly install new services. This could be lucrative enough to make Estonia a very wealthy country, and then attract competition from other countries (such as nearby Finland, which is attempting to follow Estonia's path). Yet, unlike a private sector product or service, governance just does not value efficiency or productivity to this extent. The State of California alone could save billions of dollars per year, and either spend the taxes on other things, or (preferably) pass the savings on to the taxpayers.

Before long, the ATOM will force even the largest nation-states to improve their productivity of government services. But that process will be messy, and government officials may take a scorched-earth approach to defending their own rice bowls. Let us hope that Estonia inspires at least a few other countries into voluntary modernization.

ATOM Award of the Month, January 2018

With the new year, we have a new ATOM AotM. This is an award for a trend that ought to be easy for anyone to recognize who is at all familiar with Moore's Law-type concepts yet is greatly overlooked despite quite literally being in front of people's faces for hours a day.

The most crude and uninformed arguments against accelerating technological progress are either of a "Word processing is no better than in 1993, so Moore's Law no longer matters" or "People can't eat computers, so the progress in their efficiency is useless" nature. However, the improvements in semiconductor and similar technologies endlessly finds ways into previously low-tech products, which is the most inherent ATOM principle.

The MONTICELLO-Model 211-CD-90
EARLY AMERICAN LOWBOY TV
- 21" Tube (Overall diameter) 260 sq. In. viewable picture
- Pull-push, On-Off, stay-set volume control
- New super-power chassis
- New RCA long-range tuner
- Improved mirror-sharp picture
- Simplified color-quick tuning
- RA security sealed circuits
- 3-Speaker panoramic FM sound

$795

The concept of television has altered cultures across the world more than almost any other technology. The range of secondary and tertiary economies created around it are vast. The 1960 set pictured here, for $795, cost 26% of US annual per capita GDP at the time. The equivalent price today would be $15,000. Content was received over the air and this was often subject to poor reception. The weight and volume of the device relative to the area of the screen was high and the floorspace consumed was substantial. There were three network channels in the United States (while most other countries had no broadcasts at all). There was no remote control.

There were slow, incremental improvements in resolution and screen-size-to-unit-weight ratios from the 1960s until around 2003, when one of the first thin television sets was available at the retail level. It featured a 42" screen, was only 4 inches thick, and cost $8000. Such a wall-mountable display, despite the high price, was a substantial improvement above the cathode ray tube sets of the time, most of which were too large and heavy to be moved by one person, and consumed a substantial amount of floor space.

But in true ATOM exemplification, this minimally improving technology suddenly got pulled into rapid, exponential improvement (part of how deflationary technology increased from 0.5% of World GDP in 1999 to 1% in 2008 to 2% in 2017). Once the flat screen TV was on the market, plasma and LCD displays eventually gave way to LED displays, which are a form of semiconductor and improve at Moore's Law rates.

Today, even 60-inch sets, a size considered to be extravagant in 2005, are very inexpensive. Like any other old electronic device, slightly out of date sets are available on Craigslist in abundance (contributing to the Upgrade Paradox). A functional used set that cost $8,000 in 2003 can hardly be sold at all in 2018; the owner is lucky if someone is willing to come and take it for free.

TV screens are getting bigger and bigger
Percentage of global television unit sales accounted for by 40+ inch TVs

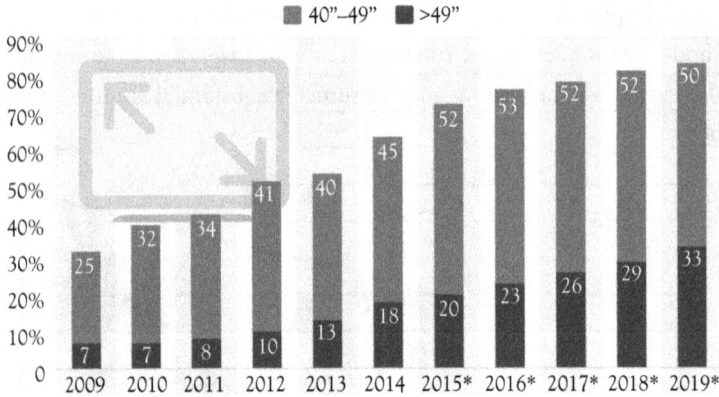

Since once ATOM-speed improvements assimilate a technology, the improvements never stop, and sets of the near future may be thin enough to be flexible, along with resolutions of 4K, 8K, and beyond. Sets larger than 240" (20 feet) are similarly declining in price and visible in increasing numbers in commercial use (i.e., Times Square everywhere). This is hence one of the most visible examples of ATOM disruption, and how cities of today have altered their appearance relative to the recent past.

This is a large ATOM disruption, as there are still 225 million new sets sold each year, amounting to $105 billion/year in sales.

ATOM Award of the Month, November 2017

For this month, the ATOM AotM goes outward. Much like the September ATOM AotM, this is another dimension of imaging. But this time, we focus on the final frontier. Few have noticed that the rate of improvement of astronomical discovery is now on an ATOM-worthy trajectory, such that this merited an entire chapter in the ATOM publication.

Here at The Futurist, we have been examining telescopic progress for over a decade. In September of 2006, I estimated that telescope power was rising at a compounding rate of 26%/year, and that this trend has been ongoing for decades. 26%/year happens to be the square root of Moore's Law, which is precisely what is to be expected, since to double resolution by halving the size of a pixel, one pixel has to be divided into four. This is also why video game and CGI resolution rises at 26%/year.

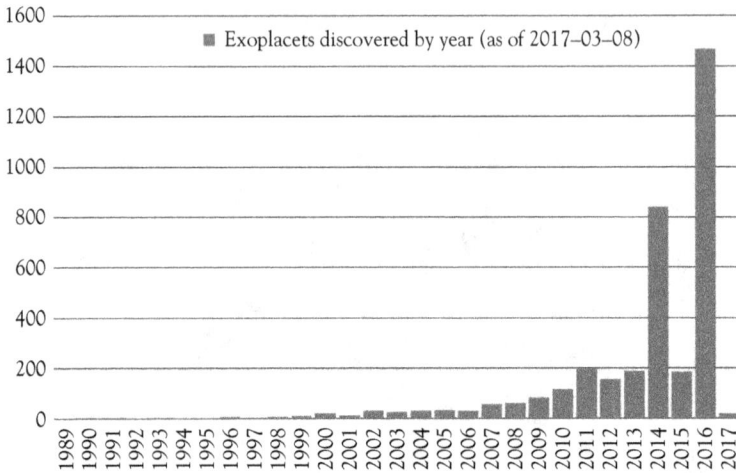

Rising telescope resolution enabled the first exoplanet to be discovered in 1995, and then a steady stream after 2005. This estimated rate led me to correctly predict that the first Earth-like planets would be discovered by 2010–11, and that happened right on schedule. But as with many such thresholds, after initial fanfare, the new status quo manifests and people forget what life was like before. This leads to an continuous underestimation of the rate of change by the average person.

Then, in May 2009, I published one of the most important articles ever written on The Futurist: SETI and the Singularity. At that time, only 347 exoplanets were known, almost all of which were gas giants much larger than the Earth. That number has grown to 3693 today, or over ten times as many. Note how we see the familiar exponential curve inherent to every aspect of the ATOM. Now, even finding Earth-like planets in the 'life zone' is no longer remarkable, which is another aspect of human psychology towards the ATOM—that a highly anticipated and wondrous advance quickly becomes a normalized status quo and most people forget all the previous excitement.

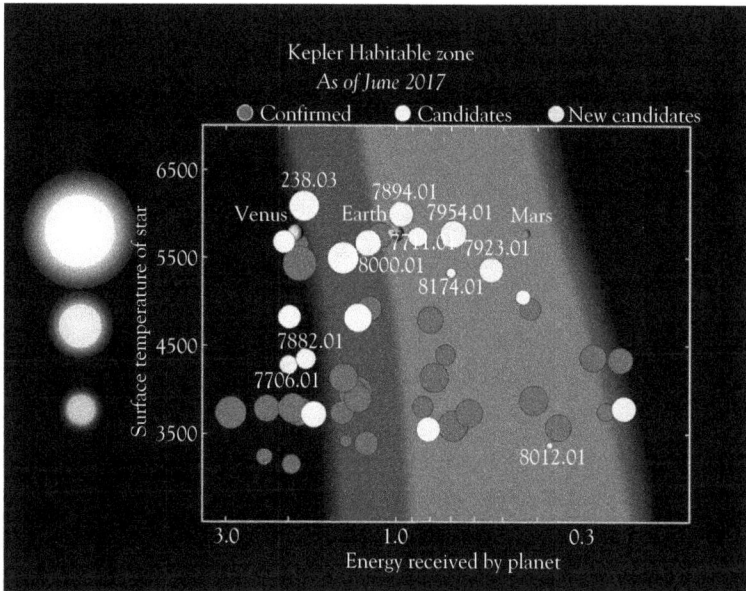

The rate of discovery may soon accelerate further as key process components collapse in cost. Recent computer vision algorithms have proven themselves to be millions of times faster than human examiners. A large part of the cost of exoplanet discovery instruments like the Kepler Space Observatory is the 12- to 18-month manual analysis period. If computer vision can perform this task in seconds, the cost of comparable future projects plummets, and new exoplanets are confirmed almost immediately rather than every other year. This is another massive ATOM productivity jump that removes a major bottleneck in an existing process structure. A new mission like Kepler would cost dramatically less than the previous one, and will be able to publish results far more rapidly.

Given the 26%/year trendline, the future of telescopic discovery becomes easier to predict. In the same article, I made a dramatic prediction about SETI and the prospects of finding extraterrestrial intelligence. Many "enlightened" people are certain that there are numerous extraterrestrial civilizations. While I too believed this for years (from age 6 to about 35), as I studied the accelerating rate of change, I began to notice that within the context of the Drake equation, any civilization even slightly more advanced than us would be dramatically more advanced. In terms of such a civilization, while their current activities might very well be indistinguishable from nature to us, their past activities might still be visible as evidence of their existence at that time. This led me to realize that while there could very well be thousands of planets in our own galaxy that are slightly less advanced that us, it becomes increasingly difficult for there to be one more advanced than us that still manages to avoid detection. Other galaxies are a different story, simply because the distance between galaxies is itself 10–20 times more than the diameter of the typical galaxy. Our telescopic capacity is rising 26%/year after all, and the final variable of the Drake equation, fL, has risen from just 42 years at the time of Carl Sagan's famous clip in 1980, to 79 years now, or almost twice as long.

Hence, the proclamation I had set in 2009 about the 2030 deadline (21 years away at the time) can be reaffirmed, as the 2030 deadline is now only 13 years away.

> If we do not find any evidence of extra-terrestrial intelligence by 2030, then we can confirm with some certainty that such civilizations are not as common as the proponents had hoped. Additionally, each subsequent year without a discovery makes the probability exponentially less likely.

Despite the enormity of our galaxy and the wide range of signals that may exist, even this is eventually superseded by exponential detection capabilities. At least our half of the galaxy will have received a substantial examination of signal traces by 2030. While a deadline 13 years away seems near, remember that the extent of examination that happens during 2017–30 will be more than in all the 400+ years since Galileo, for Moore's Law reasons alone. The jury is out until then.

(All images from Wikipedia or Wikimedia.)

ATOM Award of the Month, October 2017

For this month, the ATOM AotM goes to an area we have not visited yet. Enterprise software and associated hardware technologies may appear boring at first, but there is currently a disruption in this area that is generating huge productivity gains.

Amazon web services (in millions)

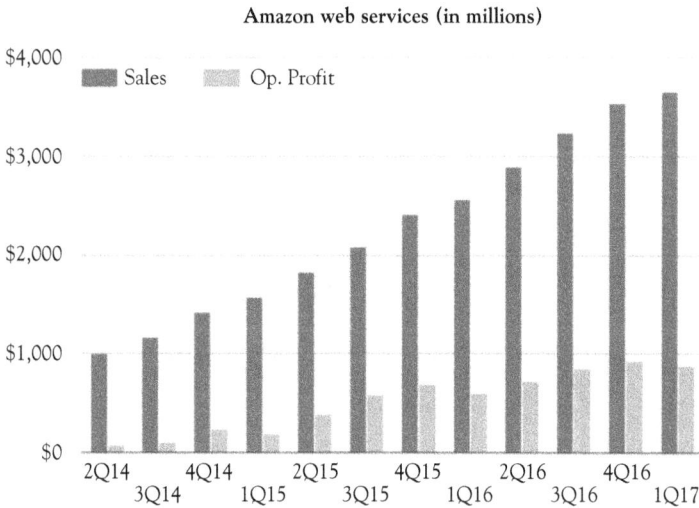

Amazon Web Services (AWS) is an ever-growing list of services that replaces computing, storage, and networking expenditures at client companies. At present, over 90 different services are available. Here is a slideshow of the various companies and sectors being disrupted by AWS.

Cloud computing itself is relatively new, but this revolution by Amazon as taken direct slices out of the existing businesses of Microsoft, IBM, and Oracle, which were slow to deploy cloud-based solutions since they wanted to extend the lives of their existing product lines. Their anti-technology behavior deserves to be punished by the ATOM, and Amazon obliged. AWS is set to register $14 billion in revenue for 2017, most of which has replaced a greater sum of revenue at competing companies.

The biggest value is the lower cost of entry to smaller companies from the on-demand flexibility enabled by AWS. Now that IT Security and Compliance is far more cost-effective through AWS, the barrier to entry for smaller firms is lowered. This is particularly useful for clients in far-flung locations, enabling a decentralization that facilitates greater technological progress. Upgrades across computing, storage, software, networking, and security are disseminated seamlessly, and since far less hardware is used, the upgrade process is far more materially efficient. This removes a variety of smaller bottlenecks to technological progress, mitigating the corporate equivalent of the Upgrade Paradox.

Another great benefit is elasticity, where a company does not have to worry about estimating hardware capacity needs in the future, which can often lead to overbuying of rapidly deflating technologies, or underbuying, which can cause customer dissatisfaction due to slow speeds. All of this can now be scaled dynamically through AWS.

For the productivity gains inherent to the scale and dynamism of AWS, it receives the October 2017 ATOM AotM.

ATOM Award of the Month, September 2017

For September 2017, the ATOM AotM takes a very visual turn. With some aspects of the ATOM, seeing is believing.

Before photography, the only image capture was through sketches and paintings. This was time-consuming, and well under 1% were prosperous enough to have even a single hand-painted portrait of themselves. For most people, after they died, their families had only memories via which to imagine faces. If portraits were this scarce, other images were even scarcer. When image capture was this scarce, people certainly had no chance of seeing places, things, or creatures from far away. It was impossible to know much about the broader world.

The very first photograph was taken as far back as 1826, and black&white was the dominant form of the medium for over 135 years. That it took so long for b&w to transition to color may seem quite surprising, but the virtually non-existent ATOM during this period is consistent with this glacial rate of progress. The high cost of cameras meant that the number of photographs taken in the first 100 years of photography (1826–1926) was still an extremely small. Eventually, the progression to color film seemed to be a "completion" of the technological progression in the minds of most people. What more could happen after that?

But the ATOM was just getting started, and it caught up with photography around the turn of the century with relatively little fanfare, even though it was notable that film-based photography and the hassles associated with it were removed from the consumer experience. The cost of film was suddenly zero, as was the transit time and cost from the development center. Now, everyone could have thousands of photos, and send those over email endlessly. Yet, standalone cameras still cost $200 as of 2003 and were too large to be carried around everywhere at all times.

As the ATOM progressed, digital cameras got smaller and cheaper, even as resolution continued to rise. It was discovered that the human eye does in fact adapt to higher resolution, and finds previously acceptable lower resolution unacceptable after adapting to higher resolution. Technology hence forces higher visual acuity and the associated growth of the brain's visual cortex.

With the rise of the cellular phone, the ATOM enabled more and more formerly discrete devices to be assimilated into the phone, and the camera was one of the earliest and most obvious candidates. The diffusion of this was very rapid, as we can see from the image that contrasts the 2005 vs. 2013 Papal inaugurations in Vatican City. Before long, the cost of an integrated camera trended toward zero, to the extent that there is no mobile device that does not have one. As a result, 2 billion people have digital cameras with them at all times, and stand ready to photograph just about anything they think is important. Suddenly, there are countless cameras at every scene.

But lest you think the ubiquity of digital cameras is the end of the story, you are making the same mistake as those who thought color photography on film in 1968 was the end of the road. Remember that the ATOM is never truly done, even after the cost of a technology approaches zero. Digital imaging itself is just the preview, for now we have it gener-ating an ever-expanding pile of an even more valuable raw material: data.

Images contain a large volume of data, particularly the data that asso-ciates things with each other (the eyes are to be above the nose, for exam-ple). Data is one of the two fuels of Artificial Intelligence (the other being inexpensive parallel processing). Despite over a decade of digital images being available on the Internet, only now are there enough of them for AI to draw extensive conclusions from them, and for Google's image search to be a major force in the refinement of Google's Search AI. Most people don't even remember when Google added image search to its capabilities, but now it is hard to imagine life without it.

Today, we have immediate access to image search that answers ques-tions in the blink of an eye, and fosters even greater curiosity. In a matter of seconds, you can look up images for mandrill teeth, the rings of Saturn, a transit of Venus over the Sun, the coast of Capri, or the jaws of Carcha-rocles Megalodon. More searches lead to more precise recommendations, and more images continue to be added. In the past, the accessibility of this information was so limited that the invaluable tangents of curiosity just never formed. Hence, the creation of new knowledge speeds up. The curious can more easily pull ahead of the incurious.

Digital imaging is one of the primary transformations that built the Internet age, and is a core pillar of the impending ascent of AI. For this reason, it receives the September 2017 ATOM AotM.

ATOM Award of the Month, August 2017

For the August 2017 ATOM AotM, we will bend one of the rules. The rule is that a disruption already has to have begun, and be presently underway.

But this time, a conversation in the last month's comments brought forth a vision of a quad-layer disruption that is already in the early stages and will manifest in no more than 15 years' time. When fully underway, this disruption will further tighten the screws on government bodies that are far too sclerotic to adapt to the speed of the ATOM.

To start, we will list out the progression of each of the four disruptions separately.

Electric dreams

Manufacturing capacity Gigawatt-hours per year — 2017 2020

Panasonic* (Japan); CATL (China); BYD (China); LG Chem (South Korea); Samsung SDI (South Korea)

Battery cost Woldwide, $/kWh — FORECAST

Battery energy density Watt-hours per litre

2008 10 12 14 15   20 2022 target

Sources: Cairn ERA; US department of energy   *Included tesla gigafactory

(1) Batteries are improving quickly, and while electric vehicles are not yet competitive in terms of cost and charging speeds (partly due to the true cost of imported oil not being directly visible to consumers). At the same time, an electric car has far fewer moving parts, and fewer liquids to deal with. By many estimates, an electric car can last 300,000 before significant deterioration occurs, vs. 150,000 for an internal combustion engine car. Now, under the current ownership model, a car is driven only 12,000 miles/year and is parked 90% of the time or more. The second half of an electric vehicle's lifetime (150,001–300,000 miles) would only begin in year 13 and extend until year 25 of ownership, which is not practical. If only there were a way to avoid having the car remain idle 90% of the time, occupying parking spaces. It may take until 2032 for electric cars

to compress the cost delta to the extent of being superior to ICE cars in total ownership costs for the early years, which then leads to the dividend available in the later years of the electric car's life.

(2) Autonomous vehicles are a very overhyped technology. Stanford University demonstrated an early prototype in 2007. Yet even a decade later, a fully autonomous car that operates without any human involvement, let alone the benefit of having a network of such cars, seems scarcely any closer.

Eventually, by about 2032, cars will be fully autonomous, widely adopted, and communicate with each other, greatly increasing driving efficiency through high speeds and far less distance between cars than humans can manage. Uber-like services will cost 60–80% less than they do now, since the earnings of the human driver are no longer an element of cost, and Uber charges just 20–30% of the fare itself. It will be cheaper for almost everyone to take the on-demand service all the time than to own a car outright or even take the bus. If such a car is driven 20 hours a day, it can in fact accrue 300,000 miles in just 5 years of use. This effectively is the only way that electric cars can be driven all the way up to the 300,000 limit.

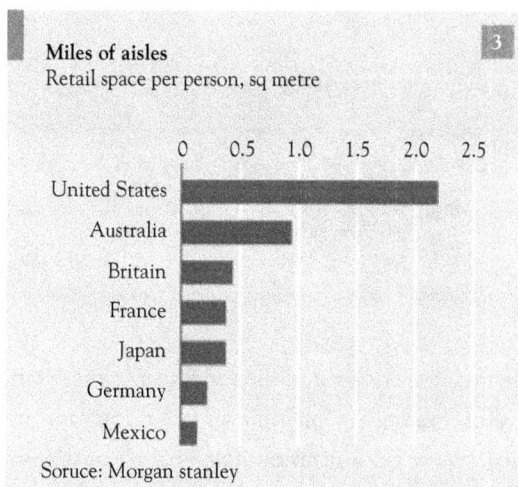

Miles of aisles
Retail space per person, sq metre

	0	0.5	1.0	1.5	2.0	2.5
United States	████████████████████████					
Australia	██████					
Britain	██					
France	██					
Japan	██					
Germany	█					
Mexico	█					

Soruce: Morgan stanley

(3) The displacement of brick-and-mortar retail by e-commerce has far greater implications for the US than for any other country, given the excessive level of land devoted to retails stores and their parking lots. The

most grotesque example of this is in Silicon Valley itself (and to a lesser extent, Los Angeles), where vast retail strip mall parking lots are largely empty, yet are within walking distance of tall, narrow townhouses that cost $1.5M despite taking up footprints of barely 600 sqft each.

As the closure of more retail stores progresses, and on-demand car usage reduces the need for so many parking spaces, these vast tracts of land can be diverted for another purpose. In major California metros, the economically and morally sound strategy would be to convert the land into multi-story buildings, preferentially residential. But extreme regulatory hurdles and resistance towards construction of any new housing supply will leave this land as dead capital for as long as the obstructionists can manage.

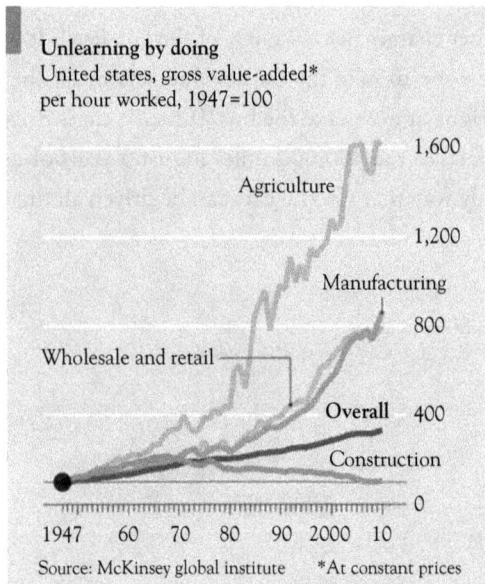

Unlearning by doing
United states, gross value-added*
per hour worked, 1947=100

Source: McKinsey global institute   *At constant prices

But in the vast open suburbs of the American interior, land is about to go from plentiful to extremely plentiful. If you think yards in the suburbs of interior cities are large, wait until most of their nearby strip malls are available for redevelopment, and the only two choices are either residential land or office buildings (there are more than enough parks and golf courses in those locations already). Areas where population is already flat or declining will have little choice but to build even more, and hope that ultra-low real estate costs can attract businesses (this will be no problem at all if the ATOM-DUES program is implemented by then).

This disruption is not nearly as much a factor in any country other than the US and, to a lesser extent, Australia, as other countries did not misallocate so much land to retail (and the associated parking lots) in the first place.

4) This fourth disruption is not as essential to this future as the first three, but is highly desirable, simply due to how overdue the disruption is. It is quite shocking that the least productive industry in the private sector relative to 50 years ago is not education, not medicine, but construction. US construction productivity has *fallen* over the last 50 years. Not merely failed to rise, mind you, but outright declined in absolute terms.

But remember, under ATOM principles, the more overdue a disruption is, and the more artificial the obstructions thwarting it, the more sudden it is when it eventually happens. China is not held back by the factors that have led to the abysmally low productivity in US construction, and when there is so much retail land to repurpose, pressure to revive that dead capital will just become too great, even if that means Chinese construction companies have to come in to provide what the US counterparts cannot. This pressure could be the catalyst of the long overdue construction productivity catchup. This topic warrants a lengthy article of its own, but that is for another day.

Hence, the first three factors, and possibly the fourth, combine by 2032 to generate a disruption that will be so comprehensive in the US that the inability of government to change zoning laws and permitting at anything close to the speed of market demand will be greatly exposed.

The first disruption, batteries, alone could be an ATOM AotM, but this time, the cumulative disruption from these multiple factors, even if it will take the next 15 years to accomplish, gets the award.

ATOM Award of the Month, July 2017

The ATOM AotM for July 2017 reminds us of the true core principles of the ATOM. Whenever anything becomes too expensive relative to value provided, particularly if done so through artificial government intervention in markets, a technological solution invariably replaces the expensive incumbent.

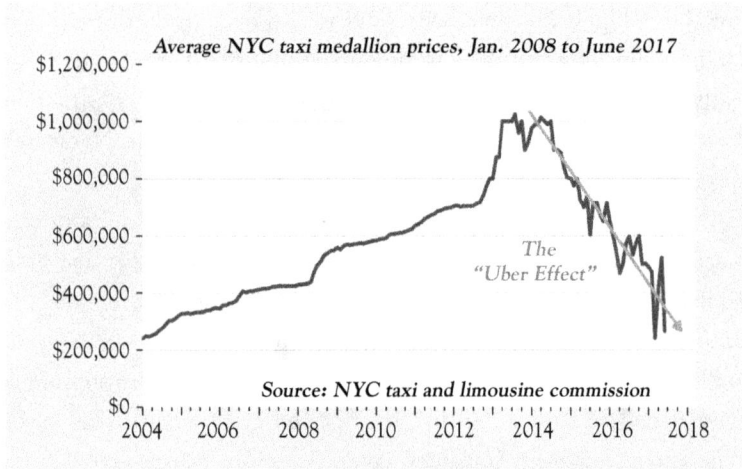

Average NYC taxi medallion prices, Jan. 2008 to June 2017

The "Uber Effect"

Source: NYC taxi and limousine commission

Taxi medallions, particularly in New York City, are just the crudest form of city government corruption. Drunk with its own greed, the city ratcheted up the price of taxi medallions from $200,000 in 2003 to $1 million in 2013, which is far faster than even the S&P500, let alone inflation. Note how there was no decline at all during the 2008–09 recession. This predatory extraction from consumers, much like high oil prices artificially engineered by OPEC, created a market window that might otherwise have not existed until several years later. This induced the ATOM to address this imbalance sooner than it otherwise might have and gritty entrepreneurs swiftly founded companies like Uber and Lyft, which provided a dramatically better value for money. As a result, the price of taxi medallions in NYC fell by 80% from the inflated peak. The ATOM was at a sufficiently advanced level for the technological response to be as rapid as it was (unlike with, say, expensive oil in the 1973–81 period, when there was almost no ATOM of macroeconomic significance).

Remember that the reduction in cost for a certain ride and demolition of a seemingly intractable government graft obstacle is just the first of several ATOM effects. The second is the security of each driver and passenger being identified before the ride. The third is the volume of data that these millions of rides generate (data being one of the two core fuels of Artificial Intelligence). The fourth is the ability to dynamically adjust to demand spikes (the surge pricing that the economically illiterate malign). The fifth is the possibility of new service capabilities altogether. Recall this excerpt from Chapter 11 of the ATOM:

> Automobile commuters with good jobs but lengthy commutes have joined Uber-type platforms to take a rider along with them on the commute they have to undertake anyway. The driver earns an extra $200–$400/week (against which an appropriate portion of car and smartphone costs can be applied as deductions) with no incremental input time or cost. Meanwhile, other commuters enjoy having one less car on the road for each such dynamically generated carpooling pair. The key is that a dead commute is now monetized even by corporate-class people, increasing passengers per car and reducing traffic congestion, while replacing dedicated taxicabs. For the macroeconomy, it also creates new VM where none existed before.

The creation of an entirely new sub-economy, with entirely new velocity-of-money (VM), is where new real wealth creation is the purest. This effect of these ride-sharing platforms is still in its infancy. When autonomous vehicles replace human drivers, the loss of driver income is matched (indeed exceeded in post-tax terms) by savings to passengers.

It does not matter which company ultimately wins (Uber is having some PR problems lately), but rather that the disruption is already irreversible and woven into the fabric of the ATOM and broader society. Maybe Uber and Lyft will just be to transportation services what Data General and Commodore were to computing. The point is, this is a superb example of how the ATOM works, and how the transformation is often multilayered.

ATOM Award of the Month, May 2017

For May 2017, the award goes in a direction that not many associate with technological disruption. Remember that the ATOM relates to not merely products that themselves have a rapidly improving cost/benefit profile, but also towards technological improvements in products, processes, and services that themselves may not be high-tech.

The standard shipping container is just an inert box, and most people rarely ever see one. It is not improving from one year to the next in any meaningful sense. The real innovation was in the process technologies enabled through this standardization, and the immense deflation derived through these technologies.

Malcolm McLean, a trucking tycoon, envisioned the idea of standardized container sizes and generously decided to give his idea away for free rather than patent it and seek profit. After the first experiment was a success, rapid adoption and port standardization followed.

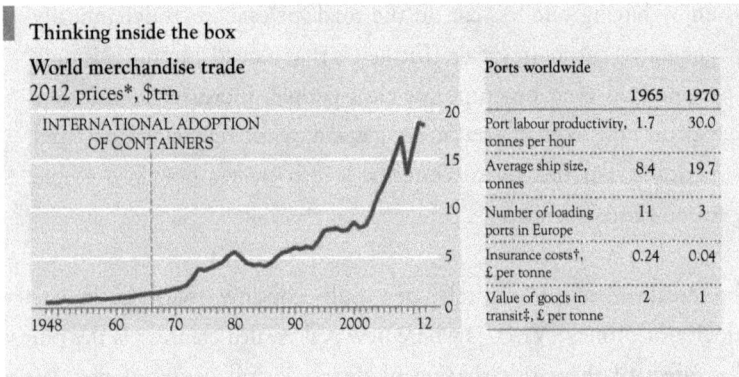

Thinking inside the box

World merchandise trade
2012 prices*, $trn

INTERNATIONAL ADOPTION OF CONTAINERS

(chart x-axis: 1948, 60, 70, 80, 90, 2000, 12; y-axis: 0, 5, 10, 15, 20)

Ports worldwide

	1965	1970
Port labour productivity, tonnes per hour	1.7	30.0
Average ship size, tonnes	8.4	19.7
Number of loading ports in Europe	11	3
Insurance costs†, £ per tonne	0.24	0.04
Value of goods in transit‡, £ per tonne	2	1

As we can see from the table (click to enlarge), the introduction of the shipping container swiftly led to an almost 20-fold increase in unloading rates from 1965 to 1970, an unusually rapid improvement of any productivity metric for such an early era. This increased speed led to larger ships, and this in turn led to larger and fewer ports. From an ATOM perspective, these productivity gains introduced a great deal of deflation in the prices of the goods themselves. A broader range of goods could be traded internationally, leading to many more countries being able to compete for the same export demand. New countries could merely join existing supply chains, rather than build entire industries from scratch. China's entry into international trade could not have been as rapid as it was, without the shipping container, and the advantages it conferred onto large countries over smaller ones, and to low-cost production countries over expensive ones. This advantage is ongoing, as countries poorer than China are still in the process of integrating the low-hanging fruits of benefit that the shipping container provides.

Despite this introduction having begun almost 50 years ago, the full ATOM effect continues to increase. The precise logistics of the entire container-shipping ecosystem demands more powerful computation, sensors, and other innovations like RFID tags and GPS tracking. Furthermore, supply chains transporting trillions of dollars of goods each year generate a huge amount of data, which for the longest time was not even being utilized. Any large and ever-growing collection of data will attract Artificial Intelligence onto it, and this AI will generate additional productivity gains for participants in the supply chain, and hence price reductions for end-users.

Since shipping containers are produced in such volume, there are ideas emerging to use them elsewhere, such as a building block for modular construction, or as simple pop-in swimming pool enclosures.

For this reason, the shipping container, an inert metal box that transformed the entire award, receives the May 2017 ATOM AotM.

ATOM Award of the Month, April 2017

It is time for the ATOM AotM for April 2017, for which we return to an article I wrote way back in 2009. That article is titled 'The Publishing Disruption', and at the time of writing, we were on the brink of a transformation in content publication as seismic as the invention of the Gutenberg printing press. Since that time, the anticipated sequence of events unfolded as expected.

To excerpt from that article, consider how many centuries of background evolution occurred to get us to where we were in 2007:

> What a unique thing a book is. Made from a tree, it has a hundred or more flexible pages that contain written text, enabling the book to contain a large sum of information in a very small volume. Before paper, clay tablets, sheepskin parchment, and papyrus were all used to store information with far less efficiency. Paper itself was once so rare and valuable that the Emperor of China had guards stationed around his paper possessions.
>
> Before the invention of the printing press, books were written by hand, and few outside of monasteries knew how to read. There were only a few thousand books in all of Europe in the 14th century. Charlemagne himself took great effort to learn how to read, but never managed to learn how to write, which still put him ahead of most kings of the time, who were generally illiterate.
>
> But with the invention of the printing press by Johannes Gutenberg in the mid-15th century, it became possible to make multiple copies of the same book, and before long, the number of books in Europe increased from thousands to millions.

But then, note how incredibly low-tech and low productivity the traditional publishing industry still was well into the 21st century:

> Fast forward to the early 21st century, and books are still printed by the millions. Longtime readers of The Futurist know that I initially had written a book (2001–02), and sought to have it published the old-fashioned way. However, the publishing industry,

and literary agents, were astonishingly low-tech. They did not use email, and required queries to be submitted via regular mail, with a self-addressed, stamped envelope included. So I had to pay postage in both directions, and wait several days for a round trip to hear their response. And this was just the literary agents. The actual publishing house, if they decide to accept your book, would still take 12 months to produce and distribute the book even after the manuscript was complete. Even then, royalties would be 10–15% of the retail price. This prospect did not seem compelling to me, and I chose to parse my book into this blog you see before you.

The refusal by the publishing industry to use email and other productivity-enhancing technologies as recently as 2003 kept their wages low. Editors always moaned that they worked 60 hours a week just to make $50,000 a year, the same as they made in 1970. My answer to them is that they have no basis to expect wage increases without increasing their productivity through technology.

An industry this far behind was just begging to be disrupted. As we have seen from the ATOM, the more overdue a particular disruption is, the more dramatic and swift the disruption when it eventually occurs, as the distance to travel just to revert to the trendline of that particular innovation, is great. Proceeding further in the original article:

> The Amazon Kindle launched in late 2007 at the high price of $400. Many people feel that the appeal of holding a physical book in our hands cannot be replaced by a display screen, and take a cavalier attitude towards dismissing e-readers. The tune changes upon learning that the price of a book on an e-reader is just a third of what the paper form at a brick-and-mortar bookstore, with sales tax, would cost.

As of 2017, an entry-level Kindle 8 costs just $80 (with 3 GB of storage), yet is far more advanced than the $400 Kindle of 2007 (with just 250 MB of storage). Cumulative Kindle sales are estimated to be over 100 million units now.

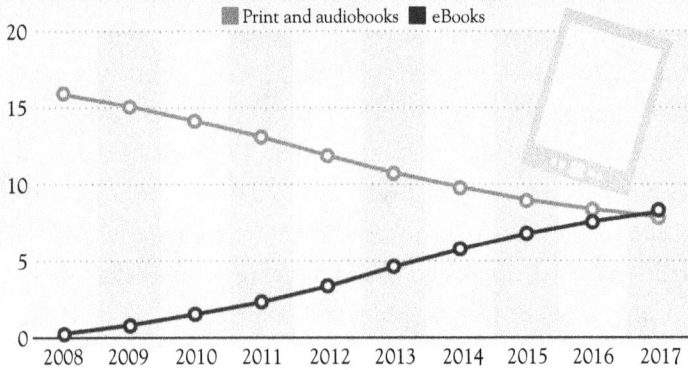

U.S. eBook sales to surpass printed book sales in 2017
Consumer book sales in the United States from 2008 to 2017 (in billion U.S. dollars)

But the Kindle hardware is not the real disruption, as it is a new pur-chase imposed on people who needed no such device to read paper books. The real ATOM disruption is in books themselves. Now, an author can publish directly on Kindle, and at a $10 sales price, immediately begins to receive a 70% royalty. Contrast that with the 10–15% royalty on a $20 sales price in traditional book publishing, that too after a 12-month waiting period even after the manuscript is complete. While bound books may still make sense for famous authors, the new market created by the Kindle has enabled the publication of many books that only expect to sell 10,000 copies. There is no material involved, so the production and distribution cost of any such publication has literally fallen by a factor of millions. A hefty cost is now no cost, precisely as the ATOM predicts.

2017 is the year where e-book sales have surpassed print and audio book sales, as per the chart. Since the previous article, brick-and-mortar bookstores have seen a torrent of closures. Borders Bookstores has completely shut down all of its 511 bookstores in the United States. Barnes & Noble still exists, partly due to capturing the residual Borders revenue, but a growing share of B&N's in-store revenue is now from the coffee shop, magazines, and certain specialty book sales.

The unshackling of the bottom 99% of authors and aspiring authors from the extreme inefficiency of the traditional publishing industry has unleashed more content than was ever possible before, and is a mar-ket upgrade just as significant as that of the Gutenberg press in the

15th century. It is also a perfect demonstration of the accelerating rate of change, for while it took centuries for the diffusion of printed books to manifest, the e-book transformation was in mere years. For this reason, the Amazon Kindle and e-book ecosystem are the winner of April 2017's ATOM Award of the Month. I need more candidate submissions for future ATOM AotM awards.

ATOM Award of the Month, March 2017

It is that time of the month again. For our third ever award of the ATOM AotM, we return to an article I wrote over 10 years ago about the lighting revolution. At that time, when the disruption was still in the future, I highlighted how the humble status of the light fixture leads to an associated disruption going widely unnoticed. That continues to be true even today, despite the important product transition that most people have already undertaken.

Average lighting efficacy (light output per unit of energy consumed) and cost per bulb

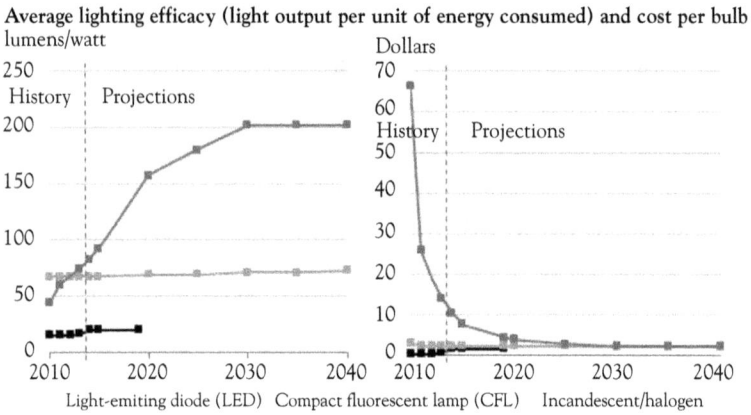

Light-emiting diode (LED)   Compact fluorescent lamp (CFL)   Incandescent/halogen

So the ATOM AotM award for March 2017 goes to the LED lightbulb. Something that most people do not even notice is a major engine of the ATOM, as it has introduced rapid price/performance improvements into what used to be a stagnant product.

Charge of the Light Brigade: Remember that the average household has about 25 light bulbs on average. From the chart, we can see that light output per until of energy and cost per watt of LED lighting are both improving rapidly, leading to a double-exponential effect. Lighting is hence now fully in the path of the ATOM and is seeing progress at a rate entirely beyond what the predecessor technology could have experienced, and is indeed one of the fastest technology shifts ever (see the second chart). Bulbs are now purchased in packs of 4–12 units, rather than the single-unit purchases of the recent past. The expected electricity savings worldwide are estimated to be over $100 billion per year in the near future.

Exhibit 19: The rapid adoption of LEDs in lighting marks one of the fastest technology shifts in human history.
LEDs for general lighting were commercialized only recently, but will dominate sales by the end of this decade

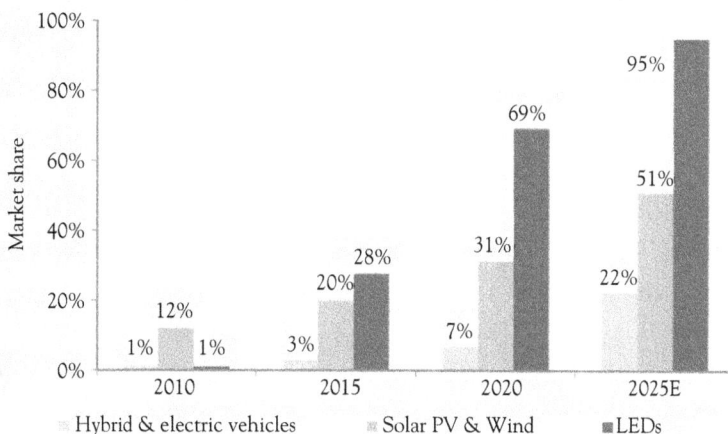

The domino effects of this are immense. Follow the sequence of steps below:

- LED bulbs are reducing the electricity consumed by lighting.
- This reduction in demand more than accommodates the proliferation of electric cars. The first 100 million electric cars worldwide (a level we are still extremely far from) will merely offset the loss of electricity demand for lighting.
- The spread of electric cars with no net rise in electricity consumption nonetheless reduces oil consumption and hence oil imports. The United States already has a trade surplus with OPEC, for the first time in half a century, and this force is strengthening further. Even if the price per barrel of oil had not fallen through fracking, the number of imported barrels still would have plunged.
- So even though most lighting is not fueled by oil, it created a puncture point through which a second-degree blow to oil demand arose.

That is truly amazing, making LED lighting not just a component of the ATOM but one of the largest disruptions currently underway.

ATOM Award of the Month, February 2017

After the inaugural award in January, a new month brings a new ATOM
AotM. This time, we go to an entirely different sector than we examined
last time. The award for this month goes to the collaboration between the
Georgia Institute of Technology, Udacity, and AT&T to provide a fully
accredited Masters of Science in Computer Science degree, for the very
low price of $6,700 on average.

The disruption in education is a topic I have written about at length.
In essence, most education is just a transmission of commoditized information, that, like every other information technology, should be declining in cost. However, the corrupt education industry has managed to
burrow deep into the emotions of its customers, to such an extent that a
rising price for a product of stagnant (often declining) quality is not even
questioned. For this reason, education is in a bubble that is already in the
process of deflating.

What the MSCS at GATech accomplishes is fourfold:

- Lowering the cost of the degree by almost an order of magnitude compared to the same degree as similarly-ranked schools
- Making the degree available without relocation to where the
  institution is physically located
- Scaling the degree to an eventual intake of 10,000 students, vs.
  just 300 that can attend a traditional in-residence program at
  GATech
- Establishing best practices for other departments at GATech,
  and other institutions, to implement in order to create a
  broader array of MOOC degree programs

After a slow start, enrollment now is reported to be over 3,300 students, representing a significant fraction of students presently study-
ing MS-level computer science at equal or higher ranked schools. The
only reason enrollment has not risen all the way up to the full 10,000 is
due to insufficient resourcefulness in shopping around and implementing ATOM principles to greatly increase one's living standards through
ATOM means. Aside from perhaps the top two schools like MIT and

Stanford, there is perhaps no greater value for money than the GATech MSCS, which will become apparent as the slower adopters drift towards the program, particularly from overseas.

Eventually, the sheer size of enrollment will rapidly lead to GATech becoming a dominant alumni community within computer science, forcing other institutions to catch up. When this competition lowers costs even further, we will see one of the most highly paid and future-proof professions being accessible at little or no cost. When contrasted to the immense costs of attending medical or law school, many borderline students will pursue computer science ahead of professions with large student debt burdens, creating a self-reinforcing cycle of ever-more computer science and <u>ATOM</u> propagation. The fact that one can enroll in the program from overseas will attract many students from countries that do not even have schools of GATech's caliber (i.e., most countries), generating local talent despite remote education.

Crucially, this is strong evidence of how the ATOM always finds new ways to expand itself, since the field most essential to the feeding of the ATOM, computer science, is the one that found a way to greatly increase the number of people destined to work in it, by attacking both cost thresholds and enrollment volumes. This is not a coincidence, because the ATOM always finds a way around anything that is inhibiting the growth of the ATOM, in this case, access to computer science training. Subsequent to this, the ATOM can increase the productivity of education even in less ATOM-crucial fields medicine, law, business, and K–12, since the greatly expanded size of the computer science profession will provide entrepreneurs and expertise to make this happen. This is how the ATOM captures an ever-growing share of the economy into rapidly-deflating technological fundamentals.

ATOM Award of the Month, January 2017

With the new year, we are starting a new article series here at The Futurist. The theme will be a recognition of exceptional innovation. Candidates can be any industry, corporation, or individual that has created an innovation exemplifying the very best of technological disruption. The more ATOM principles exhibited in an innovation (rising living standards, deflation acting in proportion to prior inflation in the incumbent industry, rapid continuous technological improvement, etc.), the greater the chance of qualification.

The falling cost of U.S. shale production

Wellhead breakeven oil prices

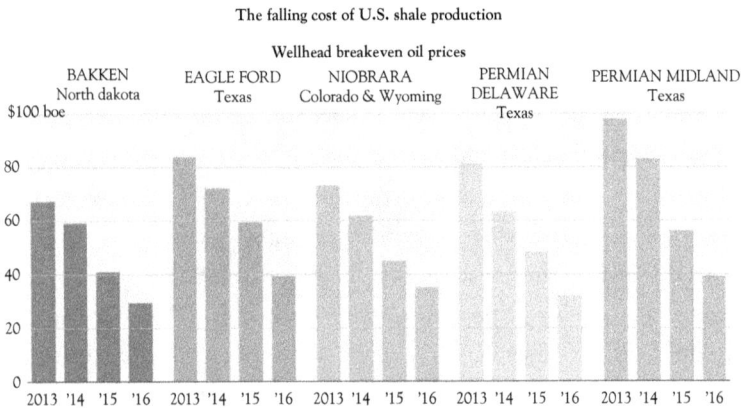

The inaugural winner of the ATOM Award of the Month is the US hydraulic fracturing industry. While "fracking" garnered the most news in 2011–13, the rapid technological improvements continued. Natural gas continues to hover around just $3, making the United States one of the most competitive countries in industries where natural gas is a large input. Oil prices continue to fall due to ever-improving efficiencies, and from the chart, we can see how many of the largest fields have seen breakevens fall from $80 to under $40 in just the brief 2013–16 period. This is of profound importance, because *now even $50 is a profitable price for US shale oil.* There is no indication that this trend of lower breakeven prices has stopped. Keep in mind that the massive shale formations in California are not even being accessed yet due to radical obstruction, but a breakeven of $30 or lower ensure the pressure to extract this profit from the Monterrey shale continues to rise. Beyond that, Canada has not yet begun fracking of its own, and when it does, it will certainly have at least as much additional oil as the United States found.

This increase, which is just an extra 3 million barrels/day to US supply, was nonetheless enough to capsize this highly elastic market and crash world oil prices from $100+ to about $50. Given the improving breakevens, and possibility of new production, this will continue to pressure oil prices for the foreseeable future. This has led to the United States turning the tables on OPEC and reversing a large trade deficit into what is now a *surplus*. If you told any of those "peak oil" Malthusians that the United States would soon have a trade surplus with OPEC, they would have branded you as a lunatic. Note how that ill-informed Maoist-Malthusian cult utterly vanished. Furthermore, this plunge in oil prices has strengthened the economies of other countries that import most of their oil, from Japan to India.

Trading places
U.S. trade balance with OPEC nations, billiions

Under ATOM principles, technology always finds a way to lower the cost of something that has become artificially expensive and is hence obstructing the advancement of other technologies. Oil was a premier example of this, as almost all technological innovation is done in countries that have to import large portions of their oil, while almost none is done by oil exporters. Excess wealth accumulation by oil exporters was an anti-technology impediment, and demanded the attention of a good portion of the ATOM. Remember that the worldwide ATOM is of an ever-rising size and comprises of the sum total of all technological products in production at a given time (currently, about 2% of world GDP).

Hence, all technological disruptions are interconnected, and when the ATOM is freed up from the completion of a certain disruption, that amount of disruptive capacity becomes available to tackle something new. Given the size of this disruption to oil prices and production geography, this occupied a large portion of the ATOM for a few years, which means a lot of ATOM capacity is now free to act elsewhere.

This disruption was also <u>one of the most famous predictions of mine here at The Futurist</u>. In 2011, I predicted that high oil prices was effectively a form of burning a candle at both ends and such prices were jolting at least six compensating technologies into overdrive. I provided an equation predicting when oil would topple, and it toppled well in accordance with that prediction (<u>even sooner than the equation estimated</u>).

This concludes our very first ATOM AotM to kick off the new year. I need candidate submissions from readers in order to get a good pool to select from. Criteria include the size and scope of the disruption, how anti-technology the disrupted incumbent was, and an obvious improvement in the quality of a large number of lives through this disruption.

About the Author

Kartik Gada is widely renowned futurist with a lengthy career in investment banking, hedge funds, and technology product management. As a futurist, he has 14 years of archived predictions at his blog (www.singularity2050.com), with a high degree of accuracy. He teaches finance and technology classes at Stanford University, and has delivered over 100 conference keynotes worldwide to audiences of up to 3,000.

Index

www.ingramcontent.com/pod-product-compliance
Lightning Source LLC
Chambersburg PA
CBHW061154220326
41599CB00025B/4476